# The Directors Guild of America Oral History Series

*David H. Shepard, General Editor*

1. Byron Haskin. 1984.
2. Worthington Miner.
3. Curtis Bernhardt/Henry Koster.
4. King Vidor.
5. David Butler.
6. Stuart Heisler.

A Directors Guild of America Oral History

# BYRON HASKIN

Interviewed by Joe Adamson

The Directors Guild of
America and
The Scarecrow Press, Inc.
Metuchen, N.J., and London
1984

**Library of Congress Cataloging in Publication Data**

Haskin, Byron, 1899-1984.
  Byron Haskin.

  (The Directors Guild of America oral history
series ; 1)
  Includes indexes.
  1. Haskin, Byron, 1899-1984.  2. Moving-picture
producers and directors--United States--Interviews.
I. Adamson, Joe.  II. Title.  III. Series.
PN1998.A3H336  1984    791.43'0233'0924 [B]    84-14080
ISBN 0-8108-1740-3

Copyright © 1984 by Directors Guild Educational and
Benevolent Foundation

Manufactured in the United States of America

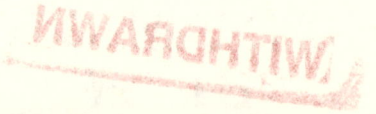

## TABLE OF CONTENTS

| | Preface | v |
|---|---|---|
| I | Early Background | 1 |
| II | The Twenties | 30 |
| III | England | 78 |
| IV | Reminiscences About Early Hollywood Personalities | 86 |
| V | The Thirties | 106 |
| VI | The Forties | 130 |
| VII | The Fifties | 166 |
| VIII | The Early Sixties | 240 |
| IX | THE POWER and After | 283 |
| X | Epilogue | 295 |
| | Title Index | 301 |
| | Subject Index | 304 |

## PREFACE

Byron Haskin belonged to that small group of filmmakers who began work before the studio system fully defined an industrial pattern for the production of motion pictures and remained active from silent film into the era of filmed television. His experience is a microcosm of Hollywood's salad days.

These pages vibrate with life, for Byron Haskin had the greatest gift to which a director can aspire: he was a storyteller. The reader will see that he was modest about even his most impressive achievements (he never bothers to mention his Academy Award or nominations) and critics are probably correct when they describe Byron Haskin as a highly gifted craftsman rather than as an _auteur_ who carried a personal vision from one project to the next. Nonetheless, this is a wonderful book because of Haskin's insight into human nature, his astonishing recollection of detail, his vivid language and his wise perspective on a career of immense and varied accomplishment.

This oral history also benefits from empathy between the subject and his interviewer. Joe Adamson had authored three books of film history, written a television special and a low-budget feature, and produced an award-winning short; however, he had never met Mr. and Mrs. Haskin when I sent him to Montecito in quest of a consent to tape. All barriers of age tumbled and as they spoke, they became close friends.

The Oral History of Byron Haskin was transcribed and edited by Adele Field. Joe Adamson continued to extend close attention at every stage, and Mr. Haskin did much of the polish work for the published version, reading and approving page proofs less than two weeks before his death on April 16, 1984. To Terry Haskin, herself a published novelist, we extend ten thousand thanks for as many good ideas and amenities.

-- David H. Shepard

Chapter One

**EARLY BACKGROUND**

ADAMSON: About your family background --

HASKIN: My family tree is pre-Revolutionary on all four basic roots. My father's name, Haskin, was English. He was a direct descendant from the first and only Haskin that came to America in the colonial days. He married a relative of George Washington's wife, from the gentry. He was a peddler.

My father's mother was a Guiberson. She was descended from the original Dutch settlers of New York in pre-Revolutionary days. My grandfather Harry Haskin homesteaded a section of land in Ventura County, to do some farming. Grandfather Harry's cows kept getting sick from drinking out of the creek, and eventually he sold it to his neighbor, and father-in-law, Guiberson. He (Haskin) had married Margaret, one of the Guiberson women. After the sale of the ranch Grandpa Haskin moved to Arroyo Grande, where he became postmaster.

Later, oil was discovered in Ventura County, on Guiberson's and (what had been) Grandpa Haskin's land. That's what made Grandpa Haskin's cows sick -- the oil seeping up into the creek! This land became the center of the great Ventura oilfields. The Guibersons developed their holdings to form the Pan-American Oil Company. What Grandpa Harry Haskin thought about this blow of fate is unrecorded.

My mother's father was Ephraim Francis Conrad, a Presbyterian minister. He was a descendant of the original Pennsylvania Dutch colony -- actually German -- pre-Revolution. He married a Mary Bryan, of Irish descent. She was a first cousin to William Jennings Bryan, also a direct descendant of Daniel Boone. So, it's a kind of bonafide American background. A cousin of mine, from a different branch of the family, Elmer Haskin, saw an old Bible at a relative's funeral, in which there was the full family tree. The only thing of note to me was that the original Haskin was not of the gentry, but that he married gentry. (Laughs) Hell, that and two bits will get you a cup of coffee nowadays, but it seemed to be of great importance in colonial times!

Grandpa Haskin had a peculiar Civil War career. He was a captain of artillery in the Union forces, assigned to guard a hill in Salt Lake City, with his guns trained on the Mormon tabernacle. If the Mormons kicked over the traces, threatening to join the Confederacy, he had orders to blow the tabernacle to pieces!

Grandma Conrad, Mary Bryan as a little girl, crossed the country in a wagon train. They were the wagon train following the Donner party. When they got to the famous lake, the Donner party was encamped there, flaked out and having a good rest for themselves as well as getting all cleaned up and washing their clothes and so forth.

The wagonmaster in charge of my grandma's train made his decision: "Well, this is not a good place to camp. I'll go over the ridge before we clean up." They pressed on over the Sierra Nevada mountains. Shortly after they passed the ridge and were going down the California side, the big snowstorm began.

The Donners were still camped at the lake and were marooned. Eventually they began to starve; eventually, they had to eat each other. Well, those are bits of my family background.

All of my people were born in California. My mother was born in Arroyo Grande, north of here (Santa Barbara). My father was born in Ventura County, near Santa Paula on the ranch that was later sold. I am the only one who wasn't born in California.

ADAMSON: Why was it you were born in Portland, Oregon?

HASKIN: My father was a schoolteacher after he left the University of California. He taught in Nipomo and Sisquoc and all those little towns around there, also Oceano Beach. Some trade paper for teachers had an advertisement for a job in Portland, Oregon.

To my father, it was an adventurous prospect; like taking a job in Afghanistan. So he sent his application. They signed him up for a year in Portland. Just long enough to get me conceived and delivered, then back.

ADAMSON: Then he went and settled in San Francisco?

HASKIN: No, we came back and lived at Lake County. That's where my sister, Rowena Catherine, was born. I say Lake County because there was no town big enough to be named. After a time, we moved down to San Francisco. Father decided to give up teaching, became an employee of the Pacific Cereal Association. Pacific Cereal had a virtual monopoly on the mush sales in the western states; their leading product, Carnation Mush, was very popular. They also sold chicken feed, and other grain products.

Father settled down as secretary and advertising manager for his company.

Later, when I grew big enough, I worked in the mill nailing boxes. I also worked in the Oakland mill, after Pacific Cereal sold to Albers Brothers Milling Company, featuring Albers' Flapjacks, popular hot cakes. So, this is the little cocoon from which I sprang to fame. (Laughs)

ADAMSON: Is your name Haskin or is it Haskins?

HASKIN: Haskin.

ADAMSON: Why is it "Haskins" on a lot of the credits?

HASKIN: Never was, on a film. It's just careless reporting. I always saw to it that the title department got the "s" off. My grandfather Harry eventually gave up the struggle. As a postmaster, every new regime that came in, the "s" went back on his name on the paycheck. Finally, after years of trying, he gave up. But the rest of the family kept up the fight.

I grew up in San Francisco, went to many different schools and finally to Lowell High School. From there to the University of California.

My first vivid memories of San Francisco are of the 1906 earthquake -- April 18, 1906, early in the morning. Four days later I was seven years old, so obviously I still have a pretty active recall of what went on. It seems like yesterday. In the aftermath I went through the confusions of starting school.

ADAMSON: What do you remember about the earthquake?

HASKIN: I don't remember the actual shock. But for the fact that my father was sucker for a book agent, I would probably have slept all the way through it. My bed was in a bay window in the front bedroom overhanging the street. There was a set of shelves alongside my bed, and I was awakened by the shower of books. Father had recently bought The Book of Knowledge in twenty-four volumes, thin and square. They all fell down on me.

Father was up at the time, in the kitchen, cooking, of all things, a big kettle of mush! Usually he got up a little after four o'clock and went to the kitchen at the back of our third floor flat, and put on this big kettle of mush. He got it free, working for the Carnation Mush Company. The rest of the family never would eat the damn stuff. He'd cook enough for an army -- there was only my mother, my sister, and myself to do away with all this gloop. We hated it. But he would always cook it and leave the kettle full for us. We'd dispose of it some way by the time he'd get home that night.

So, when the earthquake hit, he was already in the kitchen, with the mush bubbling. He tried to run along the narrow hallway to reach the bedrooms -- but he was knocked around like a pea in a shell, battered from one side to the other. While the quake lasted, he never made it. He didn't arrive in my bedroom until after the deluge of the books. The bed was still sliding around the room. My sister was in her next room screaming.

The building was three stories high; it jumped out into the street eight feet, to the edge of the sidewalk, and leaned over thirty-eight degrees. The chimney went down through the floors and made an awful clatter.

My father was not a conventional thinker. He first thought of us, of course, and got us out of the building, planting us in a vacant lot next door; then his chief concern became his duty to the mush company. The company mill was at 3rd Street and Townsend downtown at that time; our flat was out at 3rd Avenue and B Street in the Richmond District. That meant he had to cross the entire city to get to the mill. As secretary, he figured that saving the records of the company was vital in this kind of a disaster. It certainly was. Because of his foresight, Pacific Cereal was one of the few companies in San Francisco that had any continuity of records, so they could collect their bills and so forth. It was a big help in continuing business; afterwards they moved into a new mill at 450 Bay Street, on the North Beach waterfront.

His adventures, as he told us, were something. He left in pre-dawn darkness, and when he got back, it was dark at night. He had been all day getting across the city and back to us in the Richmond District. In transit, he had been impressed into laboring in the coalyards three times by the military. The city was dotted with coalyards, it being the only heating fuel at the time, and they figured they ought to shovel the coal back and forth, I guess, or whatever the hell they were trying to do with it, to prevent the fires.

While he was gone, Mother concluded that we weren't safe in the vacant lot. Besides she was curious to see the downtown city, so she got us kids into some clothes and took us all over into Golden Gate Park. We were living near the peacock pens in the park; the characteristic thing I remember from the whole period of the earthquake and fire is the screaming of the peacocks. They sounded like sirens. That was the whole aura of the damned earthquake -- these peacocks. They started screeching when it first began shaking, and kept it up for days. (Laughs)

Mother led us up the slopes of the Twin Peaks after crossing the park. In the high wild oats and barley growing in the open fields, the biggest aftershock hit. I remember that the whole sea of grass looked like a million snakes. It knocked us down, it was so severe. Of course, my sister and I cried. Mother dragged us on up to the top of Twin Peaks. We could see the whole city spread before us. There were sporadic little spires of smoke here and there. The city had not caught fire yet. Here and there, we'd see a little puff of smoke starting up in the wreck of some building. From where we were we could look down Mission Street, into the backs of the hotels, with the bricks all fallen off and beds sticking out of the rooms. Down in the front of us where the Civic Center is today, there had been a thirteen-story reinforced steel and concrete earthquake-proof building, which had been praised in the newspapers. Well, this building went up the first couple of floors straight, then the next two of three floors began to bend over, then split at the top of the structure, like a busted firecracker. It had heaved pavement blocks all over the neighborhood. It was standing on one of the epicenters of the quake -- this wonder-of-wonders they called "earthquake proof" . . .

The fires began to spread. We could see clear to the Fairmont Hotel up on the top of the hill. In between was just flat debris. The fire hadn't yet harmed the city -- the earthquake had knocked it flat. It was a city of masonry, and there it was, laid out in rubble; piles of bricks. With tiny people scattering through it, running, and trucks driving their teams of horses frantically.

Around noon we went back to our home. Mother sneaked in and got something to eat. By noon, the sky was black -- you could look right up at the sun. Up the streets, thousands of people were coming out of the city, with baby carriages loaded with goods and stuff, heading for Golden Gate Park. It went on like that for days and days, and nothing could be done by man to stop it. Van Ness Avenue just happened to be a very, very wide street, which the fire did not hop and so did not come out into the Richmond District where we were living. It burned the whole city to Van Ness Avenue.

There wasn't any water -- all the mains burst and the gas mains ruptured, feeding the fires. Right in front of my father on the way back from the mill, a gas main went up like a bomb, and blew horses and a beer truck filled with barrels all over him.

At 3rd Street and Townsend was the Southern Pacific Railway depot. It was deserted. Father sent the last telegraphic message out of San Francisco before the fire engulfed the district and burned the wires. There was a telegraph instrument, and the operator had left to parts unknown. (Laughs) The mill was right next door, and my father paused long enough to go into the depot and use the Morse code, in his fumbling way, and send out a message. My grandfather received it in Arroyo Grande.

ADAMSON: The wires burned down?

HASKIN: Shortly after, they did, and the whole city was cut off. My father got out of there with practically his coattails on fire. He had secured the company books. He also had armloads of silver spoons and forks and knives. As advertising manager he'd had a program of putting a fork or a knife or a spoon in each package of mush -- you'd keep buying the stuff, and eventually you'd get fifty spoons and one fork. I don't know how it was ever figured out. (Laughs) But we had those things for years afterwards. After the fire, we later went over to the site of the mill, and bundles of these spoons which were stacked in boxes, had all been _fused_ into one unit with the heat of the fire. They were still spoons, but they were all just burned together.

ADAMSON: One giant composite spoon!

HASKIN: (Laughing) Yes. Our street, 3rd Avenue, in the Richmond District split open about eight or nine feet. We kids used to sit on the edge of the crevice and throw pebbles down, and we couldn't hear them hit the bottom, it was so deep.

We all finally took up life out on the curbstone. It became against martial law to be in the house, to have a light. They wouldn't fool around -- the soldiers would go by, and if you had a light in the house, they'd give you about two seconds. "Put out that light!" If you didn't, they shot it out. Bang! My father, with some ingenuity, got a grocery box and put it against the window with candlelight out the back. He'd light that and then we'd creep around in there, because it rained for a couple of days after the earthquake, and we had to go inside or drown. An emergency crew of workers put a big 6 x 6 timber up against our building, as a prop, so it didn't fall over on us.

There was an amusement park called the Chutes nearby which had a sort of carnival group of animals, and they all broke out of their cages -- an elephant and monkeys, all running around the streets. It was a real wild time. Nothing whatever normal. Everything was goofy! (Laughs) The grass was wobbling, buildings were jumping out in the streets, and we had coal stoves to cook with on the curbstone. Mother was the chef. We got our water from the Masonic Cemetery, which was over near the Presidio. I used to have to go over there with buckets and bottles. I thought it showed the biggest impact of the earthquake of anything. This little cemetery was surrounded by a six-foot stone wall. Six feet high, six feet wide, and down into the ground. This thing had been yanked in the air and twirled like a piece of string by the force of the earthquake. Obviously right on the epicenter.

We were issued clothing -- nothing fit. Kids would get shoes size nine, flapping as we walked. Mother was busy sewing all the time, trying to alter the stuff.

Eventually, after life settled down, my father, who had salvaged the books of the company, got a little bonus, and bought a place over in Hayward. We moved. I began school in earnest over there.

ADAMSON: So that was some seventh birthday, I guess!

HASKIN: That was a P-Dinger, yes.

ADAMSON: Was there any problem with looting? You were living outside of the house.

HASKIN: Not in our district. I remember a very impressive thing happening the night before the earthquake. My father was a sort of orator of the old style, and at that time was a very strict man morally. . . .

I remember this as if it were this room. The night of April 17th, for dinner, we had some friends in. After the meal, my father was wont to hold forth on the iniquity of San Francisco -- what a hellhole it was. And it <u>was</u> really something, if I remember my history! My sister and I never paid much attention to him -- he was always declaiming about graft and sin. But this I remember -- he stood up at the end of the tale and said, "God will strike this city dead for its sins!" He hit the table -- BOOM -- and the Welsback gas burner in the chandelier collapsed and dropped onto the table with a crash. My sister and I yelled, and got sent off to bed. That was the last we knew until -- BALOOM! -- the world was being shaken to pieces. So I knew my father had done it, you see.

Of course, I remember distinctly, too, that the year previous to the earthquake was punctuated regularly with small earthquakes, fore-shocks. Mother kept all the cups in the cupboard on hooks, and she had sort of little sea-rails around the cupboard shelves that kept the dishes from sliding off. There was plenty of warning for the big earthquake.

It was an outstanding event in my life. I don't know what influence it had on me any more than on anybody else, but it caused me to maintain a pattern of hundred-percent recall of all the things in my life in visual terms. It stands out so vividly -- I can visualize it right in my head.

ADAMSON: You don't describe any physical pain or carnal torment.

HASKIN: No, it was the excitement and the curiosity of seeing life from a perspective I'd never seen before, you know -- weirdos out in the park and the things they were doing. Us kids were typical peepers -- looking in on things, and discovering behavior we would never have discovered had it not been for this derangement caused by the terrible catastrophe. We even learned about sex. We learned about everything up there in the park!

The overall memory is pure nightmare, that's all I can recall. It was not a normal human experience -- it was Nightmareville-plus. Everything out of control. You can't look back and analyze, because the sounds and the effects were too far-out. I tried to create in WAR OF THE WORLDS a similar feeling that there was nothing normal left to see, or hear.

I think that more or less covers the early years of my life. I became an "A" student and number one in the grammar school class throughout, without ever cracking a book. I became the consummate con-man, as a student.

ADAMSON: That's the way to do it!

HASKIN: I learned all the tricks -- that the quickest way not to have to answer a teacher's question was put your hand up first. My early primary school education was very hit-and-miss. I don't recall details of anything I learned or preferred to know as a student, because of the early gypsy existence we followed, moving constantly. I began school in Oakland, then we moved to Alameda. I went to school in Hayward, after they'd built one there. All I remember vividly about Hayward is chasing kids. They made fun of me. I was bigger than they were, and I had white hair. It was blonde, white as a sheet. The kids all picked on me, stealing my tops, and marbles, and so forth. I remember my early education mostly as a torment.

ADAMSON: Isn't that part of what comes from being the outsider all the time?

HASKIN: Yes, yes. Well, I should have started school before the earthquake, but I didn't. My father was a schoolteacher, and he thought, Well, no need to rush getting into school. I was about six months or a year late. As a result, I was bigger than the other kids. Anything that's off the norm to kids is something to torment. I never won any fights because I couldn't run fast enough to catch anybody.

When eventually we moved back to San Francisco, I entered the Ingleside School. That was an experience! The teacher had only one ear -- it had been cut off in some mysterious way we never found out. I now know that much of his eccentricity was because he drank pretty heavily. We didn't know it at the time. We just thought that he was occasionally over-jolly. He had all eight grades in the one room. There were a few kids in each grade. It was a traditional little one-room schoolhouse. From where we lived in Parkside it was a hell of a walk through the sand dunes -- it must have been three or four miles, at least. I didn't have a bike when I went there. I'd walk through the wilderness, finally getting into civilization and this little district of Ingleside with the school.

There was a civic-pride group which put on children's plays in a sort of park called the Trocadero, near Sloat Boulevard. All the neighboring kids would take part as angels and what-have-you. I participated in that, playing an elf in one of them; embarrassed because I was twice the size of the other elves.

ADAMSON: These were put on by adults and the kids would have minor parts?

HASKIN: Yes, they were put on by Helen Hokinson-type ladies of the district. Mostly pantomime things. I don't remember ever having any lines or anything, but we'd go galloping through the eucalyptus trees in the glade there, all us fairies in costume. I was too big for most of them, and it broke my heart, because I wanted to be an actor at that time. (Laughs)

ADAMSON: When did you see your first motion picture?

HASKIN: Now, my first acquaintance with live theatre was seeing Maude Adams in *Peter Pan*. My father took the whole family to see it. It opened up a life that I had never dreamed of -- it was crazier than the earthquake, because I was completely transported.

ADAMSON: When was it roughly?

HASKIN: It was sometime after the earthquake. Maude Adams was on tour. It was my first theatrical experience.

I used to attend the Pantages Vaudeville later on, the Orpheum, sometimes the opera. I saw Tetrazzini sing in Market Street, at Lotta's Fountain, and Caruso, and all the great singers of the day. San Francisco was quite a center of culture. I had no theatrical background in my whole family, that I know of. My principal interest was as a spectator at that time.

ADAMSON: San Francisco was still "Sin City?"

HASKIN: Well, yes. The two were not inimical -- the culture and the sin. It seemed that there was a lot going on behind walls up on Russian Hill, too, that wasn't according to Hoyle. But it was quite a city. Holy cats! At one time -- just where in my life, I don't recall, it's between the earthquake and high school somewhere -- when I was in grammar school -- we lived on the slopes of Russian Hill in a flat overlooking the Bay, and I could look down below and see Bartlett Alley, in North Beach, on the Barbary Coast. Bartlett Alley was the most infamous crib house street of the whole tenderloin district. I could also look out the bay window and see Alcatraz and all the steamers going in and out of the Golden Gate. It was really one of the thrills of my life to overlook this port of adventure, great ships sailing in and out. It gave me a longing -- I suppose eventually it was the foundation for my travels all around the world, making films.

ADAMSON: What exactly is a crib house?

HASKIN: Whorehouse -- the cheapest kind. Just a small room, with a bed and a chair. The whores sit in the doorway, enticing the sailors in.

ADAMSON: Was that legal at that time?

HASKIN: Yes, when I was a kid, prostitution on the Barbary Coast was legal.

ADAMSON: When did that cease to be true?

HASKIN: Later, in my teens, I remember the warfare between the city and the vice lords about closing up Barbary Coast and stopping the whores from peddling in the streets. There was always a row going on in San Francisco between the ladies of sin and the bluenoses. The general run of people in the city couldn't have cared less, but there was always a faction around that -- all us kids thought -- was a bunch of bluenosed bastards.

ADAMSON: In Philadelphia they had taken over, but not in San Francisco. This is the interesting thing about the difference between San Francisco and L.A. -- that there's a tradition and a culture up in San Francisico --

HASKIN: Ye gods! Right from the time of the Gold Rush, you know, they had the greatest operas as well as whorehouses and everything else going on -- when potatoes were fourteen dollars apiece. Talk about inflation! Brother, they saw some inflation. A cup of coffee was five dollars in the Gold Rush days. Everybody was loaded with money, and so goods went up according to the demand. That's the tradition and history of the City.

I saw my first movie on North Beach in the Barbary Coast. It was while we were living at the flat on the side of Russian Hill. My sister Rowena was attending a school on the North Beach, mostly Italian kids, some Chinese. I, even today, can remember a few of the Italian songs that she used to sing while she was a student down there. . . .

Anyhow, this little friend of mine and I wandered down to the Barbary Coast with some fear and trepidation. He knew some kids in the district. There was a gang known as "The Forty Strong" at that time, progenitor of the Mafia, I guess, and all the Forty Strong had little kid brothers. My friend was a pal of a lot of them, and we used to go down there. I knew some of the Chinese kids.

This particular day we wandered down the main street of the Barbary Coast. There were lights on a small storefront, bulbs flickering in front of it -- it was a movie, a nickelodeon.

ADAMSON: This is at night now?

HASKIN: No, no, this was in the afternoon. The nickelodeon was open for business. If either one of us had been alone, we wouldn't have had guts enough to go in, but between the two of us we mustered up courage, paid our nickel each, and went in.

ADAMSON: Were you scared because of the area?

HASKIN: Yes, it was a real rough place, not far from Bartlett Alley, where you could be killed for a dime, and where cops would only walk in pairs -- no single cop would ever enter the district. And here we were wandering around! (Laughs) We went into this nickelodeon and sat down -- I remember it distinctly -- it's another outstanding event, like the earthquake. Inside there was an aisle, between seats like a railroad coach, wicker-backed. They could be flipped back and forth, like a streetcar. At one end of the coach was the screen. At the other the projection room. As we took our seats, there was a scenic film taken from a moving train running on the screen. Like the view from an observation car.

ADAMSON: Oh, was this one of the Cook's Tours things?

HASKIN: Well, I don't know whose tour it was -- it was probably some predecessor of Burton Holmes, the great scenic man who shot every place in the world from the back of the train. It was like being on the train -- you sit down and there's the rails receding, and it's traveling through South America or some such place.

I suppose the show was about a half or three quarters of an hour, no more, but we stayed there for hours; seeing it over and over. (Laughs) Absolutely couldn't believe it. We were world travelers!

Eventually, they closed for dinner or something and threw us out. As we came out, it was dark! Well, that immediately meant trouble. Kids weren't supposed to be out after dark. Trouble at home, I mean. Big trouble.

We hurried up the hill toward home. Finally my friend split from me, and I'm all alone, going up to my residence, and I'm trying to be quiet about climbing the back steps. My father had been quietly following me, and grabbed me. "Where the hell have you been?" He gave me a whack. I told him some lies. . . .

That was the first movie I ever saw.

ADAMSON: Was that long after the earthquake?

HASKIN: Not very long. I think it was about 1908, somewhere in there.

ADAMSON: So that's well before anything really interesting. Well before Mack Sennett or Griffith or --

HASKIN: Oh, nothing of organized drama was being made at that particular time. Shortly after, shorts began to appear. I remember THE GREAT TRAIN ROBBERY and the first "big features." It was not too long after the nickelodeon episode that this all happened. The early Keystones and all those things.

ADAMSON: So, did you become a pretty regular movie fan, following this stuff?

HASKIN: Yes. I did. It built up to that. Of course, I loved vaudeville and I used to go religiously. I had the type of memory that I could go right home from a vaudeville show and recite every word that was said. (Laughs) All the bum jokes and the comments and everything else. Much to the annoyance of my folks, no doubt.

ADAMSON: I guess the main question I would have about how you got into films was -- Why did your father end up with this movie camera you told me about?

HASKIN: Well, I said originally, he was not only secretary of this cereal company, but he was advertising manager. He used to put on all kinds of campaigns. After Albers Brothers bought in, the scene expanded. We moved into quite an expensive apartment in downtown San Francisco.

ADAMSON: When he was still advertising manager?

HASKIN: Yes, he was advertising manager of Albers Brothers with aggressive campaigns of all kinds. I had studied art. I remember that I redesigned some of his ideas about billboards, and I showed some ingenuity. Previously, all billboards or signs painted on buildings had a conventional border, with the pictorial matter and the printing inside of it. He was still featuring Carnation Mush with a spray of carnations as decoration. I conceived of having the carnations sticking out through the border, as if they penetrated the frame. This broke one of the solid conventions of the advertising of the day.

He also featured ads for Albers' Flapjack Flour, and he had a symbolic figure of a miner kneeling by a fire with a frying pan, flipping a flapjack in the air, as keynote of his ad campaign. He conceived an idea of having this miner on round bulletins on a sort of easel, and distributing them along the right of way of all the railroads in the west, even up in the Sierras, and the Cascades in Oregon.

ADAMSON: Visible to passengers.

HASKIN: So that while you're gazing out the window of the train, you come around the curve and this miner floats by, with the printed legend: "Look for the miner." I, along with a friend, traveled the West, helping place many of these easels.

It was always my opinion that my father had been born many generations too late. He loved adventure. He should have lived during the time of Daniel Boone. With his usual switch-thinking, he conceived the idea of scoring a big mark in the world by making an advertising film.

ADAMSON: When was this?

HASKIN: I went into the University when I was sixteen, and it was just before that, so I was probably around fifteen, the time of the World's Fair in San Franciso. It was just after that he got very many kudos and rewards for his exhibits in the Industrial Building -- for the Albers Brothers Mush exhibits, and the mechanical miner flipping the lead flapjack. That turned his head, I guess.

Shortly after that he came up with this idea of doing an advertising film. He'd had certain film excerpts made for the exhibits in the fair, that's what started him. He made a connection with a chap named Ralph Radnor Earle who had a commercial movie lab and producing unit under a hotel on Eddy Street. He got this idea that he was going to make a film that would more or less, in his thinking, conceal the fact that it was an advertising film, expecting to peddle it commercially.

ADAMSON: It could go out as a movie?

HASKIN: Yes, whatever. He was mistaken, badly.

ADAMSON: Why didn't he just go to this guy that made them? Ralph Earle? I mean, presumably, this guy made them regularly.

HASKIN: Earle? No, he shot scenics. Of Yosemite. Period. (Laughs) You know, every spring, Ralph Earle would be the first one in after the tough winter, in his Buick with his Universal camera and his faulty lens.

Anyhow, Father made a trip to Hollywood, contacting an agency -- English and Erlanger or something like that, kind of a talent agency. He engaged a whole movie crew. After returning to San Francisco, he found out that there was a studio in San Rafael, where Beatrice Michelina had been a star in the early days.

ADAMSON: One of these things with a glass roof, or open at the top?

HASKIN: Diffusers -- sunlight studio. Anyway, he had a weirdo named Hale Ayres as director, an aged matinee idol named Jimmy Johnston as leading man, with Enid Markey, a has-been star of the day, along with a lot of character people. The film was about "Look for the miner" -- the guy with the flapjack. He was the sort of Tom Mix/Gene Autry of the whole deal. All the rest of them were sort of villains. My father elected himself to play the miner.

I don't know what the hell it was all about, but I got a job in this lab processing the film because of the pressure my old man put on them. That began my movie career. I did everything. It was a ramshackle joint, the quarters were no bigger than a small bungalow, with developing tanks, drying drums, film racks, a little printing press, cutting rooms, storage vaults, and everything. Above was a fleabag hotel whose patrons were mostly skid row types. There was no protection against fire, and we were working with the highly flammable nitrate film, too, and all smoking like chimneys -- no regulations. We could have had a nice sanguinary fire, but we never did. One day, at the cutting bench, there was a young guy named Bud Hooper, who later moved to Denver, and he's still there, R.B. Hooper, owning his own movie outfit. He was cutting film one day, and he had film barrels on each side of him, and his rewinds here, on the table above the barrels. He was the fastest splicer I ever saw in my life. ZOOM! -- he'd cut two films, lay the ends together, swish the film cement across on a brush, and wind it in! He had it hopped up; the minute the cement touched, it was joined.

      This day, he was getting a news item together for a theatre downtown, meanwhile smoking Bull Durham as he worked. The ashes dropped out of the end of his cigarette paper into his apron. He slapped the apron and the hot coals jumped into the barrel full of film, and this went WHOOSH! -- right up to the ceiling curling past all the ends hanging on the rack in front of him. It was so fast, and of course, he grabbed at the barrel to pull it out and drag it outside, but the handle of the rewind was hooked into it. I passed by about that time, got my eyebrows singed off, and managed to yank the barrel out from under the rewind. We quickly threw it out in the street. He slapped out the few ends that had caught, and so we were saved.

      Our drying drum was certainly a pip. We would photograph stuff, process it, often have it in the theatre in less than an hour. That included the shooting, taking it to the lab, developing it, drying, printing, processing the print, editing, making titles, putting it in the can and roaring downtown in the flivver, into the theatre, onto the projector, all within that time.

ADAMSON:    What was Earle's connection with the theatre?

HASKIN:    An agreement with the newsreel, for inserts of local events. He'd supply them with local headline events, cut them into the newsreel. A typical event was the San Francisco bombing of the Preparedness Day Parade. I photographed that -- people blown to bits all over Market Street. I think within forty-five minutes we had that from blood to screen.

ADAMSON:    What was it that happened?

HASKIN:    A famous case. It was a Preparedness Day Parade to alert the area for the imminent entry of the U.S. into the

First World War. Tom Mooney and other anarchists were arrested later and charged with the bombing. Downtown Market Street was loaded with spectators as the parade passed. The bomb was detonated right among the crowd.

The organizers of the parade were trying to get the U.S. to prepare -- William Randolph Hearst, particularly. Of course, the I.W.W. and all the radical elements were violently against it. So somebody put this big suitcase full of nails and bolts and dynamite against the wall and set it off. I don't remember how many were killed, but pieces of them were flying all over the street, hit by the bolts and nuts and crude shrapnel of the bomb. Well, we got word of it and raced to the scene, and photographed it, and tore back and got it in the developer. To hell with the quality -- it was no more than fairly dry when it was in the theatre! (Laughs)

But those were the beginnings of my movie career. During this time I did everything: I printed, I developed negative, I wound film on racks, then onto the drying drum. Photography no longer held any mystery for me.

ADAMSON: On editing: Did you edit negative, like they finally did on the newsreel, or did you edit after you printed it?

HASKIN: No, we edited the print. I think it was quicker. But we made out titles on white cards with black letters, using the negative in the segment.

ADAMSON: But then, the spliced print was the one you took down to the theatre.

HASKIN: That's right. It went clickety-clack through the gate.

Our drying drum was really a work of art. It was about eighteen to twenty feet long and about ten feet in diameter, with a big axle down the middle, and all these slats lengthwise. We'd start on one end and wind wet film from the racks onto the damn thing, and before it was even finished we'd light the burner. A gas jet of raw flame would blow out through the middle of it. We'd start it rolling. (Laughs).

I tell you, if that drum had even slowed down with the film half dry, it would have blown up like a bomb. This big flame in the middle of the drum of nitrocelluloid, wheeling madly around -- crazy! So hot you could hardly breathe.

ADAMSON: Well, it sounds wild enough now. What did you think at the time?

HASKIN: At the time, it was just routine -- the way it was done. I didn't know any different. Who would?

During all this excitement, my father had bought another camera. Remember, he had hired a crew in Hollywood and brought them to San Francisco to film his advertising film. A guy named Gabe Nathan was the cameraman.

ADAMSON: This wasn't a feature, then.

HASKIN: Yes, it was -- eight or nine reels -- a real grandiose concept!

ADAMSON: Was it ever finished?

HASKIN: I think so, eventually. But it certainly was never released anywhere.

Anyhow, during my labors in the laboratory sweeping the sidewalks and printing the film, and all kinds of jobs, my father bought a Universal camera. It was a box that you opened up and loaded inside.

The second units needed for the film were shot by our lab staff. Because the new camera belonged to my dad, I did much of this work. The new camera happened to have a good lens, and my stuff would stand out sharply. Particularly compared to stuff shot by Earle. The difference between Earle and me as cameramen was that he was a better one, but he had a lousy lens! (Laughs)

From the beginning, though, I will say this, I was a natural cameraman, I don't know why. Just had a good sense of composition and fundamentals. Of course, I'd studied art; matter of fact, I was still studying art. After I learned how to gauge the exposure on exteriors, all my stuff looked professional. Toward the end of shooting, I did most of the stuff for the movie. Then it went into the doldrums of editing.

During this phase, I was in high school. I soon entered the University of California. Came the war, shortly after, I joined the Navy. With the training units for the services, the academic atmosphere had become disorganized at the University. I began to think, This is a waste of time. I arranged my program so I'd have no morning classes, and very little heavy stuff -- I took mostly art or lectures I could snore through. It was a waste of time. I had entered at age sixteen, and I was a student two or three years.

I was finally assigned by the Navy to Bremerton, Washington. On the eve of departure from Berkeley I broke my arm. End of military career.

By this time my father had crews of demonstrators, young women traveling around the various cities and towns in the West, setting up exhibits of the product in the stores -- the mush, flapjacks, etc. So Harry Hagenah, who had been assistant director on the film, and I -- he was several years older -- took the job of managing these groups, which wasn't tough. We'd get rooms for them, book them into markets, department stores, and arrange transportation, look after them.

After a while, Harry said, "I'm going down to Hollywood, you want to come along?"

I had never been there. It was 1919. I said, "Why not?" I hopped in the car with him, and away we went.

I had no regrets about leaving an academic career at all. The real thrust of my study had always been art -- I was a good painter, I was potentially a top cartoonist, and I could have made a good living. I had done jobs on and off around the San Francisco newspapers. I got a background of that from the San Francisco Daily News. I felt I could make a go of it. But the glamour of Hollywood was pulling strongly. I simply opted to drop school.

In 1919, I guess it was late spring, we stopped first in Santa Barbara. Harry wanted to see some friends of his in the American Film Studio, on State Street. The studio no longer exists, but it was a big going place then. It happened that everybody he knew was in L.A. for the weekend. We went on down south.

My taking up life in Hollywood was like discovering a new world. Driving in a car, you entered San Fernando Valley over the Santa Susana Pass, which wound around through willows and laurel and wild looking brush-jungles. As we rounded one curve a sign in the midst of this wilderness read "Los Angeles City Limits"! (Laughs) We asked each other, "Where are the Indians and the bears?" Five minutes later we broke out in the clear. My first glimpse of Utopia was this huge valley stretched out like a fairyland. Even before that, the scent of orange blossoms had given warning of the miracle.

ADAMSON: There were more orange trees in the L.A. area than outside?

HASKIN: Oh, yes. The scent loaded the air.

So we broke out of the weeds and bushes into the clear, between big rocks surrounding us 1,000 feet high -- into the valley. It was no ordinary valley, it was covered end to end with little pennants flying.

Why should the valley be covered with little flags? Well, they were having one of the earliest of the L.A. real estate booms! All over the valley were the little pennants, and here and there a tiny real estate office.

San Fernando Valley was a network of ancient Indian dry creeks. No flat land, except where the highway went through. It was these meandering dry creeks which, come winter, got very wet!

That didn't deter the real estate guys. To create lots they filled the creek beds in with a roadscraper, pounded the ground, put a flag up, and sold them. Of course, when the first rain came -- BOOM! The owner's house floated into Long Beach! (Laughs) Down the L.A. River.

Anyhow, we saw this wonder of wonders, the San Fernando Valley, from up above Chatsworth. Driving into Chatsworth, we could see a huge Sugar Loaf boulder with some strange activity going on -- tiny figures up on top of it, running around, flashing lights -- reflectors, etc. Harry knew what it was. He said, "A movie company."

At the foot of the boulder, trucks were parked. He inquired, found out it was Douglas Fairbanks, Sr., shooting THE MAN FROM PAINTED POST. The San Fernando Valley at that time was serving as a background for the Far West. (Laughs) Now it's got a million buildings in it!

So, we drove on, down the old Cahuenga pass to Hollywood Boulevard.

Big red streetcars ran down the middle of the street. It was all one-story buildings, except the Hollywood Hotel, which was three or four. Out past La Brea, the streetcar turned out through Gardner Junction toward the beach. It seemed to be the end of civilization -- nothing beyond there, except mustard fields.

There were two restaurants on the boulevard: John's Cafe, a Greek place, and across the street, Frank's -- later to become Musso & Frank.

ADAMSON: They keep saying, "Since 1919 -- Musso & Frank." In 1919 it was just Frank's?

HASKIN: Yes. It was Frank's, when I first got there. And at the corner of Hollywood and Cahuenga was a big drugstore, I've forgotten the name.

On going out to location in the valley, companies would stop there to buy sticks of Stein's makeup for the stars. The prop man would run in and get some for Mary Pickford, who'd put her own makeup on. It was before all the luxuries of big departments and unit makeup men. Many crafts of present-day filmmaking grew up out of nothing but these barnacle beginnings. Grips? Never heard of them then. The onstage floor crew of a movie company in those days was about nine guys -- a few electricians and general laborers. There was no still man, no grips, no makeup, nor all the wardrobe people. Actors took care of themselves, in those days, even the big stars in the features.

ADAMSON: Much more of an independent set-up.

HASKIN: I stayed at the hotel down on Pico Street with Harry for probably six months and finally I got a job and went to work. It wasn't that I couldn't get a job right away. I didn't want to -- I wanted to see what the place was all about. I went to my first Hollywood party. In San Francisco, all us young guys used to think of Hollywood as a cesspool of vice, with dope on every street corner.

ADAMSON: Even in San Francisco?

HASKIN: Yes, we thought that's what Hollywood was. And bejesus, the first party I went to, at the bungalow of a minor Western star of the day in silent films -- everybody was loaded on grappa and raisin brandy. It was during Prohibition. I wandered out into the dining room, where the light was off. There was a bowl on the table full of little papers. Cocaine! All of my worst anticipations were brought to life on my first party.

I was a gate crasher with a guy named Jack McDermott, and Harry Hagenah. During the evening, a well-known star of the day came in, Wally Reid, with his gang. He was in the advanced stages of morphine addiction at the time. He died not too long afterwards. Oh, he had been a big star at Paramount -- was at that time.

ADAMSON: He died in '21?

HASKIN: Yes. This was '19. He was pretty well along with his dope.

ADAMSON: Do you still think that it was more decadent or more sinful in L.A. than in San Francisco at the time?

HASKIN: No, not at all. San Francisco had good commercial vice -- there was no fooling around about it. In Hollywood, it was amateur stuff.

The movie business had not yet gone behind walls. It was out in the open. If you wanted to see a star drunk, go down to the old Alexandria Hotel. Before that, there had been the Rosalind Hotel, but it had gone out of fashion.

The Alexandria was the new Peacock Alley where you'd have all the fun and get loaded. You'd take your own booze in a flask. I carried one down to my knee in my back pocket!

During the first few years, they were trying to enforce Prohibition, and it was _real_ rotgut you drank, the weirdest kind. Ed Pinaud's Lilac Vetal was a favorite . . . pure grain alcohol with some flavors in it that tasted pretty good. They had drinks with physic in them, and God knows what. At the time, they hadn't poisoned the stuff yet, but of course the dear old prohibs introduced wood alcohol, and practically killed everybody! (Laughs)

As to vice, it was a loose society, a society that was an illusory fairytale life, and there were few strictures. Lee Francis, a famous madam, ran the most popular whorehouse. We all went to nightclubs -- a whole circuit of them, Jahnke's Tavern, Club Royale, Tait's-at-the-Beach, Nat Goodwin's, the old

Cotton Club, etc. Driving from one to the other, drunk, and not knowing where the hell you would end up. There was no traffic much at night, and you might land in the ditch or back at home. Who knew? Or cared?

I took ZaSu Pitts to her first nightclub. She was a young chick around town, and we went out to Club Royale. Colleen Moore used to go around with us, too. She hadn't really scored in movies yet, not until the flapper era later. She was cast mostly as a sensitive young flower. Who the hell knew the truth of the matter? (Laughs) We accepted people as they were -- there was no front -- none of the chi-chi or crap that is now going on.

The evening would begin generally in the ballroom of the Alexandria with two reprobates falling down the main staircase: Buster Keaton and Lew Cody, both acrobats. They'd do 108's down this stairway -- KA-RA-LA-BOOM! -- into the middle of the dance floor. You knew the evening had begun! The dance floor was so solidly packed every night that you could lift your feet and still stay up. Jammed with people -- Mae Murray and Prince Mdivani -- all the movie characters. I met Jack Warner one night and said I wanted a job from him. Next morning I started a twenty-year tour with him. But, they were all out in public, not at house parties behind walls, with guards and parking attendants, and all the coke and hash and heroin that goes on today. It was an uninhibited society, to say the least.

ADAMSON: The hierarchy hadn't really stratified.

HASKIN: No, there was no onus attached to being a rounder, you see. It wasn't until later, when Wall Street moved into Hollywood, where budgets began to be -- what the hell was a budget? Nobody knew what a budget was, you know. A guy like Marshall Neilan, who was a famous director of the day, didn't pay any attention to what things cost. His imagination was his limit; he had accountants who got money for him, and it didn't take too much money, either.

He had his own studio. I worked with him as an assistant cameraman. We went up to the Sierras for ten days' work. He got a yen for somebody back in the city, so we worked seventy-two straight hours, and went home. With the whole thing finished. He kept a blimp at his studio, and one day disappeared in it for a week, off on a tear somewhere. He was a big director-producer of the day.

Tired of fooling around, I worked first at some studio out on Figueroa, where the old ballpark was. I've never heard of anybody who ever worked there, but I played an extra, the first job I ever had. They slapped a bed sheet on me, threw Bole Armenia all over me and placed me behind a camel. I knew enough about cameras to know that the camel was blocking me out of the shot! So I just sat there and collected the money, five dollars a day, in costume!

Finally, I thought, hell, I better go to work. I borrowed somebody's Ford roadster and went to the old Brunton Studios on Melrose Avenue, a half mile west of Western Avenue. It is now Paramount. It wasn't set back -- they sold the front on Melrose later.

I walked right into the studio; nobody cared. I went into an office and the secretary said, "Yes. What can I do for you?" There was a guy standing there.

I said, "Well, I'm looking for a job as an assistant cameraman. I know about cameras."

She said, "Well, this is Lyman Broening, our cameraman. We're starting a picture. Talk to him."

I talked to Lyman about fifteen minutes, we liked each other. He could tell that I knew photography, at least a bit -- I was an amateur, of course, as far as Hollywood movies went.

He said, "All right, you're in. You'll get twenty-five dollars a week." I never looked back from there on. I was an assistant for about eight months on the first stretch. After another three or four months, I ended up with a three-year contract as first cameraman. (Laughs) And you know the obstacles today -- the unions and various knickknacks!

ADAMSON: I know you couldn't do it today!

HASKIN: It's absolutely ludicrous.

ADAMSON: I didn't know you started shooting that soon.

HASKIN: Just about a year. Believe me, what I didn't know would fill a book.

Chapter Two

**THE TWENTIES**

HASKIN: During the short period that I was assistant cameraman, I worked with many picturesque people. Raoul Walsh was one, on a picture called KINDRED OF THE DUST, a Peter B. Kyne story. We made it in the redwood country, in Mendocino County. The art director was from New York, doing his first job in movies. He'd been an advertising sketch artist, named Bill Menzies -- William Cameron Menzies.

Raoul was producer-director, and Jack O'Brien, who had directed Mary Pickford, was second unit director. Some famous prizefighters were handymen around the set. Who the hell the actors were, I don't remember.

Walsh was married to Miriam Cooper. His company starred her at Brunton Studio. He was an independent. George Loane Tucker, whose company starred Betty Compson, was also at Brunton Studio. Sidney Franklin starred Conrad Nagel, Naomi Childers, and such celebrities of the day.

On a particular film I was assistant cameraman for Sid Franklin. They kept watching me running around the set with film cases for a week or so. Later I found out Sid had been considering casting me as the juvenile in the show. They had a kid in there about my age already cast in the role, but he was lousy! They were debating throwing him out and putting me in the part. Which would have changed my whole life, I'm sure. Probably, I'd have been dead long years since. I came close enough to it without being an actor.


ADAMSON: You were a very good-looking guy -- I found a picture of you in my digging around.

HASKIN: Yes, I have one hanging in my wife's bathroom when I was at Brunton Studios -- in a Foreman and Clark suit! (laughs)

Let's see, Allan Dwan also had his company at the Brunton Studios. There was Lewis J. Selznick, father of the whole Selznick tribe, David and Myron and the others. I went to work for him, my first real job, as assistant to Lyman Broening. Tom Moore and Matt Moore, big stars, Kathleen Perry, Eugene O'Brien. A fellow named Robert Ellis was directing the first film I ever worked on. It was his first directorial job. He had been a screen writer.

Afterwards, I went with Lyman to work with Marshall Neilan, who had his own studio, where the General Service Studio is, on Santa Monica Boulevard near Seward. That was Marshall Neilan's studio first. I could set up the camera outside the stage door, look off and see only mustard fields between there and the beach except for a startling phenomenon: palm trees that would go wafting across the landscape every once in a while -- full grown palm trees! The Howard Nursery was down there somewhere at the end of Fairfax Avenue. The street cut across, hidden by the high mustard in between. You'd never even see the trucks, just those trees floating across the scenery every once in a while!

ADAMSON: Could you see the ocean from there?

HASKIN: No, it was beyond the hills. There was only an occasional house here and there -- and the highway winding all around, just like it does today--Sunset Boulevard.

ADAMSON: What about Santa Monica Boulevard and Wilshire -- did they go down to the ocean?

HASKIN: I believe, yes. They all went through. I remember the beaches quite well. The best beach of them all was Ocean Park -- that's where we all swam every Sunday. It was the only one that had good waves that you could body surf.

I worked for the Rockett Brothers, Al and Ray, down in Selig's Zoo Studios. Louis B. Mayer had a company there; Marshall Neilan was working for L.B. when they had their famous fist fight. Neilan, who was about to direct a film for Mayer, would drive into the studio. Mayer'd come with his, "Ah-ha, there you are!" Neilan would drive out, disappear for another couple of days! Eventually Mayer trapped him, and the fight was on.

ADAMSON: Mayer had a habit of doing that, didn't he? He also knocked Chaplin down in a very famous incident.

HASKIN: Yes, he was a tough guy. Chaplin was working at his own studio on La Brea. Rollie Totheroh was his cameraman. A more mediocre cameraman never lived.

ADAMSON: Why do you say that?

HASKIN: Well, he just had little sense of art.

ADAMSON: It looked that way even at the time -- in 1919?

HASKIN: Yes, it did. But Charlie liked him, so I guess it was the way he wanted it. There were some great artists among the cameramen then. Charles Rosher, Karl Struss and -- oh hell, a whole flock of them were not only artistic but very innovative.

Early in my career, the movie business was the most innovative industry in the world. As a cameraman, there were no limitations. You were on your own. Inventing a means for doing the shots as the need arose. There were few rules. Of course, one maintained consistency, but the effects were your own. You did as you felt, that's all. Even when I was top cameraman at Warner Bros., photographing Barrymore, I never followed any set style. I never copied anybody else. It was a highly satisfactory craft. In fact, I prefer the camera as a profession. A fulfilling occupation.

ADAMSON: To directing?

HASKIN: Yes. By far. The business of directing films, particularly today, but even in the early days, was so hamstrung by barnacle intelligence -- or lack of it --that one had to fight to the death to achieve any autonomy. If you weren't born a hardnosed bastard, I mean <u>bastard</u>, you'd have very little chance to rise above the crowd as a director. That doesn't mean there haven't been a lot of weak-kneed saints who succeeded, but they had to do it another way: they conned people, or wheedled or had a girlfriend who shacked up with the owner. It's a real rough go. I never made the money directing that I made on camera.

ADAMSON: Why was that? Was that just because you could do more pictures a year as a cameraman?

HASKIN: Yes, and I also made a very good fee on the camera. The problem was, of course, that you were a social leper as a cameraman in the hierarchy of the town. If you were a married man with wife and family, eventually they'd get you to change. (Laughs) Leon Shamroy, who was my assistant for a long time, was one of the few who stuck it out. He remained a cameraman. Leon got his fee up to $25,000 or more -- on CLEOPATRA.

ADAMSON: Per picture?

HASKIN: Yes. He got good money. By osmosis it broke down the social barricades against cameramen, you know, as third class citizens.

ADAMSON: Was it harder to raise a family as a cameraman? Your children couldn't get into good schools or -- ?

HASKIN: No, no. It wasn't that. It was the pressure. Your wife would say, "It's beneath you to be on the camera."

ADAMSON: Could you give me a thumbnail portrait of some of the people that you knew and worked with -- McDermott, Raoul Walsh, the major figures. What were your impressions of them?

HASKIN: Well, Raoul Walsh, in those days was a free soul. Miriam Cooper, his wife, was all for trying to tie him down. But he fought to remain a free spirit. There was a row every minute. She'd throw things at him on the set, and he'd disappear and be gone for a day or two.

I remember at the boxing matches at Vernon, she'd come in and yell, "Raoul, you son of a bitch, where are you? I know you're here!" He'd be leaving at the far end, while she was at the other end. (Laughs) Pretty wild!

I remember Walsh used to have half of the fighters from the ring in Vernon on the payroll for some damn reason; as well as a couple of jockeys. What they did, nobody knows. Mostly they'd wander around the darkrooms, prop rooms and other places. They'd get up and lift something if you wanted them to. I remember receiving a warning from Raoul. I was a real go-getter, wanted things done quick. A couple of these jerks were assigned to the camera crew, when I was first camera assistant. I tried to roust them into action, got a little goaty with them. Raoul pulled me aside, said "Hey kid. Watch it. These guys will take you all apart." Most of them were little Mexicans, whose next fight probably would be for the championship.

I listened to many of Raoul's stories, too. He'd had a tremendously colorful life. He was a wonderful guy personally, he was not over-impressed with himself. He had a flair for the kind of adventure films he liked to do, but occasionally he made a bomb. God, he did some of the worst flops ever made! For high budgets too.

He loved action with stuntmen. Give him a ship, with mast falling -- guys jumping over the side, the fight going on, the deck collapsing, and all that kind of stuff, which is precision staging -- it goes to a beat. Well, Raoul would stand alongside the camera and yell, "Roll! Action!" And from then on, "Keep going, keep going!" No matter that everything collapsed and stopped. He'd still imagine it was going on! Screaming, "Come on you bastards. You bunch of -- !" Nothing against Raoul, but he kind of got overwhelmed with the excitement.

I began work as a cameraman for a director-producer worse than Raoul ever thought of being -- Alan Holubar. He started as an actor at Universal Studios, where he'd eventually directed a couple of things during the First World War. When I joined him, he had his own company, allied with First National. The first film he made when I was with him was the most awful bomb ever made in Hollywood, a thing called MAN-WOMAN-MARRIAGE. It was shot concurrently with FOUR HORSEMEN OF THE APOCALYPSE, made by the Metro Company. It cost the same amount of money, used the same amount of people, took as much effort, or more, and hardly ran to the ushers. THE FOUR HORSEMEN was a classic. So how can you tell?

He picked his location in Chatsworth where we camped for six weeks. We housed 450 women, and 450 cowboys, along with the necessary wranglers. God knows -- thousands of people it seemed. Trucks filled the San Fernando Valley on the way up there. We slept and stayed up there. It was planned so carelessly that our drinking water was right out of a fresh cement tank. We had dysentery in no time. Everybody was running to the can all the time we were up there! (Laughs)

We staged the battle of the Amazons on what is now the L.A. reservoir. We had a castle built up among the rocks. It was supposed to be the Amazons' castle.

I'll never forget the big moment of the Amazon forces leaving the castle. They opened the gates and the cavalry came roaring out of the courtyard into open country to ride to the battle -- 450 women, mostly Mexicans, some pregnant -- aboard these spooky horses bareback.

The cameras were high on platforms with many decks. I was on the highest deck with Holubar, cranking my camera by hand. He was so excitable that when the moment came for him to give "Camera!" -- he went crazy -- "EEEEEEEEHHHHHHHHHH!" -- and began shooting off his signal pistol. Three times he walked right out into the air, ninety feet above the ground. I had to grab the seat of his pants and pull him back. All the while with the other hand still cranking. The horses dashed out of the big gates, and spread like a fan, bucking everybody off all over the countryside. (Laughs) Women rolling in the ditches, pregnant or not, knocked everyway -- Jesus! The craziest scene I ever saw.

Later, in the battle of the Amazons, I don't think we got five good shots out of it, because of the cowboys on the sidelines. If their girlfriend began getting the worst of things, they'd ride in, in full Western regalia, and rescue their lover. Crazy!

Holubar was one of many D.W. Griffith imitators of the day. He wore the same big kind of Panama hat, smoked a cigar, and sat in a chair slouched down, and looked like Griffith a great deal -- even had the long aquiline nose. The only thing he didn't have was Griffith's talent.

Anyway, the cast of the film, besides Dorothy Phillips, included James Kirkwood, and -- Oh God, everybody in town I guess. The cast was as big as THE FOUR HORSEMEN. The production was along the INTOLERANCE/"little-hand-that-rocks-the-cradle," style, but offered little else.

ADAMSON: Including disaster.

HASKIN: Yes. The disaster was the picture.

ADAMSON: Well, Griffith had kind of set the style at that time, right?

HASKIN: Yes, Holubar was emotionally arrested at the point of being D.W. Griffith, never developed a style of his own. When this picture was finally released, they spent a lot on advertising, but it just didn't take -- it was silly. He suffered disgrace for over a year. That's when I went back to assisting. I had been signed by Holubar as first cameraman for a period of three years. Now my director had no films to make. Finally he got a bankroll together again, and he went right back to the solid stuff -- melodrama. He made a picture called HURRICANE'S GAL, starring Dorothy Phillips once more.

ADAMSON: HURRICANE'S GAL in 1922?

HASKIN: Yes. Robert Ellis played the lead. Same guy who'd directed the first picture I was on, now turned to acting. Wallace Beery was in it. I don't remember who else.

ADAMSON: I have here that it was photographed by you and William McGann.

HASKIN: I made the American negative and Bill shot the foreign negative.

The action of the story called for the services of the United States Navy -- a destroyer down off San Diego, coming alongside the lugger, the sailors all jumping aboard, grabbing the villains.

Typical of Holubar, and his excitement as the shooting began: We'd given the skipper of the destroyer orders to have all four stacks puffing out black smoke. The ship circled four or five miles away, then came on course to make a run at us at flankspeed head on, and come alongside. Then the sailors would jump down aboard.

Well, both cameras were set together, McGann next to Holubar inboard, me on the outside with McGann in between.

As the distant destroyer was maneuvering for the run, I'm thinking about things in general. I hear a big yell. It's Holubar. "Camera!"

I checked. The goddamn destroyer has just come about four miles away, and is beginning to put out smoke. It looks like a pinpoint, utterly of no use to us.

I said, "Hey, what for?" Well, Holubar went nuts. He grabbed McGann, forcing him to start cranking his camera. (Laughs)

I refused to roll. He tried to get past McGann, shooting off a pistol, going crazy. That signaled the foreground action down on deck to start. I yelled to the assistant director, Harry Bucquet, "For chrissakes, hold that action till the ship gets close enough!"

The bit players were firing, and you couldn't even see the target. Finally, Holubar got past McGann, forced me to begin cranking. The camera held only 400 feet of film. As the destroyer loomed bigger, I stopped and reloaded. I thought Holubar was going to shoot me.

By the time the destroyer was looming big, coming like hell, I was cranking again. It maneuvered smoothly alongside. I got the avalanche of the sailors jumping aboard. McGann ran out of film at that crucial point while the boys were in midair! (Laughs) Oh Jesus!

ADAMSON: What followed that?

HASKIN: Next was BROKEN CHAINS, at the Goldwyn Studio in Culver City. It is now MGM. At that time Mayer was still at Selig's Zoo and Metro was another major studio on Cahuenga under Joe Engel.

ADAMSON: What was Selig's Zoo?

HASKIN: Principally, a big zoo. Downtown, near the end of Sunset Boulevard. Somewhere near Chavez Ravine.

ADAMSON: Combination of a zoo and a motion picture studio?

HASKIN: Yes. In that order! (Laughs) Anyhow, we made BROKEN CHAINS at Goldwyn Studio in Culver City, with Holubar directing. It was a dog if there ever was one. The "story" has to be in quotes. I never did know what the hell it was about, even when we were making it. (Laughs) We did it in the Sierras near Huntington Lake. I remember, we had to ride horses to the location.

In the cast were Ernest Torrence and Colleen Moore. I don't remember the others. Torrence, an ugly guy, was playing a villain. He was famous for playing the heavy in TOL'ABLE DAVID, with Richard Barthelmess.

I remember that I had a horse who didn't like me. It would never get out of a trot. At night, when we'd finally ride up from the location to the railroad tracks, there was about three miles more to get to the lodge. Every night, I'd be mounted on this nag, clumping along, shaking my insides out at the trot, arriving a half hour after the others. One night, I recall a streak of cruelty I hadn't suspected. This horse, jogging slowly along, turned its head and looked at me leering. I kicked him right in the face. (Laughs) Which surprised him so that he broke into a canter. I quickly caught up to the others!

Max Fabian was with me on that film, shooting the foreign version. Later, he became a famous photographer for MGM.

ADAMSON: You said Metro was on Cahuenga in Hollywood?

HASKIN: Yes, The Metro Company. Later, I went there with Holubar for another film. While waiting, I had the experience of working with Rex Ingram as extra cameraman.

While preparing some script, Holubar read a newspaper one morning informing him that the Navy was going to sink an obsolete battleship, the Iowa, off Panama in a Navy exercise. The Iowa had been a unit of the Great White Fleet that Teddy Roosevelt had sent around the world, after the Spanish-American War.

I saw this fleet in San Francisco as a child with my mother and father and baby sister Rowena. On a Sunday, Father bought tickets on one of the shore boats to tour the fleet at anchor in San Francisco Bay. I don't recall seeing the Iowa at that time, but I do recall the Oregon which had made the famous historic trip all the way from the Pacific Ocean, to get to Cuba in time to help blow the Spanish Fleet out of the water when it sailed from the Harbor. (Laughs) One of the fantastic tales of the U.S. Navy.

Well, anyhow, this old battleship Iowa was to be maneuvered under radio control off Panama. The whole combined Atlantic and Pacific Fleets were to form a lane of columns on each side of the area, steaming along with the old battleship zigzagging in between.

I was to be aboard the flagship, USS California. Hull down over the horizon at 18,000 yards would be the battleship Mississippi. She would steam at right angles to the course, firing turret salvos down into the lane of battleships at the Iowa.

While cruising through the Caribbean aboard a United Fruit vessel on the way to Panama, we ran into a hurricane. Well, this was quite an experience. It caused us to be a day late. When my ship docked in Panama, the Panamanian customs authorities impounded my cameras, mistaking them for machine guns. Next morning, to free my equipment, I boarded the USS California to clear the situation. Immediately, the battlewagon sailed with me aboard, hands in my pockets and no equipment. (Laughs)

ADAMSON: Watching the Iowa get sunk?

HASKIN: Yes. It was a beautiful sight. (Laughs) Lovely.

Ashore again that night, I bought a copy shot of the sinking from a newsreel guy for $450, so I didn't miss the assignment altogether.

Then I sailed to San Pedro on the USS California for eighteen days. We'd had a little rough weather, and the heavy ship pitched not only during the storm, but for days after; with the sea as calm as a lake. (Laughs) It was a terrible ship. That was just one of my small assignments. If you just hung around a studio doing nothing, you'd be liable to get one of those assignments any time.

ADAMSON: And they might take a shot like that and build a story around it?

HASKIN: Oh, yes. Holubar had no story in mind when he sent me. I remember especially that if I'd had a camera that day, I could have got some fantastic shots of the fleet steaming along in a line of ships as if under fire.

It was a much less complicated world in those days. To get the use of the United States Navy, one would send a postcard to some guy in the service, and he'd send you a reply and you went aboard. They'd feed you, and wash your clothes, and everything else.

There was a mob of guys, reporters, feature writers and so forth, living with the fleet like a flock of locusts. Some of them had been with the fleet out to New Zealand, others to the Middle East. They had it made. Even their laundry was done weekly. Geez, it was something. Some of them even lived in the Admiral's quarters....

What brought memories of this back was that eventually, Mayer and the Metro Company joined Goldwyn to form Metro Goldwyn Mayer Studios.

While I was at Goldwyn making BROKEN CHAINS, it was a prestigious kind of group, but they didn't make many pictures. There was a certain amount of snobbishness as well.

I remember a guy named Louis Physioc, who ran the Goldwyn Studio film laboratory before the merger. I was shooting Colleen Moore. He hauled me on the carpet one day because I shot flat-light close-ups of Colleen Moore. Holubar insisted on it. That's what he wanted: the spotlight right over the top of the magazine.

So Physioc took me to his office, showed me a series of still pictures, 8 x 10's he had personally lit and photographed, of statues. He'd lit a broad light on one side, as crosslight. They had definition, I'll admit. Looked great on a statue, but hardly commercial with live actors. As head laboratory and camera man also, Physioc maintained a group of apprentices. There were no unions at that time to prevent such practice. He would light their sets for them, and turn them loose for a while. He'd show up every hour to check progress. If they got into trouble, they sent for him. He more or less had the whole thing in his hand; a group of five or six incipient cameramen. Who they were, I don't remember. Later, they became the famous MGM photographic corps. Ace cinematographers, but at that time, just stooges for Physioc. (Laughs)

ADAMSON: Did he take credit on the pictures?

HASKIN: Oh yes. Big credit -- "Louis Physioc." And the unit man would have some minor credit.

He viewed me as an interloper. He was a vengeful sort of a bastard, too, and my style was dictated by the director I was working for, and to whom I was on contract. I was not about to violate what he wanted in favor of Physioc's exercise in statue photography. So Physioc stirred up the Production Department. Additionally, he hopped his negative developer bath a little bit. My close-ups of Colleen got whiter and whiter. She had a funny little round face anyhow, with big eyes, and it looked like somebody had frightened her on Halloween.

I had my own laboratory guy from previous films. The finest laboratory man in the history of film: Roy Davidge. He ran his own laboratory -- an independent. He was greater than Joe Aller really, and entirely foolproof. If you had nothing on the film, he would try to get something on it. He had a bath that he could leave it in for an hour without fogging it over. Or, if you had forgotten to stop down, he would yank it out early to save it.

So to counteract Physioc's conspiracy, I almost torpedoed him. I shot two takes of each close-up of Colleen. At the end of the day, one roll went to Physioc, and one I smuggled out to Davidge.

Next day, I slipped the Davidge print to the projectionist, and said, "Put this on with the regular dailies." Jesus Christ! Davidge had done himself proud. Colleen's face was smooth like liquid gold, beautiful flesh. Flat lighting takes a special kind of lab treatment anyway. Davidge was a master.

When Physioc's roll popped on, the snowbank again! The production manager, Joe Cohn, and some of the people who became big wheels later when it was MGM were there.

Seeing Physioc's dailies first, they complained, "Oh, God. Well, we better make a change." Then Davidge's roll came on. They jumped up. "Hey, what's this? What's this? Where'd this come from?"

I said, "That, my friends, is two takes of the same scenes. Each done by a different laboratory. One, your own laboratory; the other from Roy Davidge."

Physioc managed to weather that one somehow, but just barely. (Laughs)

ADAMSON: Great.

HASKIN: I completed the picture, much to the chagrin of Mr. Physioc.

ADAMSON: In terms of what we were discussing earlier, didn't you mention that the movies at that time were oriented toward the director -- the star director who had his company?

HASKIN: Oh yes. It was a time prior to the rot setting in: the Wall Street invasion, with its economy wave, its henchmen. There were no producers, per se. The big wheels were the great directors of the day -- Ince, Griffith, combining work of the producer with that of the director. Raoul Walsh learned from Griffith as an assistant director.

I learned about this whole routine from a friend, Duncan Mansfield. He had been editor for Tom Ince, and later for Harold Lloyd.

The pictures were made by the director. Ince would get C. Gardner Sullivan, writer, and tell him a story line he had in mind. C. Gardner would write the screenplay. Ince would study it, trim it to his taste, prepare it, and then shoot it himself.

He became rich, as they all did. They began to hate the slogging work, so they chose go-fors as delegates of minor authority. This function and that function, particularly the accounting, they would slough off. How they got money together anyway, I have no idea. Probably just went to a bank and said, "I'm making a movie." The banker opened the vault, I guess. There were no money problems. No big outfits from New York controlled financing. I remember when this changed. A studio named FBO was the first to come under the baleful spell, under a head accountant named H. O. Davis.

Previous to that, these fat cat director-producers like Mickey Neilan usually had their own studios. Neilan made his pictures the way he wanted. I remember we'd sit around for weeks, and no Neilan. We're in the middle of a picture, he's somewhere on a tear. Nobody to hold him to account. Occasionally, there'd be rumbles from the bank. We'd hear about it vaguely and we'd laugh. Neilan made his own schedules, his own pictures. They had a dashing sort of melodrama to them. They were distinctive and made money.

ADAMSON: When you say you would all be there, you mean on salary? Getting your paychecks every week?

HASKIN: Yes, indeed.

ADAMSON: Was it California money?

HASKIN: Well, it was money from the bank. Security Savings -- I don't think Bank of America even had gotten in. Motley Flint for years was head of Security Savings Bank, and he operated as a funding source for films. They had a qualifying board, and this, that, and the other, but the exact method of financing films, I don't know. In those days, before the blight of Wall Street set in, I do not think there was any firmly established budget of what a film was going to cost. It was a speculative venture and the bank would be venturing capital on the reputation of the particular director. There was a very lucrative field of releasing, it wasn't all the gamble one might think.

ADAMSON: Wasn't it fairly certain that if you had a picture, it would at least bring in money, even if it wasn't a phenomenal success?

HASKIN: Yes. The big releasing corporations such as First National -- others existed -- came later.

When the first economy wave came along, we asked each other, What the hell is this? It was so contrary to the ordinary way of operating a studio at that time.

ADAMSON: Was this sometime in the twenties?

HASKIN: Yes. . . . After BROKEN CHAINS I shot a film for Colin Campbell, director.

ADAMSON: Oh, that was THE WORLD'S A STAGE.

HASKIN: I don't remember anything about it. I guess it was with Dorothy Phillips.

ADAMSON: Yes. Colin Campbell directed and Dal Clawson did the foreign negative. A company called Principal Pictures produced it.

HASKIN: Yes. We shot a lot of it on location in Santa Barbara I remember. That's about all I do remember, that we used the Samarkand Hotel.

ADAMSON: Is it still here?

HASKIN: Yes. Shortly after that, one night dancing at the Alexandria Hotel, I talked Jack Warner into giving me a job and I began my twenty-year hitch at Warner Bros.

ADAMSON: I couldn't find any credits for you for 1924, after SLANDER THE WOMAN.

HASKIN: What was SLANDER THE WOMAN?

ADAMSON: Something you did with Holubar that First National released in '23. That was the only credit I could find for '23.

HASKIN: We probably made it as THE WHITE FRONTIER, if that's the one. The last time I worked with Holubar was on the picture he died on. It was never completed. We were at the old Metro Company, over on Cahuenga. It was a story called THE BISHOP OF COTTONTOWN, laid during the Civil War. We went down to the historic location in Tennessee for pre-production scenes. We had carloads of uniforms with powder-men and equipment to stage the Battle of Franklin, Tennessee.

ADAMSON: What was the Battle of Franklin?

HASKIN: Historically, one of the turning points of the Civil War. The South was beaten back in this battle -- they lost the Battle of Franklin.

It was fought in open countryside, a sanguinary battle -- thousands of people killed. Well, that was to be the crux of our story. We had brought boxcars of guns and uniforms, ammunition, and all kinds of equipment. We picked a location very close to the actual site of the battle. A little town had grown up around the actual site. There, we worked at preparing the fields for the battle, about six weeks.

In scope, from the point of the camera to the horizon on the hill, was about two miles. I used a 40mm wide angle lens, that took in a lot of territory. We planted it all with powder shots connected to a master switchboard alongside a camera. Carl Hernandez was the chief powdermonkey, borrowed from Goldwyn. He brought from Hollywood six assistants, and hired twenty-five crackers from Nashville who were to do the digging for the explosives. Additionally, mortars lined the sidelines. Firing these into the air would simulate shrapnel effects. Literally, thousands of explosions were installed, marked with branches and small red flags to warn the troops to avoid them.

Finally, it was all set up beautifully. We staged the dry rehearsal; no firing. The powder board proved quite efficient.

Meanwhile, the assistant directors under Harry Bucquet had been drumming the countryside for troops. They hired some 1500 crackers from the hills of Tennessee, most of whom had never seen a paved road in their lives. Fugitives from Dogpatch. (Laughs) These characters were the weirdest bunch of alleged humans I ever saw in my life.

At dawn, they met near the battlefield, marched to the location, singing along the way. With the first sound of the approach in the distance, every black man in our whole crew left suddenly over the hill. That ended any further preparation. The ragged mob came in. Most of them didn't even wear shoes. These guys -- straight out of Hee-Haw!

ADAMSON: This was in Tennessee?

HASKIN: Yes. Real hillbillies -- moonshiners and tough. We had invited thirteen actual veterans of the Battle of Franklin, and had built a little grandstand for them, to watch the shooting. There were six first aid tents near the battlefield, with doctors from Nashville.

At last, we got our troops in uniform, placed 300 of them in Union uniforms in the foreground. The rest were ready to march to the hilltop two miles in the distance. A number had been mounted as cavalry.

The action, according to history, was for the Southern forces to advance toward the camera, get beaten off by the Northern troops, retreat in confusion.

ADAMSON: Did you have to put shoes on the Southerners?

HASKIN: Yes, we put shoes on them with the uniforms. Then we issued the rifles. The final preparation was to issue blank ammunition.

As soon as they got the blanks, a whole gang of them sneaked around the grandstand behind these thirteen veterans. They'd shoot their whole ration of blanks under the asses of the old heroes. The old guys came unglued. (Laughs) Teeth, wigs and everything flying. No respect for the veterans at all!

Finally, we got the troops together with enough ammunition and marched them off to their positions, there to be given the final instructions.

Mainly, they were warned about the powder shots, how to avoid them. Came the great moment, a silence settled over the whole valley. All was ready. As cameraman with me, we had my old mentor, Lyman Broening.

I nodded quietly to Mr. Holubar, alongside me on the platform. He went crazy, exploding, "Camera! Blow up everything!" On the powder board there were thousands of different shots ready to be triggered carefully to avoid killing everybody. The only instruction Holubar ever gave during the scene was, "Blow up everything!"

Above the din, I yelled to Carl Hernandez, "Pay no attention to the bastard, you take charge." About halfway through the battle, a big clod hit Holubar in the head, and knocked him stiff. That saved the rest of the troops from annihilation.

Through the smoke and fire we could see that, contrary to history, our foreground Union guys were all falling dead, on the principle that the only good Yank was a dead Yank. And these were the troops who historically won the battle!

Down the hill raced our crackers, whooping the Rebel Yell. The cavalry paid no attention to them, running over them, galloping along swinging sabres. Quickly the troops ignored warning flags on the powder shots. They'd blow black dirt fifty feet in the air filled with rebels.

At one point, I saw a guy running, giving a Rebel yell, tumbling into a bush, getting blown into the air thirty feet, circling slowly, coming down -- BALOOM! -- bouncing, then jumping up and running on. (Laughs) By the time they gained the foreground, screaming and yelling, there were no Yanks left alive to drive them back!

Our bugler blew Retreat. Not one Reb would retreat. They decided to stay where they were -- the way the battle should have been fought in the first place!

With bruises, bloody cuts, not one of the whole 1500 would go into any one of the six first aid tents at all -- too damn tough. Ears hanging, eyes closed, like they'd been through a war. And they had been!

So we paused and regrouped, attempted to organize a shot of the retreat. Wouldn't work. By then it was lunchtime.

The prop men issued the box lunches. These guys ate, belched, and simply said, "We've seen all we want to see. We goin' home." And they went home! With our uniforms, guns, etc. The hills were loaded with deputies from Nashville trying to wrestle back our property.

ADAMSON: Had they been paid?

HASKIN: Yes. The pay was issued when they first came in. We lost a baggage car full of uniforms and guns and stuff. That was the end of the battle -- we couldn't muster anybody after that.

ADAMSON: So you never got a retreat?

HASKIN: No. It was all moot anyhow, because Holubar became sick from riding eighty-five miles a day over bumpy roads; he had a kidney stone, which descended halfway. He turned yellow. We sent him up to Chicago. They examined him, and quickly shipped him out to the Coast for the operation. He died.

ADAMSON: So the film was never finished?

HASKIN: No. Never made. I saw the rushes of that battle. It was the most grandiose scene ever staged. It really looked like the Civil War, particularly the first and middle stages of it: a screen filled with men being blown to pieces! (Laughs)

These damn helpers on the sidelines, these crackers we'd hired to operate the mortars, got in the spirit of the battle and kicked the props out from under the mortars and began aiming at the troops. I saw one rebel get a mortar shot right in the belly -- BOOM! -- flying like a bird, then up and start running again. Unbelievable!

ADAMSON: These were just blanks they were shooting?

HASKIN: Well, the mortar fired a ball of highpowered fireworks. It'd go off with a hell of a whack. Knocking a guy right off his feet. They'd blow his eyes out if they ever hit him in the face.

ADAMSON: So they were almost shooting real stuff?

HASKIN: These mortars, yes. But they had been propped up to go into the sky to simulate shrapnel. You see it in all the illustrations of the Civil War. These guys said to hell with shrapnel -- they kicked the props out, started following these guys with the mortars like using a gun on rabbits, knocking them off.

ADAMSON: Were there any other cameras getting closer shots?

HASKIN: No, no. This was a master scene with close shots left to be shot later at the studio. We had two cameras. That's all. Lyman Broening used a 40mm lens. I shot with a 50mm. Camera movement had not come in yet. They were set shots.

ADAMSON: When you cranked those cameras by hand, were you looking through the viewfinder, or was there a viewfinder?

HASKIN: Yes, there was a viewfinder. I used a Bell and Howell camera in the beginning, and there was a small finder, about an inch square, showing the picture upside down. A little unit mounted on the side of the camera. The Bell and Howell was an excellent piece of machinery, but it was certainly not designed for any facility of moving around or anything of the sort. If you used the Bell and Howell on Westerns, sometimes you'd free the head on the tripod, and tape a stick to the magazines and keep the magazines lined up on the galloping horse. That's why I said that it was a period when you solved contingencies as you met them.

ADAMSON: Presumably, there were advances going on all the time.

HASKIN: Absolutely, yes. Even as late as when I was in photographing at Warner Bros. -- after I had been to England, so that would make it in the thirties -- it was near the finale of the Golden Age of invention in motion picture technical facilities. I personally have a string of patents as long as your arm for things I worked out at Warner Bros. Of course, they own them all. I even invented a traveling matte camera that bypassed the Technicolor patents as a 3-color camera. Eight basic claims allowed. I couldn't take out patents in my own name, because I was working for Warners on contract.

When I started in movies, there were no grips on the set; assistant cameramen kept the lights from shining at the camera lens. Then the mill built black frames to place along the sidelines for the purpose. They were first called "niggers," but that brought objections from certain minorities, so they renamed them gobos. We constantly improved these stands, and made them more mobile.

When I started a film called GREEN LIGHT, starring Paul Muni, a talkie, I invented a whole series of attachable shields for the studio lamps, to control the light. It was a matter of advancing technique all the time. We were sort of figuring it out as we went along. Later, the lampmaking companies made these ideas into permanent attachments.

All of which stopped with television. Television shot Cock Robin. The Golden Age bit the dust with the advent of the boob tube.

ADAMSON: The great leveler, right?

HASKIN: Yes. Cynically, it's been said that most TV directors watch the actors' feet instead of what's going on in the scene. If the actors hit the marks, "Print it!"

The actual creative effort put into many TV series, you could put in a thimble. The actors acquire a standard group of expressions, reactions, knickknacks and gimmicks, and occasionally the director may say, "Oh, why don't we try this?"

"Who, me?"
"Well, yes."
"All right."

A big innovation, you know! Big deal!

ADAMSON: O.K., let's see -- the first credits I have for Warner Bros. are 1925.

HASKIN: I doubt that. It must have been earlier.

ADAMSON: In 1925 you did BOBBED HAIR.

HASKIN: BOBBED HAIR was with Marie Prevost and Kenneth Harlan. It was a real hoodoo, that picture, we all have scars on us. Once, we were doing a follow shot from a camera platform on the front of a car full of the heavies. Duke Green was to drive down the Arroyo Seco in Pasadena -- about fifty miles an hour. Unbeknownst to anybody, the grip had lashed the camera platform to the steering knuckles in front! The car wouldn't steer. The first turn we went off into the rocks!

Another time we were on a platform on the front of the car for a shot up Benedict Canyon, a winding road. The grip had fixed the platform good and sturdy -- you could have stood an elephant on it. But he forgot to tie it down. When we went around the curves -- WHOO! -- the whole thing flipped in the air and the cameras went flying. I ended up hanging on with a tire roaring between my legs! (Laughs) Kenneth Harlan driving -- thank God he didn't panic. If he hadn't braked to a stop, I'd have been a capon!

BOBBED HAIR was a book written by eleven famous authors. Each of them wrote a short individual segment in the progression, leaving the story in suspended animation and daring the next writer to figure how to get out. Each author tried to make his bit more hairy than the rest. Naturally, it became a terrific chase, pure melodrama. I have scars on me to this day from that picture. Look here. On my shins and everywhere. One location was in San Diego. Even going there on the train, the engineer had a heart attack; the train was wrecked. Some jinx!

ADAMSON: What happened to that grip who tied the platform to the steering knuckles? Was he fired?

HASKIN: No. He tied the platform on, went to lunch and mysteriously never came back in his life. I don't know where the hell he went. (Laughs) He damn near killed the whole bunch of us! We went over a curbstone twelve inches high, catapulting into the bottom of the Arroyo Seco filled with big boulders -- how we got out alive, I'll never know.

Then this train -- the Santa Fe -- the engineer fainted in Del Mar. We hit the Torrey Pines fourteen-mile grade at seventy-five miles an hour. It was raining heavily, at night. The cars peeled off and buried themselves in the mud-bank. Every car went off the track but the observation car, in which we were seated. Lucky!

ADAMSON: Why did you go down to San Diego?

HASKIN: Well, we were to shoot the next day aboard a yacht chasing around the harbor -- part of the chase that one of the authors wrote.

After the wreck, a relief train came, picking us up, taking us to San Diego. We finally got working. A stranger came up alongside our barge in a shore boat. He was a representative of the railroad with a suitcase full of checks for everybody in return for signing a release. Several people were killed, although none of our outfit. The engineer died.

The fireman died later and several passengers in the smoking car got it. There wasn't anything left of that smoking car. All of our cameras were in the baggage car, which had gone off following the engine -- you could have swept them up with a broom (laughs) -- a bunch of nuts and bolts! I'll tell you, to be a cameraman in those days, you really were a stuntman. I kid you not. . . .

I remember now, BOBBED HAIR was not my first photographing job for Warner Bros. Before that I photographed a film with Millard Webb -- starring Huntley Gordon and others.

ADAMSON: Not WHERE THE WORST BEGINS?

HASKIN: No. WHERE THE WORST BEGINS was an awful bomb; written and directed by Jack McDermott, starring Ruth Roland. It was Co-Artist Productions, Truart Film Corporation -- probably names they invented one night over a drink. I don't think there was any such corporation! (Laughs) They financed it on Ruth Roland's name. Her serials were long over, but her name was still important.

ADAMSON: Jack McDermott was some kind of colorful character wasn't he?

HASKIN: Very. He was one of the celebrities of Hollywood in the silent days. He was a director of sorts, for Al and Charlie Christie. He was a writer of sorts, too, for MGM, Harry Carey, and other stars. He was a pal of Sam Marx and all the guys in the Culver City Studio. He owned a little house on the top of Cahuenga Pass, up in the hills, remote from everybody else. He had built it with the aid of all his friends out of pieces that he had managed to high grade out of movie sets.

ADAMSON: That's what I heard.

HASKIN: Yeah, the place was more or less Oriental design. One outhouse looked like a mosque. The only way to get into it was to put up a stepladder and climb through a hole in a dome. Inside, it was a kind of studio.

I traded latchkeys with Jack on my wedding night. It was something scary. The fireplace looked like a small temple. A slide was built inside of it so that he could dive headfirst into the fire -- BOOM! -- and he'd come up two floors below in the patio. One of his bits of magic straight out of Omar Khayyam! Talk about moral turpitude -- everything that happens today was invented at Jack's place!

As I said before, these early silent days, when I first came to Hollywood, were completely uninhibited. You think that things are free and easy now -- life with Jack McDermott makes today look like a church picnic. Really!

ADAMSON: This was in terms of dope that was going around, or sex or -- ?

HASKIN: Not particularly dope, although there was easy access to every kind. More sex and free living. Stealing, what have you.

I remember a house we rented, a group of us guys -- there was Jack; Norm McLeod, later a director; Jim Tinling, later a director; Jack King who was a drug salesman whose beat was the Orient; a guy named Hookie Quinn, a drifter; and his brother Eddie, a piano player who couldn't read music.

The owner of the house was an artist, Russell Iridell; his wife was a fortune teller. We all had to laugh. Why didn't she know we would never pay the rent if she was so smart at forecasting? (Laughs)

We had an amusing several months there with all the whoopee that was going on in the house above us owned by Barbara La Marr, with her friends, Jack Pickford and Harry Sweet, and other places around. We managed to keep our own place fairly lively as well.

We furnished our place from the lobbies of the apartment houses on Hollywood Boulevard and around Franklin Avenue, etc. Apartment houses were usually open. The lobbies were furnished beautifully. Eddie and Hookie, who felt that everything that was loose belonged to them, would borrow a car, usually my Ford, and cruise at night; coming home with pieces of furniture. We even got a few choice items from the lobby of the Hollywood Hotel....

Eventually, we ran into the harsh facts of life, foremost of which was the gas company. It was the beginning of the end for us. They came and presented the bill, demanding immediate payment. Naturally, we ignored it. Then they sent a closing notice. We ignored that too.

Eventually, they shut off the gas. That was simple: Hookie went down and turned it on as soon as the guy left. Finally, they sent a wrecking crew that took all the gas pipes out of the house, and plugged up both ends -- one at the street, and one at the house. That was the end of the little sojourn.

ADAMSON: Are you serious when you say you never paid any rent?

HASKIN: No, we never paid any rent. My money that I would get as assistant -- twenty-five or thirty dollars a week -- would go for groceries. I was the only one employed at the time.

ADAMSON: Feeding everybody?

HASKIN: Yes. It would feed the whole group. Occasionally, some of them would get a piece of loot. Jack would do a Christie Comedy and get $250 for directing it, and he would spring it for useless items of food -- jars of marinated herring or some such delicacy.

This Whitley Heights place was the culmination of our lifestyle formulated at another place -- we had a flat on

Argyle. We were sitting around one day -- I don't think Jack was living there, but Tinling and Norm, and Norm's brother Bonner, who'd come down from Seattle, were there. We were all starving to death. I was unemployed, waiting for a job to start. We hadn't any money at all.

A throwaway newspaper landed out front on the lawn. We waited until the coast was clear and fetched the paper. All the blinds were down; we never answered the doorbell. That'd be the worst thing in the world, you know. Our laundry was all jammed into the closet and locked up.

Jim Tinling began reading the throwaway newspaper with mounting interest. On an inside page was a big ad -- Walsh and Mackie, fine groceries. Listing many delicacies. There was a quote: "Just have your wife phone and open an account." (Laughs) Tinling's eyes bugged. Our phone was still operative. Tinling called Walsh and Mackie using a falsetto, representing himself as Mrs. Tinling who wished to start an account. By God, they casually started an account! Jim had made a list of staples you wouldn't believe! That afternoon, the delivery boy left the groceries after several rings of the doorbell on the back porch. For five days we got more and more goddamn food out of this Walsh and Mackie. Finally, the grocery boy didn't leave it on the porch. He took it back with him as he went.

A couple of friends drove from Seattle in a Cunningham car, which was a tremendously big limousine. They were friends of McLeod's and Tinling's. Jim, still thinking fast, got a great idea and asked them to lend him the car for a few minutes. He took it around the block in front of Walsh and Mackie, smoking a cigar. Like he'd come into sudden wealth!

That was good for three more days of food. Needless to say, Walsh and Mackie quickly went out of business. Hollywood was a place where you couldn't do that kind of thing. All of which had little to do with movies, I guess, but it was the way the town operated at that point. . . .

Back to WHERE THE WORST BEGINS -- it was shot at Universal Studios. I don't know how it could ever have been released, but I suppose it was. At Warners, I did whatever came along, even some of the RIN-TIN-TINs.

ADAMSON: Yes, I was going to ask you if you had done any of those. Those were really the studio's --

HASKIN: -- bread and butter. Well, I actually declined the credit for those RIN-TIN'S.

ADAMSON: Why?

HASKIN: They didn't want them well photographed, in the first place. Frank Kesson, my assistant, rose to the great job of being the cameraman for the dog, and he was pretty rough in his photography. I shot one, but I didn't take credit. What my actual thinking was, I really don't recall.

ADAMSON: There's one thing here -- a picture called ON THIN ICE. Was that one of those? Zanuck and Mal St. Clair did it.

HASKIN: That was not a RIN-TIN-TIN. It was a feature film with Tom Moore starring. What the heck is THE GOLDEN COCOON?

ADAMSON: It's a film you shot at Warners, released December '25.

HASKIN: I don't remember anything about it. ACROSS THE PACIFIC was with Monte Blue. We had a swamp built on the backlot. It was a story about the Philippines. It made them quite a lot of money. In fact, they remade this later in Burbank with Bogie. As a talkie. . . . The first picture I did with Barrymore was THE SEA BEAST.

ADAMSON: Yes. Which I just saw last night.

HASKIN: Really. Is it still together?

ADAMSON: Most of it.

HASKIN: It was a real cornball.

ADAMSON: There were a few jumps in it, but most of it is still around.

HASKIN: But it was a good photographic job in a lot of places, as I remember.

ADAMSON: Oh, yes. There were some wonderful shots, especially all the stuff on the ship. I thought it was a good picture of the whaling life. I don't know how accurate it was, but it seemed very authentic.

HASKIN: The special effects were nothing.

ADAMSON: (Laughs) They didn't all work!

HASKIN: No. I remember that. But Dolores Costello and John were beautiful subjects. I got really turned on in a lot of the scenes as I remember. That's where Jack first met Dolores. I had been pretty much on the make for her, but of course, with someone as big as Barrymore, that was the end of me.

ADAMSON: Sounds like the plot of the movie.

HASKIN: Yes!

ADAMSON: I had one big question about this film. I was really in love with the shots you had from the top of the mast, I guess in the crow's nest, with Barrymore sliding all the way down the rope. Was that really Barrymore doing that?

HASKIN: Yes.

ADAMSON: That was an incredible angle. Were you up in the nest?

HASKIN: Yes. There was a camera also at the bottom of the stay. Barrymore was a gutsy guy, and he was half loaded anyhow. He had the monkey on his shoulder and he volunteered to slide down. Nobody had investigated that it was a steel cable which must have been on that old lugger since its launching. It was rusted, with sprays of sharp edges sticking out all the way down. It was a high mast -- it must have been 100 feet or 120 feet, with this diagonal stay down to the bowsprit. I suppose we just assumed that because he was going to do it, it was all right. (Laughs)

So the guy took off from the top with the monkey on his shoulder. Halfway down, I could see that his hands were bleeding, cut to ribbons. But he came down, jumped off and twirled the monkey in the air and ran out of the shot.

We had to hurry him into first aid to replace the meat on his hands. God, he could easily have been killed if he'd let go.

ADAMSON: There were a lot of these high angles in THE SEA BEAST that were really great -- I wonder if POTEMKIN was the inspiration?

HASKIN: I don't think so. It was expediency on my part. I have been all my life a good sailor; not affected by sea sickness. I didn't mind getting up in the tops. I was in pretty good shape at that time, however, toward the end of THE SEA BEAST, I collapsed physically. I took off several months to recoup.

On the ship Barrymore would get stewed to the eyes on booze. The greatest scene in THE SEA BEAST is when he first tried on the crutch, after his leg had been amputated. He fell on it, and was in agony. It had plunged into his ribs. It was real!

ADAMSON: Did you take off from San Pedro Harbor every day with the ship? Was it a long time that you were out there?

HASKIN: Yes. We'd leave the dock and pull out to sea.

ADAMSON: There's supposed to be a story of the time he had gone to a costume party the night before as a hobo, and went straight to San Pedro at six in the morning and fell asleep and nobody recognized him. Everybody was waiting around until noon, till he showed up, and he'd been there all the time, sound asleep.

HASKIN: Well, I don't remember that one, but I remember he used to have his damn monkey, on his shoulder and it would shit all over. His limousine was absolutely a craphouse in the back.

ADAMSON: Because of the monkey. Isn't that monkey in THE SEA BEAST?

HASKIN: Yes. He used to go to Marion Davies' parties with this monkey with his makeup and his costume still on, from San Pedro. I know apocryphal stuff about his deals to buy Dolores from her mother. I had believed them, but I had no proof.

ADAMSON: Buy her? Was that because her father didn't approve -- ?

HASKIN: Well, Barrymore promised to make her a star if the old lady let her take a trip on the yacht with him, that kind of business deal . . . .

During the making of DON JUAN, Warners signed up with Western Electric for sound pictures. It was with Mary Astor and Barrymore.

ADAMSON: Why was that selected -- do you know -- to be the picture to introduce Vitaphone with?

HASKIN: It was the big film that was being made at the time with John Barrymore, their top star. There was no other reason. If it had been THE SEA BEAST or any other film that had top priority in the studio, that would have been it. DON JUAN was supposed to be a prestige picture -- Bess Meredyth wrote the screenplay. It was with Myrna Loy, Warner Oland, Estelle Taylor, Helene Costello, Joe Swickard, and on and on. I have a still photo with the cast and art director and production managers and all. It's a real classic. In the photograph, I had lent Myrna my coat. It was cold on the stage and she was shivering, and I threw my coat around her. I was down to 123 pounds, believe it or not. (Laughs)

DON JUAN -- now it would have been a classic photographically, but dear old Jack Warner with his grubby mitts -- I was going as fast as possible -- the show was not really being delayed photographically at all. I was a very fast cameraman. But because of delays for other reasons, Warner lit on me, and focused on me as the heavy, blaming me for the time it was taking to get this show finished.

So I, in a snit, very foolishly said, "All right, I'll show this sonuvabitch." And I started really racing through the shots. Reflections of lights in windows, anything -- to hell with it -- you know.

The problems with things you do to show people -- Jesus, they look like they're the whole picture when they get cut in, those lousy shots. But there was a lot of pretty good photographic stuff in the film, particularly around the dungeons.

ADAMSON: Yes. And the guy had a kind of laboratory, and was doing his alchemy --

HASKIN: Yes, yes.

ADAMSON: The stuff at the beginning was very dramatic, too. Were those the first things shot?

HASKIN: Yes. But the stuff in the round set where he lived -- I raced through, and the hell with it. Worse than RIN-TIN.

Following that though, I did a nice one about the Manon Lescaut story, WHEN A MAN LOVES, with Dolores and Jack again. It was a sort of French Revolution type of thing, I remember.

ADAMSON: Tom Santschi was in it too. It came out in '27, and there's a mutiny at the end of it.

HASKIN: Yes, that was a nice subject to photograph. Now, I don't remember what the hell was after that, but anyhow, I became quite a friend of Barrymore -- in a professional way. We didn't become personal friends, but mutually respectful. He gave me a Cadillac automobile and he thought I was the greatest thing since sex.

It was a pleasure working with him, although I realized that he was just on the verge of going under through his carousing. It was from him that I learned about the tradition of the theatre, and got the feel of Broadway and all that.

But he was a madman, really. The whole family strain was tainted with some kind of disregard for any ordered process of behavior or consideration. They had no logic -- very akin to the royalist king idea: that they do no wrong, and have license to do anything to anybody.

I invented a lot of things to keep him from looking collapsed. In DON JUAN, I had a spiderweb inner wig made out of tapes. We put it over the top of his head and pulled his face up supported by the tapes. Then we clapped the wig on top of this. We had pads for his calves and his legs. The only trouble with the wig was that by the time the long shots and medium shots were over, he was half stewed, and he'd stretch his muscles and his face would drop. Then we'd be in for close-ups. (Laughs)

ADAMSON: How old was he then? Wasn't he in his forties?

HASKIN: He evidently was.

ADAMSON: Was it the evidence of a dissipated life that you were trying to hide?

HASKIN: Yes.

ADAMSON: More than his age?

HASKIN: He was a real rakehell, and a boozer. He had the bottle of Coke and Rum on the table all the time, the dressing table.

ADAMSON: When you say Coke and Rum, you mean Coca Cola?

HASKIN: Yes. He went on to MGM after Warner Bros. and he made some creditable films -- GRAND HOTEL and others. I could have gone with him at the time, but I had some fatheaded idea of my destiny and I didn't pursue it. Actually, I realized it was very close to the end of his career. He got mixed up with that crazy broad, and chasing her around, he became a clown.

It was a great tragedy to me, because at the time I was working with him at Warner Bros., he was universally respected as the world's greatest actor. He certainly was the world's greatest living Hamlet at that time. He had proven that in London and at Stratford. There was prestige in being connected with Mr. Barrymore.

All the perquisites of the theatre were followed out on the set. It was an over-polite atmosphere, you know.

ADAMSON: What was Erpi?

HASKIN: Erpi was Electrical Research Products Incorporated. That was the division of Western Electric that had the synchronous motors and amplification that made talking pictures possible.

ADAMSON: Now, Sam and Jack were out here, right?

HASKIN: Yes. Sam was on the West Coast, and he heard about it, and rushed back to New York, and got ahold of H.M. -- Harry, the older brother -- and Abe, and forced them to re-open negotiations with Erpi. Erpi had by then been turned down by everybody, and so they got a hell of a deal out of it. An exclusive for twelve features, or one year, whichever. Each one of these they made millions on. That set them up as a top rank production company. Up to that time they were really a third-rate outfit.

ADAMSON: Not even second-rate?

HASKIN: No, they had two prestige commitments -- one Ernst Lubitsch, the other Jack Barrymore, and Barrymore was fading rapidly. Lubitsch, of course, was at his most creative.

ADAMSON: Lubitsch was on the rise, too.

HASKIN: Yes.

ADAMSON: Didn't they have to close up shop from time to time during the twenties?

HASKIN: Yes, they did. I remember many times that word would come out onto the stage, "Get ready, the stockholders are coming. H. M. is bringing a group of potential investors out." We would get every camera out of the vaults, set it up on a phony set, and grab a few of the extra people around. Anybody was the director, anybody was the cameraman. There'd be twelve or fourteen companies going on simultaneously on the same stage. Nothing was actually happening; no film in the cameras or anything. Then H.M. would take them walking through and Jack would tell them, "Well, here's Monte Blue, and here's Marie Prevost," and they'd shake hands and so forth. Then they'd go through the laboratories.

Of course the last pièce de résistance -- they would go down to the toilet and take a look at Freddie the office boy's whang, which was world-record size. We used to lay nineteen nickels on top of it. That would generally be the convincer. A star named Bill Lewis and Jack Barrymore were sponsors of the Freddie exhibition.

ADAMSON: Was this "O.K. Freddie"?

HASKIN: Yes.

ADAMSON: Where did that expression come from?

HASKIN: Well, all you had to do to see it was say, "How about it, Freddie? Let me take a look, O.K.?" ZING! He popped the thing out. (Laughs) Never refused. I used him in a film called THE POWER in 1967. He played bits and all, and made money with his tool, I guess. He was a nice guy, sort of flaky, and he died shortly after. He was always stooped over and you wondered what the hell he was doing. He was walking along the sidewalk looking for coins in the gutter. That was his hobby, he picked up dimes and quarters, pennies and things. He used to make quite a little money that way.

ADAMSON: You'd have to be awfully busy! Or was there really gold in the streets then?

HASKIN: No, I don't think so.

ADAMSON: Can you tell me a little bit about Alan Crosland? You worked with him even before DON JUAN.

HASKIN: The Elder. Yes. Well, Alan Crosland was one of Warner Bros.' top directors. He had a high reputation. He was a famous director name. He had been with Hearst, making WHEN KNIGHTHOOD WAS IN FLOWER, with Marion Davies, and was a big wheel. He did not take the lousy assignments that most directors got around there. Lehrman and those characters would do anything, you know.

ADAMSON: Could we talk a little about THE SINGING FOOL?

HASKIN: THE SINGING FOOL was with Jolson -- it was Jolson's next film after THE JAZZ SINGER, and it technically had a lot more class than THE JAZZ SINGER. THE SINGING FOOL was part talkie.

ADAMSON: It switches from silent to talkie more times than I've ever seen -- about eighteen times -- and subtitles come up where you don't expect them.

HASKIN: It had no particular style or thrust or anything to it. Jolson didn't look like much, and he couldn't act his way out of a paper bag. He was a trial to Lloyd Bacon, the director.

ADAMSON: He did most of his acting while he was singing.

HASKIN: Yes. He had kind of a bag of tricks he'd use, like singing "my heart is breaking," while he's thinking of a racehorse.

ADAMSON: He was a good live audience entertainer, wasn't he?

HASKIN: Oh, yes. Yes. I'd seen him many times in stage plays. He'd get near the end of the show -- the audience were his aficionados, you know -- he would say, "Shall I finish the play ... or do you want a song?" They'd yell, "Sing, Sing!" He'd just throw the play away, and sing his medley of numbers. (Laughs) He could really hold them!

ADAMSON: One thing I noticed about THE SINGING FOOL was that the real elaborate production shots were in the silent sequences, because I guess in the talkie scenes you had to hold three or four cameras riveted on Jolson.

HASKIN: Yes. Backstage I accomplished what hadn't been done previously. I took the camera in a circle around through the dressing room row and back to where it started -- flying lights in and out.

ADAMSON: Just circled it around the dressing room?

HASKIN: Yes. Like going around the perimeter of this house -- all past the dressing rooms and backstage. I became pretty accomplished at multiple-camera type shooting. In fact, that was one of the attractions to the British people who hired me to go over to England and install multiple-camera shooting over there in 1929. The highest number of cameras I ever ran at one time was eleven.

ADAMSON: Was that here?

HASKIN: Yes. With Warner.

ADAMSON: Which picture?

HASKIN: ON TRIAL. With Pauline Frederick. The sequence showed a nightclub from the sidewalk, through the foyer, into the cafe, to a table, into the manager's office, and back on out -- all in one take. It was seven and a half minutes. Eleven cameras. That was before the days of dubbing.

ADAMSON: So the music had to be going?

HASKIN: Yes, whatever it was that the band played. But most pictures were put out in a lot of small reels.

ADAMSON: Oh, for each scene?

HASKIN: Yes. Dubbing did not come in for almost the full first year we had sound -- I think the whole first year. I don't know of any dubbing facilities at all. That first year, we never did get out of the booth into any kind of a barney or a blimp. We were always in the booth the first year of the talkies.

ADAMSON: Did you have anything to do with that technology? Of improving the mobility of the camera with sound?

HASKIN: Oh yes, sure. I was not instrumental but I was in on the committees establishing the basic rate of speed for sound, and all the problems that came up. I helped to solve the problem of the intrusion of microphones into the scene. Of course, these sound engineers who came out to start sound pictures had an oldstyle carbon mike on a box, and they wanted to put that so the actors could touch it. Well, this limited the shot badly. Finally, I fought them to get a one-foot pipe -- the mike is down in the scene, and the box is a foot above it, with a pipe to the mike, and then we could hang little pictures on the mike and so forth. I designed a whole technology -- we got it up to where the pipe was about three feet long, and the mike was a unit down at the bottom of it. I also designed and had built for each production company, sheaths, of varying stages of grey. Generally, you'd have five or six mikes in a shot -- behind them would be a medium grey wall -- the prop man would take the cart back and clip on a sheath in a little shield of a certain grey, and if it matched the back wall, it was O.K. I've lost as many as eleven mikes with these -- blend them in with a little powder, and a little charcoal, and dust them into the wall, and you'd lose them. It was a matter of just shading them in the proper color.

We tried to move mikes occasionally. There were pulley wires and things from the ceiling, and very crude crap. It was all Rube Goldberg junk. (Laughs) No sense to it. The major changes were, of course, in the booth. The first booths took nineteen men to move. Finally, we got a dolly booth, which would hold one cameraman. Trouble was, it didn't have any ventilation in it. Generally, at Warners, we'd put Ben Reynolds, ex-Stroheim cameraman, and quite fat, in it, and he'd fall asleep in the middle of the shot. (Laughs) After an intricate dolly shot, you'd look and Ben would be snoring against the glass, camera pointed at the floor.

ADAMSON: I just noticed something recently -- I never heard this said anywhere -- but I looked at Gary Cooper's first talkies, and I kept saying, "I wonder why they're not putting any background music to any of this?" I guess they couldn't.

HASKIN: There was no dubbing facility. You'd dub on wax and you'd pick up so much surface noise that it'd ruin the dialogue.

ADAMSON: So there was no way to mix during all that time.

HASKIN: No. Eventually, it was conquered, and of course, we at Warners were on wax and simultaneously, sound on film was developing, but Erpi held everything back and let Warners have the year exclusive on wax.

ADAMSON: It was all wax?

HASKIN: Yes. The original was wax, and then shortly after that, they began developing sound on film. Warners stayed on wax long after everybody else was on film because of their facilities -- they had a record pressing plant in the studio.

ADAMSON: Do you remember anything about ON TRIAL?

HASKIN: ON TRIAL was one of those six-day wonders that we made with multiple cameras. It took twelve days. It was shot with a four-camera set-up, and even more at times.

ADAMSON: This was done basically straight from the stage.

HASKIN: Yes, and it was shot almost like a stage play. We were in booths. We'd have close-ups on the corners, a medium shot and a long shot in the middle. That was standard as far as camera set-ups. You would whack out a hell of a lot of time and film by shooting it all together. Instead of going in for the long shot, then a medium shot, then a close-up, and breaking it up single camera, you'd cover the whole scene in one take -- BOOM. Occasionally you'd go in and shoot an extra close-up or something, but the quality, I recall, was the most miserable photographic job you ever heard of. Those long lenses for close-ups were lousy. . . .

WOLF'S CLOTHING was with Monte Blue. It's the story of a guy coming from the Midwest to New York to see Broadway, and immediately he gets a job in the subway. He doesn't see much of Broadway, because he works on the nightshift in the subway, and the first night that he gets a "day" off, he gets all dressed up and rides downtown. He's going to see Broadway and going to see New York. He comes up out of the subway, and as he steps out of the kiosk and off the curb, a car hits him in the ass and knocks him unconscious, and the whole rest of the show is a dream of crazy happenings -- of gangsters and big exaggerated sets -- a telephone receiver which is eight feet long, and he's a tiny little guy running through sets and so forth. There was a montage of trick shots which was something like 240 feet long, and I remember very distinctly that Fred Gage and Pete Steele, the lab men, and I, stood over it -- I made three takes of it, and for eight days we didn't turn in any rushes.

It was all on one piece of film going back and forth in the camera. Each night, Warner would get crazier -- "Where the hell are the rushes from this company?" "Well, we don't know." Everybody'd play dumb. Roy Del Ruth was the director. He was an ex-Mack Sennett director, and Roy's sense of humor consisted of rolling on the floor when he could blow a house fifty feet in the air with dynamite. The idea to him of Warner sitting there and seeing no rushes from a company that'd been working all day (laughs) was funny. So, for eight days we turned in no rushes, and we were shooting this damn montage day after day.

By God, years later, when I was head of the Special Effects Department of Warners in the thirties, pieces of that old montage turned up in the files in the effects library of the optical room: waves splashing, hurdy gurdies at night going around, fireworks, and everything you could think of.

I was sort of a club photographer, and in between pictures, I would hide out. Of course, I didn't want to have to shoot inserts and practically sweep the floor, which is about the way Warner regarded a cameraman's job around the place.

It was then that I met Hal Wallis. Hal had come out from the East, and was ensconced as publicity director of the studio. They'd never had one before. In my search for a safe place to hide out between pictures, I found this guy sitting in an office back by the lab, and I introduced myself, sat down. As time passed, we'd fan the breeze and we became good friends.

I remember that he was a great questioner and he was absorbing what I knew about making pictures. I was pretty sharp at the time, and we discussed many facets of picture-making, which he later utilized. In fact, he learned the fundamentals of how to make pictures from me. I was a first cameraman at the time, and in competition around town. He has always remained a good personal friend. Not that when he's in the studio this means anything, but outside he's been a personal friend.

ADAMSON: Did that help you when it came to getting directing assignments later or anything like that?

HASKIN: Actually, no. At Warner Bros. it didn't help a bit. I got some silent films to do under Zanuck, but they were dreadful things, and I really wasn't ready to take on the political internecine warfare that was necessary to get any kind of a good assignment.

My first silent film I personally stopped in mid-shooting, it was so bad. I had to walk off the stage and go into Jack Warner's office and tell him it was headed for the toilet. Really.

It was my big chance, called MATINEE LADIES. I said, "Look, the only thing we can do to save this, is to make it into a melodrama. So far, the cast is just sitting around this cafe, talking about the same stuff in subtitles over and over and I'm halfway through the film. In the second half of the script, they're in the same place talking about the same things." No action at all.

Warner said, "All right. Let's figure it out." Ray Schrock was the guy who was producing and writing it. Warner said, "First we'll fire Schrock, then find a writer and put together a finish."

So I talked it over with my friend Roy Del Ruth. He said, "Hey, there's a guy up in the third floor of the old barn that's pretty sharp. He's been writing the dog stories." We went over and talked with him -- Darryl Zanuck. The repair job on MATINEE LADIES was Zanuck's first feature film credit.

Later, I remember distinctly, Warner was sitting on the can in his office, grunting, and figuring out what was needed for my story. He said, "Hey, how about a houseboat? Let's get them on a houseboat. They're anchored in the harbor, having a party, it breaks loose and drifts out to sea." I said, "Sounds all right to me." So, that's what we had Zanuck write! (Laughs)

Later, Roy Del Ruth and I made up a plan, half as a joke, to plug Zanuck as the new head producer in the studio. Our joke became a reality. Mr. Zanuck was chosen by Warner as executive producer. For that, the first one he stabbed in the back was me. (Laughs)

ADAMSON: How did you finagle that?

HASKIN: Oh, Del Ruth was pretty strong at the time, and my testimony at the preview that the guy was a genius, that he'd saved my picture, along with Roy Del Ruth giving him a big blast of publicity and so forth, influenced Warner, who didn't care much one way or the other. Schrock had just been fired from the job, why not put Zanuck in? (Laughs) Shortly after that, I was given another assignment. It was a story called "Little Irish Girl" or something like that.

ADAMSON:   IRISH HEARTS.

HASKIN:   IRISH HEARTS, yes. Starring May McAvoy and Warner Richmond. The story depended on constant repetition of hard times for a little Irish girl. Every morning she'd go down the street and everybody would make fun of her and make life hell for her with their tricks. In the evening, she'd come back along the street and everybody'd make hell for her and play tricks on her again. This became her way of life: the butt of all the jokes; day after day. Finally, one day she is brought to realize what's happening, and this time she goes along the street and reverses the whole procedure, paying everybody back for her ignominies. It was a form of Hold Your Horses, a successful Broadway play. It depended on repetitions of the offense against her, over and over again, to be effective.

Zanuck was now a young executive producer making his name. One of the first economy waves came along. To help build his reputation, he grabbed my script and cut the middle of the story out. So what happens with my girl? She goes down the street getting into trouble; comes back along the street that night, and knocks them all off! (Laughs) It didn't play. I told him it wouldn't.

He said, "Don't buck the game." Next thing, I hear from a friend of mine who was listening at Warner's keyhole that Warner was giving Zanuck hell: "You ever do that again, I'll throw you out of here!" Zanuck said, "It's that dumb Haskin. He ruined a perfectly good story."

ADAMSON:   Zanuck said that?

HASKIN:   Yes. My next assignment was George Jessel's first film, THE BROADWAY KID, released as GINSBERG THE GREAT (1927). George Jessel, as a film comedian, was talented like a clothing store dummy. Later of course, he became a great raconteur; but that's another matter. He couldn't ever react. Slapstick comedy depends on the ability to "take it." You see the villain, you "take it big." Jessel would see a train coming toward him and he'd show no reaction.

He had not yet got news of his double-cross by Warner Bros., about being in THE JAZZ SINGER. He'd been acting in the New York play. He came out to Warner Bros. in his personal belief that he was to be in the film, but that wasn't so. Legally, they had only signed with him to star in films. He figured in what else but THE JAZZ SINGER? When THE JAZZ SINGER finally got put together, they sold Jolson the idea of doing it. . . .

ADAMSON: I always heard that Jessel demanded more money.

HASKIN: He was crossed. There was just a little gap between his playing it on the stage, and his contract as a movie star. THE JAZZ SINGER never hooked up with his picture career at all.

ADAMSON: You weren't too excited about THE BROADWAY KID?

HASKIN: It was a real bomb. I couldn't do anything at all with it.

ADAMSON: Well, we're still in '27 and there's one more picture you did -- at Columbia.

HASKIN: Oh, yes, THE SIREN. For Harry Cohn, with Dorothy Revier, Tom Moore, and Otto Hoffman -- a silent film. A fair picture, but it succeeded in getting me into trouble with Cohn. Cohn and Sam Briskin would take me up to the office every night and put me in the middle and play pingpong with me, until I got so confused that one night I went right downstairs after they'd told me to work that night -- and dismissed the company. (Laughs) I didn't know which the hell end I was standing on.

## Chapter Three

## ENGLAND

ADAMSON: We are up to your sojourn in England, then, which we have not covered.

HASKIN: I went over in '29. About two months before the stock market crashed, in summer. I arrived in August, on a bank holiday in London. It was my first trip ever, into England. BLACK WATERS, I think, was the name of the film that I was connected with in Hollywood, being made by Herbert Wilcox.

ADAMSON: Was it a British picture?

HASKIN: Yes. I don't think it ever had a release in America. Marshall Neilan directed it. That is, he was nominally the director. He was past usefulness on a movie set, but Herbert Wilcox was loyal, as British are, to the old days, and he had Marshall Neilan on this thing. He sat up in a booth and observed what was going on. I was setting the thing up and I was at the peak of my technique with multiple cameras. We used fog scenes and God knows what all. I've forgotten the cast, but the picture was, you know, acceptable.

ADAMSON: Why was Neilan past his usefulness?

HASKIN: Well, he didn't know what was going on with sound.

ADAMSON: Age or drink or just a new technique?

HASKIN: Age. And he had no technology. He never did when he was a big wheel. He seldom came down on the floor where all the directing was happening. Herbert was wandering around, and he didn't know what the hell was going on either.

ADAMSON: How did the picture get thrown together?

HASKIN: Well, I shot it. I set it up and directed the actors and rehearsed for him and everything -- I was a sort of silent butler down there, looking through cameras and jumping around, up and down off platforms. It was really a physical brute to make. They were aboard ship, and it was an Edgar Wallace story, that's all I remember about it. I think he wrote it between Chicago and New York on the New York Central one night while drunk. It had just about the expected amount of motives and continuity to it as an Edgar Wallace book -- he was one of the sleaziest of all the mystery writers. Dave Kesson was photographing the film. Dave was an alcoholic, and he was very neglectful of his duties. So, in addition to my directing and carrying on the sound and all, I had to photograph the film.

It was an example of a one-man band, really, but for what? This was the story of my life. You put out more effort with these bombs than they did on THE FOUR HORSEMEN OF THE APOCALYPSE and INTOLERANCE combined, and what do you do? You don't even get it up to mediocre-poor! It's just an outrage. But I was full of beans and I thought I was doing something, and it resulted in Herbert offering me the contract to come over and establish the American technique of shooting sound films in his new studio, which he was having built at the time -- British and Dominions Studio, at Boreham Wood. He had signed a production deal, or was at the point of signing a production deal, with His Master's Voice -- HMV -- which was the British Victor company -- RCA -- and it was the biggest sound recording company in all England.

So I packed up my trunks and my wife and little girl, and headed for England to make my life -- which ended sadly a couple of years later with coming back, having bought all the racehorses that lost the races and a few other knickknacks. It was Prohibition, and I switched from lethal alcohol (in the United States), to Scotch and good booze.

The B & D was not a successful operation. The only thing that ever paid out was one fortunate sort of a thing -- they signed up a man, Tom Walls, who had had a phenomenal series of stage plays in the Aldwych Theater -- comedies -- <u>Rookery Nook</u>, <u>Tons of Money</u>, and many others. Each one ran a year and was a hit. He had a stock company with Ralph Lynn, Winifred Shotter, etc. During the time I was over there, Herbert made a deal with Tom. I loved Tom, and we worked together. I supplied what he didn't know about movies, and we made these damned farces of his, and they all paid out. One of them even ran in America -- ROOKERY NOOK -- and made good money. But the other things, you couldn't believe. When I arrived, a thing called WOLVES was scheduled to start within two weeks. I don't think it's on the list -- my career in London is not recorded.

It was to star a young tyro from the British theatre named Charles Laughton -- his first movie -- and had an American star named Dorothy Gish, who was to be the girl. It was a story of Alaska, a sort of LIFEBOAT formula -- a group of strange, incompatible people marooned in a log cabin and snowed in for the winter, including murderers, rapists, and God knows what-all. All the bums around London who weren't working at the time were playing parts. This so-called play had been written by a Frenchman in Paris. How remote can you get from Alaska?

The screenplay was written by Sir Reginald Barclay, a puffy old futz who knew nothing about anything dramatic, but who had a big name in the theatre or something. He took the curtains out of it, and hooked it all together, and that was his screenplay -- this dreadful play, which had no motivation or anything to speak of. The director was Anthony De Courville from Paris, whose total range of experience with anything theatrical was that he put on live prologues to movies in Paris theatres. Now, he had been signed to direct WOLVES. Well, you couldn't believe it. I don't want to go into it -- I could spend days on the absolute insanity of this bloody thing. Moving into England, with the impact of the British culture on me, a more or less Flaky-Jake from Keokuk -- I did not have my cynical guard up at all.

I should have told Herbert, after I read the screenplay -- "Look, let's call this whole thing off, let's get something together," or at least, "Let's see what we can make out of this." But he said, "It's all prepared, all ready to go. . . ." Then he took me out to the studio to see the set. A big log cabin. There wasn't even room around it to get lamps in the windows, to light the thing.

ADAMSON: A four-walled cabin?

HASKIN: Yes. Of natural color logs. (Laughs) Dave Kesson was buzzed up with Scotch all the time, and he didn't know which end was up. I put in the multiple camera idea. We had such assistants to Dave on the other cameras as Freddie Young, who is now Sir Freddie, I think; he shot LAWRENCE OF ARABIA and a few other knickknacks. I brought Freddie up, actually, and Cyril Knowles and a bunch of guys just down from Oxford, who hardly knew what a camera was.

ADAMSON: What did Freddie Young do?

HASKIN: He was one of the cameramen. You see, with multiple cameras, you needed a whole flock of them. . . . Dave would be wandering around trying to get a lamp going while the scene was being shot.

Anyhow, the first morning, I couldn't believe it. I came onto the set and of course, I was not an authority, I was the American expert who was to expedite, not to handle. Well, I saw a lot of people standing around, and I asked the assistant, Jim Kelly, when the cast were going to arrive or where they were -- we should get them into costume.

He says, "They're all here. These are the cast, and they're in costume." They had on Saville Row suits tied around the knee like a navvy, with feathers in their hats. These were the costumes. It was really Alice in Wonderland!

So about midday, I went in to Herbert and I said, "Look, you've got to close this show. What the hell's the matter with you people? You've put out Antarctic expeditions, and various things -- you know what it takes to keep yourself from freezing to death in Alaska when the snow is outside covering the windows!" Well, instead of stopping the damn show then, we called the show off for ten days, and I went downtown and got it prepared. I got costumes and all the necessary things. Then it was shot and went right into the bin. That was it. They never even bothered to cut the thing, it was such a bomb.

To finish up about WOLVES, during the last six months I was there -- I was there a couple years -- Duncan Mansfield, whom I had brought over as a cutter, had nothing else to do and he took all these miscellaneous rolls of film out of the vault and spent a week cutting the bloody thing. It came out to be fifty-eight minutes long and didn't make any sense at all. (Laughs)

You found out real surprising things -- that these cameramen had buckled on the first ten seconds and hadn't informed anybody about it -- angles you expected to have from your script report just didn't exist. Also, a cameraman would have an instruction sheet, and at certain lines he's to switch to a 2-inch and pan over and get this two-shot, and then after the guy says that, he does this, and gets a close-up of him, and so on. Well, they forgot these instruction things, and they'd all end up on Laughton. (Laughs) Follow the money! He was a West End star. Or Dorothy Gish, when she was in the shot. Crazy.

That was the opening effort, and from there we went in and prepared a thing called THE LIVES AND LOVES OF ROBERT BURNS for almost six months. This was as big a fiasco. They cast for Robert Burns an anemic British tenor named Joseph Hyslop, which immediately estranged the whole Scottish race, to cast an Englishman as Burns, and such a "pouf" as this guy was, anyhow.


ADAMSON: Well, this is a pedantic question, I guess, but was the Scottish market real important to an English picture? I would think it would be.

HASKIN: Fairly so, but the question was entirely academic about the values, markets, etc., in England. In the first place, an English actor at that time, when given a Scottish part, was the equivalent of an American actor cast in a Shakespearean play for the first time: What he says on stage, you can't understand at all. Even the Scotsmen were hard pressed to find out what the hell English actors playing Scottish roles at this time were talking about. They were absolutely dreadful, made no sense. And they would not compromise to any degree in these jaw-busters!

Just one illustration of the way it was dramatized: As is known from historical fact, Burns' end was inglorious -- he got drunk in a tavern, started home, fell in a snowbank, and froze to death, or got pneumonia and died later, whatever. Now, this was translated in terms of Herbert Wilcox's glory stuff, so that Hyslop goes into the tavern and sits at a table in a booth, alone, with a candle which gets shorter and shorter during an eleven-and-a-half-minute recitative of all Burns' poems by Hyslop, looking blank. A lot of them weren't even Burns' -- "Annie Laurie" is not Burns', but that was in there. (Laughs) Finally, as he gets weaker and weaker and suffers, the candle is lower and lower, and as it gutters out, "Uhh -- " he dies. He and the candle go off together, like the hired man, the maid, and the alarm clock.

Well, finally Dunc put this thing together, and it was short. We had to send Dave up to Scotland, where it's now midwinter, which is something, to shoot a scenic of those weird-looking sheep wandering around in the snow, and the cottages half buried and things like that, clouds, glory. Dunc cut that together and played some spooky music at the beginning, and they fixed up a preview in Glasgow. They took it up there, and they ran it in the theatre, and I kid you not -- the audience threw whiskey bottles at the screen. It didn't get over halfway through. They were so outraged, the Scottish people, that they shut it off, and that was the end of it. Now there's my first two big efforts. . . .

ADAMSON: (Laughs) Well, one more pedantic question: Why Glasgow instead of Edinburgh, with a thing about Burns, which is cultural? I mean, isn't that a little bit like opening in Pittsburgh instead of Philadelphia?

HASKIN: I wouldn't know. I think Wilcox was afraid of Edinburgh. He just wanted to get into the basic Burns country or something.

I remember, on that show, he had the entire London Symphony Orchestra out one day on one stage, and the action was going on in the tavern on the other stage. The only problem was that the sound guys never connected the two up. So, the orchestra is playing over here, and they're recorded on a track, and the other people over here are singing.

ADAMSON: They couldn't mix them?

HASKIN: No, it was supposed to be piped onto a single track, but the patchwork was bad or something.

ADAMSON: Was that still going on? On THE SINGING FOOL, where there was music under a lot of the scenes, were the musicians there at the same time?

HASKIN: Oh, yes. We had no dubbing facilities, as I have mentioned. Those were individual little recordings.

Well, Wilcox then got some of the things going, some Lonsdale plays, and he made a little success, but finally, we just went into the doldrums. Nothing was happening, like early Marshall Neilan. (Laughs) For days, the boss wouldn't come around, nothing would happen. I went off to Nice for ten days, and came back and walked in backwards like I'd been there all the time, and nobody knew the difference! I'd had some adventures, practically lost my citizenship in the middle of the English Channel.

The liaison man between the gramophone company and us, Ian Javal, whom I was fairly friendly with, told me that if Wilcox could just show one quarter of profit, or only break even, they were willing to put up unlimited funds for motion picture production, but he said he could not, in any faithfulness to his board, recommend that they go on with this ridiculous type of production. So they broke up.

It wasn't until after the break between British Dominions and His Master's Voice, that we got Tom Walls and made a little money. But that wasn't due to Herbert -- Herbert hated the things.

ADAMSON: Were there other sound films being made in England at the time?

HASKIN: Yes.

ADAMSON: Did they not have partnerships with HMV?

HASKIN: No. That was a big promotion by Herbert. He was a great promoter. He would spend more time on the "trade show," which was the preview of the film, than he would on the production, and that's where his weakness lay. He was always off to some industrial town to get something lined up. But finally, I came back to America.

Chapter Four

## REMINISCENCES ABOUT EARLY HOLLYWOOD PERSONALITIES

ADAMSON: I wanted to ask you about some of the people you worked with in the early days of your career, especially the cinematographers.

HASKIN: Yes. The man who made a profound impact on me was John F. Seitz. He changed the whole course of my photographic endeavors, gave me a completely new vision. THE FOUR HORSEMEN OF THE APOCALYPSE was the first film that perfected the modern style of photography, the Rembrandt principle. In other words, you become conscious of the back wall as part of the unit of the lighting; so you leave a deep shadow on the face, and light up the back wall. You have as good a definition as you do keeping the back wall dark and blasting the subject with a lamp right over the top of your magazines. Previous to that picture, and others foretelling that type of change, the standard makeup was practically clown white, and the lighting was flat. A face looked like a white pieplate with burnt holes in it most of the time, with the contrasty developers they used in a lot of the laboratories, such as William Fox in those days. That's what made Theda Bara appear as such a weirdo -- those black eyes with the big black rims around them and white face and black lips. No gradations, no shadows, nothing.

ADAMSON: Looking back, it works best in the comedies -- the Chaplin pictures still look O.K. for that.

HASKIN: Yes, yes. Sure. Well, Rollie Totheroh persisted in that style of photography clear into the modern day.

ADAMSON: Clear into MONSIEUR VERDOUX. But wasn't that also a function of the film in a way, the orthochromatic film?

HASKIN: No, not at all. DON JUAN was shot on orthochromatic film, and it had full gradations. Also, THE SEA BEAST.

When sound came in, changes had to be made. The arc lamps we were using were too noisy, sputtering and popping. Instead, we used incandescent lighting. However, the incandescent light was no good for orthochromatic film, being too heavy in yellow, and ortho was most sensitive to blue. There was panchromatic film, sensitive to yellow, but it was very slow. The lamp units were mostly improvised from headlights, searchlights, etc.

We had to switch to panchromatic film with the coming of sound, because the arc lights we were using were too noisy. They buzzed and they sputtered all the time. The switch had to be made to incandescent lighting. These introduced a new spectrum, strong in yellow.

Ortho film was most sensitive to blue, insensitive to the warmer colors. In fact, the darkroom lamps were red. Red makeup was used on the lips -- showing black lips. Yellow was not much better. The film most sensitive to incandescent light was panchromatic. Regardless of the fact that it was very slow, it came into heavy use in the first Vitaphone shorts.

A good many of the Vitaphone shorts were shot in New York at first. Then we began shooting them out West, where there'd be eighteen to twenty-four hour per day production going. For these, we had to improvise new lights.

There was only one small stage, soundproofed with blankets and mattresses and what-have-you. To accommodate the panchromatic film, the lights were ad-libbed out of anything with a bulb. All were universally hotter than a two-dollar pistol shooting uphill. You'd come out after an hour of working in the stage absolutely dehydrated.

ADAMSON: Didn't you say once you could light a cigar on them?

HASKIN: Well, that was later. Some of the electric lamp companies began to develop units particularly for this work. The first panchromatic film was so slow it needed lots of light. We never could shoot much further from a subject than the knee figure. Finally, one company developed a 10kw spotlight. That's the one that'd light a cigar at twenty-five feet.

Ed DuPar, Willard Van Enger, Frank Kesson, a lot of us -- were called in to shoot these Vitaphone shorts in our off time, and it got to be our "on" time. We'd be eighteen hours a day in the soundstage. There was no limit to the hours, no compensation such as time-and-a-half for overtime. We were strictly slaves. We were in there as much as we could stand. And to kill the pain of fatigue, many of us were half loaded most of the time. These excessive working hours brought the unions into the business to legislate tolerable conditions. So the abuse accompanying the coming of sound brought profound alteration of the whole movie business in every way. I was in an advisory capacity on the discussions which set the standard of speed at 24 for photographing and recording. Photographing silent films had always been at the speed of 16 pictures per second.

ADAMSON: Was it known exactly how fast you were going?

HASKIN: Exactly, yes. The theatre projector was run at that 16 frames-per-second speed. Any deviation in photographing would cause the action to be slow or fast. Keystone comedies were photographed at all kinds of different speeds: 8, and 4 and 10 and 12 -- anything that the cameraman figured was needed for the particular bit of comedy. Of course, regardless of shooting speed, they would be projected at 16.

One-to-one photography -- one frame to one turn of the camera crank -- was first employed by Hans Koenekamp, who was the greatest trick cameraman of them all. He was with Larry Semon, and got this one-to-one trick so perfect that every time Larry ran down a street, when his left foot hit the sidewalk Kony would expose one picture. Semon would skid a whole block on one foot; then Kony would skip to the right foot, causing Semon to go to a right foot skid. It always got a big laugh. Fred Jackman claims he originated drop speed photography. However, I have my doubts. It could have been one of many others -- probably Koenekamp.

ADAMSON: What is drop speed photography?

HASKIN: Well, you drop from 16 speed down to 8, 10, 12, 4, 2, 1, whatever, according to the kind of zip you want to put into the action of the scene. Keystone comedies were all undercranked.

ADAMSON: Yes. What was Jackman's story?

HASKIN: Jackman originally came from the Midwest with a bit of money and his family, with an idea that he'd like to go into movies. He figured he could become a cameraman. So, he bought a camera, a Pathé, I think. It probably cost him $1200 with all the equipment at that time.

Now that he had a camera, he had to find out how you run it. He thought, The moviehouse is the place they show movies -- I'll go up and watch the projectionist and I'll find out how you do it. The trouble was that while the camera took two turns of the crank at 16 speed (sixteen pictures), the projector was a different kettle of fish: It took one turn. The projectionist was cranking by hand, sixteen pictures for one turn. So, Jackman peered in the porthole and jotted down his calculations.

Now he goes with the camera out to Mack Sennett's in Edendale, where he told them, "I'm a cameraman. I own my own camera." They said, "Fine, get your camera loaded, and get in the car and start the chase." And away they went. No argument about qualifications or anything. He shot two or three days, shooting his camera as he'd watched it done by the projectionist. When Sennett saw the rushes, he wanted to fire Jackman. "What the hell happened? What's he doing?" None of his aides knew at all. They ran it again to study it. A few people laughed. The next day, when Sennett was indignantly showing everybody what had happened, everybody broke into laughter. Being no dummy, Sennett had them hire Jackman on contract. That was the beginning of undercranking. The one turn of the crank per second equalled an 8 camera speed. It gave a supernatural kind of energy to all the comics.

ADAMSON: That must have been around 1912 or 1913.

HASKIN: It was before I came to Hollywood. All the Mack Sennett films that I remember seeing in the nickelodeons around San Francisco were -- ZIP, ZIP ZIP. So it happened probably around '13, '14, because I don't remember any Mack Sennett comedies shot at normal crank speed. Mack Sennett's was a wild and woolly place. It was an improvisation studio. These directors were really stuntmen or hoodlums, most of them. They would start with the director saying, "I've got an idea." They'd put him on the schedule, and he'd turn in two or three pages of alleged screenplay that had little to do with what eventually was shot. He'd collect a cameraman and two or three others for a crew and two comics and some stunt guys, and maybe a patrol wagon. Grover Liggon and Bill Harbaugh were in charge of the patrol with regular Keystone Kops -- Harvey Parry and the rest. Mack Swain was originally a Keystone Kop. Eddie Gribbon, and most of the stars came off the patrol.

Later, at Warner Bros., I rode the patrol downtown, with Grover Liggon driving it. He became a stuntman for Warners, a very effete sort of a position compared to being a Sennett roustabout. They would wreck the town -- they'd tie a smokepot under the patrol and fill it with Kops who fell off at every street corner, all through town, up the wrong side of the streets.

Streetcars would be jamming on brakes, and cars coming head-on would be going up over the sidewalk.

Generally, in these comedies, they'd start with the chase, while they'd think up something, and then they'd work it into some kind of a story to tie it all together. Then, day after tomorrow they'd bring it all in and there it was -- finished. It got so that railroading in Southern California was a very precarious business. No engineer liked to come around a curve to find somebody tied to the tracks, and a car crossing in front of his locomotive, and God knows what-all going on! (Laughs) Stunts of all kinds! A phony bus would be stalled across the tracks, and the engineer is supposed to run through it. They'd usually meet the train at a previous station to bribe the firemen to throw in a lot of smoke as they approached the movie location so it'd look good. Really an improvisation!

ADAMSON: That's the kind of stories I've heard. They would sort of do this without clearing it with the railroad or the police?

HASKIN: Not necessarily. It was like when I used to go out with the Navy. Feature writers, cameramen, lived with the Navy, half their life. All they needed was a little card authorizing them -- it could be printed at any print shop -- and they were guests of the Navy.

The same in town. There were no particular regulations about downtown, you could use any of the streets. They weren't too crowded. Of course, you could have killed people if you hit them with those damn patrol wagons. The movie guys were a crazy, reckless, ribald kind of a group.

ADAMSON: Why were you riding a patrol?

HASKIN: I needed some rear projection backgrounds for a chase, and I thought I'd ride it. Ed DuPar, once at Sennett's, was the cameraman at Warner Bros. on this particular assignment. He said, "Come on, take a ride. Not chicken are you? Grover will drive. You can see what we're going to get." Well, this bastard DuPar took a regular Keystone ride through town!

ADAMSON: Without a camera or anything going?

HASKIN: Yes, of course he had a camera. We were going up the wrong side of streets, ducking in between streetcars -- they'd be coming together, and would have absolutely crushed us, but we got through just in time. The damned old patrol was a wreck, too, it would hardly run.

ADAMSON: You did a lot of stuff with DuPar, didn't you?

HASKIN: Yes, he was a good friend of mine, a personal friend. He lived in Beverly Hills close to my home. We both had a fondness for liquor. Later, when I became Director of Special Effects for Warner Bros. for nine years, DuPar was one of my cameramen....

ADAMSON: Did you know John Seitz personally?

HASKIN: Oh, yes. Well, I used to go over to his set -- that's where I met Fred Gage, the laboratory superintendent at the Metro Company. I was there with Alan Holubar, as you remember.

I was extra camera on several of Ingram's films, including SCARAMOUCHE with Ramon Novarro. Rex Ingram directed THE FOUR HORSEMEN, but I didn't work on it because at the time I was with Holubar making MAN-WOMAN-MARRIAGE. Later though, I was available around the lot and worked on SCARAMOUCHE.

I knew Vic Milner, who was with Seitz the second camera on THE FOUR HORSEMEN; and I knew Seitz. Seitz was a kind of a dreamer. Fred Gage used to stand anxiously over the developing tanks at night, praying that there was something on Seitz's film, because Seitz was a very low-key light man. Fred would say, "Oh, God -- be something!" And he'd shove it back in the soup. Finally, it'd eventually show an image.

A typical scene -- Fred told me about this, I did not witness it -- Seitz had a corridor scene of the period, dusty and cobwebby. He was busy lighting it with his gaffer, the day Fred appeared on the set to report to Seitz on how the negative was the night before. Johnny was busy lighting his long hallway. Fred stood around for a while watching the lighting. Finally, he walked over to John, and said, "Well, I gotta go back to the lab. Let's turn them on and see how it looks." He figured he could convince Johnny to add a little more light. Johnny said, "Hey Fred, they're already on." (Laughs) Fred was still groping around the set! He may have been a problem to the lab, but Seitz's concepts were absolutely revolutionary for the day.

In most cases he carried them out with enough light to be able to see them, and then sometimes he didn't -- he loved dark effects. He changed the style of motion picture photography. I cannot stress this too much, that an individual man changed the whole course of this complex art. He made movie shots a composite -- background and foreground becoming a unit, an artistic concept -- the Rembrandt principle . . .

ADAMSON: Light falling off people different ways --

HASKIN: Yes.

ADAMSON: What about things like backlighting people?

HASKIN: Well, it had been employed by Bitzer for Griffith. I don't know who was first responsible. Then there was the top light from up above. Dave Kesson with Marshall Neilan used to employ 90-amp arc lights on the top of the set.

There were many innovations, but it was Seitz who made the difference, molding contours of the face, revolutionizing the whole mode of photography. I, of course, with Holubar, was tied to the old over-the-magazine spot, because his wife Dorothy Phillips was tough to photograph. He wouldn't permit anything but a nice white face on her -- not a trace of character, let alone shadows or wrinkles. Every month, when she had a period, she'd get dark streams down her cheeks here, and we'd get a bigger spot going. . . .

ADAMSON: What kind of things did Seitz do to get these mottled effects? Like putting scrims in front of the lamps, for instance.

HASKIN: Well, he used a great many silks and he'd never get so wild as to hang a Cooper-Hewitt bank over a set, because that was more light than he figured he'd need, whereas most photographers, the fire kings, would use a Cooper-Hewitt bank just to fill in the shadow! Seitz wouldn't use it because it would flood this ghastly blast of light all over his set. He used broads -- the Winfield-Kerner 2-carbon arc lights, floodlights. He would use them for a shaft of light, coming in an archway, maybe three or four of them stacked together, instead of a 150-amp arc spotlight, which most cameramen used.

Charlie Rosher was one of the fire kings. He was Mary Pickford's cameraman. Of course, Charlie made a very rounded image of Mary in her close-ups, very softly rounded, but in no way had the daring artistic concept that Seitz had.

Seitz couldn't have lasted with any star who had her or his own company. They couldn't stand for it. Throwing shadows on their faces. But Rex Ingram approved of Seitz. He overshadowed his cast. Rudy Valentino was his protégé at the time, and those gorgeous shots of him in THE FOUR HORSEMEN in the cafes and on the pampas, with the dark foreground, and the haze in the middle distance -- all these effects were a new concept completely.

It has become cliché through years of use, but at the time of THE FOUR HORSEMEN, this was all as novel as the STAR WARS special effects today.

ADAMSON: Who shot SCARAMOUCHE?

HASKIN: Seitz and Milner. Vic Milner was an unimaginative first cameraman -- he did what Seitz wanted him to. Later, he shot a lot of films of his own, but they were totally different as to character.

ADAMSON: What about some of the other cameramen working at Warners at the same time, like Tony Gaudio?

HASKIN: Tony Gaudio was an old-timer, even then. A fire king, like Arthur Edeson. Sol Polito was an old-timer, too. I worked as an assistant with Sol Polito. Later he photographed the Busby Berkeley shows. Sol was not a real top flight artistic cameraman.

There are two kinds of cameramen -- one is a natural man who sees the image immediately and then gets it to look like he visualizes. The other one is the cameraman who's there because he's getting good money. He knows the amount of exposure, and knows that a window should have a light coming through it, and works out effects with the tools at hand, without any particular vision of what he's after, or any style. Sol was the latter, but it worked out just fine for Berkeley, who wanted what is called "furniture photography" -- all the legs and the tits, and the everything, which showed up great with Sol. He'd have all the lights in the world pouring into the set. You could see under the rugs. (Laughs)

ADAMSON: Well, Polito, I know, liked these kinds of artificial things.

HASKIN: Tony Gaudio was not really of a star turn in my book, although he did consistent work which was occasionally outstanding. He photographed, for instance, some of the Curtiz films. I photographed eleven straight pictures with Mike Curtiz after he first came to this country. The first film he made was a weirdo kind of a thing. Hal Mohr shot that. Then I picked him up and shot eleven straight films with him, and a couple later on.

Curtiz was a tremendously visual man. He had no command of any language that I could find out, not even Hungarian, which he was supposed to be. His verbiage was loaded with four-letter words. He drove his Packard car one year and never knew it had any gear but second (laughs) -- let alone reverse and what not. I don't know how he got around with it.

But he did have a visual sense: "I visualize, Bunnie" -- his nickname for me. "Follow me." He was a madman on movement. Of course, he was also a madman at changing his mind after you'd laid 300 feet of dolly track. So I had my chief grip employ a set of phony tracks. He'd follow him around, and when Curtiz would look back to see that he'd already started, he'd just drop a phony track, banging on it with a hammer, until I'd give him the nod that it was going to be the shot. Owen Crump was the grip.

Curtiz was a flawed man in his dramatic concepts, but he directed a great scene, I will say that. He shot some great scenes. But he was a loser. For instance, I went to Halifax on CAPTAINS OF THE CLOUDS, for second units. It was with Cagney and the Warner stock company. I was doing the air units with bush planes.

In fact, I would follow and mop up all the things that Curtiz would drop as he was going along. It became a team, the two of us directing. I was doing the stuff at Halifax of the Hudson bombers, the Hurricanes, and shots of convoys leaving the harbor.

Every half-hour he'd call me. He could never get directions straight -- right and left, and left and right. I'd say, "Raise your right hand." I never knew which one was going up. I kept him straight as to picture geography, a good practice for my own knowledge later.

Every night he would have to call the studio back in Hollywood, and report to Warner and Wallis. If you ever saw a guy beaten to a pulp on the telephone, this guy was it. He'd finally lift the phone -- "Hello, Jack, well this is -- yeah, oh, you saw that? Well, it should -- what, Jack?" Then, after a pause: "Awwhhh, please, Jack don't talk like this. You know I am trying hard up here. Oh, it's Hal, huh? Oh, well, Hal, oh, don't talk like this, Hal." And they'd bounce him around like a pingpong ball for twenty minutes, absolutely tear him to pieces.

His stuff was generally great. He had the greatest rushes you ever saw. Sometimes it wouldn't cut together very well, but he would shoot very inspired scenes. Finally he'd hang up. "Bunnie, I jump out of the window. These guys drive me crazy."

When he worked at the studio, he'd go into Warner's office, and Warner would just mow him down -- "You bum, you creep, you wouldn't have a wife, you wouldn't have a dollar, you wouldn't have anything if it wasn't for me." Curtiz would go out under the door with a high hat on and never touch anything, and that was the end of the argument. I guess he needed it. He was a masochist, a weirdo.

ADAMSON: How do you mean, he needed it?

HASKIN: He was a freak, he had to have abuse. When they finally gave him his own company at Warner Bros., they proceeded to steal him blind. The diffusers on the lake, which had nothing to do with him, they'd charge against his pictures. Everything. He couldn't make any money at all, they were charging all the capital outlay of Warner Bros. against him.

How do I know this? I was in Jack Warner's office -- at the time we were not too friendly, and he had a hell of a lot of nerve telling Tenny Wright in front of me, "Slough that stuff over on Curtiz." Jesus. 'Twas ever thus. Movies are a vital industry, vital part of the culture. Otherwise, they never would have lasted through all the skullduggery and thievery and larceny that's gone on. It is imposssible even to conceive of the amount of money that has been stolen.

ADAMSON: Curtiz did some of their most profitable pictures.

HASKIN: He was a very innovative man, and yet there was a screw loose somewhere and he couldn't stay oriented in any kind of a workman-like way of shooting a picture. He was always in trouble with schedule and budget. He would get 500 cowboys up in the middle of the Painted Desert, and spend all day taking a close-up of the wagon wheels stuck in the sand. In the studio, Warner'd look at the rushes and say, "What the hell's the guy doing up there? Get him on the phone." And he'd tear him to pieces. (Laughs) Actually, on such films as VIRGINIA CITY, and all those Westerns and things, the big scope things that he did with Flynn --

ADAMSON: DODGE CITY?

HASKIN: Yes. I was the guy that did all the big stuff while he went down the middle, shooting his scenes.

ADAMSON: (Laughs) That fight scene in DODGE CITY? Everybody's throwing tables and things are flying through the air? Was that yours?

HASKIN: Yes.

ADAMSON: I haven't seen the movie -- I just saw that scene. It's one of the most incredible scenes I've ever seen in my life. (Laughs) Everything flying around.

HASKIN: Yes, I used to have all the stuntmen in town working for me in my department, and that was the craziest group -- Harvey Parry, Alan Pomeroy, Duke Green, Yakima Canutt, Bennie Corbett, and others.

ADAMSON: You told me a story about Busby Berkeley on Highway One which we didn't record.

HASKIN: Well, it's all in the newspapers and the annals and records of the L.A. Courts. It was toward the end of Buzz's contract with Warner Bros. Busby was a guy who couldn't drink -- two or three drinks, and he was out of his gourd. This particular night he had gone down to Bill Koenig's house in

Malibu to a party. He had some booze, and then drove off in his Cadillac in another world, down the highway with his foot on the floor, and rammed into another car head-on.

I don't remember the exact number of casualties. There were young people, teenagers in it, some killed, some suffered dreadful damage and were confined to the hospital for life. Buzz wasn't even scratched. It just blew out his tires. Being stiff, he got out and wandered away along the beach, looking for another drink.

Warners found it expedient to back him in the trial. They got Jerry Giesler, who assembled his corps of experts mostly from skid row. (Laughs) Blaney Matthews transferred his allegiance as investigator for the District Attorney to police chief of Warner Bros. So Buzz was set for trial.

I know some of the workings of the trial because, to keep Busby solvent, they assigned him to direct a picture. With Dick Powell and Ruby Keeler, who else? I photographed it. Every half hour there'd be some kind of a conference at the back of the set. Giesler would be back behind the flat beckoning him, and Buzz would grudgingly join him. He did not show a great deal of contrition about this whole thing. He claimed he was being framed, and he would get quite angry when Giesler would show up.

In the aftermath of this trial, several of the witnesses that Giesler had assembled turned up with term contracts with Warner Bros. (laughs) to work for so many hundred dollars a week. One of them I had personal experience with was the so-called tire expert who had testified that Busby's tire had a blowout which caused the tragedy. It was part of the Giesler m.o. contraption. It got Berkeley off.

This tire expert didn't know rubber from asphalt; a real idiot. They assigned him to me in my Special Effects Department. I put him in with my engineer, Bill Thomas, to spend his time -- who cared? But he couldn't keep his mouth shut. The first day he came to work, he brought a big package with him. Mid-morning, he took it up to Wallis' office, explaining to the secretary that he wanted to give Mr. Wallis a present. The secretary put him through. So when Wallis opened the package on his desk -- it's the busted tire that had been exhibited in court. Exhibit A! (Laughs) He was giving it to Wallis as a souvenir! Wallis' face was pale as he accepted.

ADAMSON: So the guy worked six weeks?

HASKIN: Yes. At $450 per. When the contract expired, they threw him out. He was typical of the witnesses Giesler assembled for the trial. Busby got off -- a not guilty verdict. Giesler was always successful. The cost, I think, was near $78,000 for legal expenses and incidentals. Including the idiot tire man. Warner put Busby immediately on assignment to fill out the rest of his contract. They garnisheed his wages. The minute they recouped $78,000, they tossed him out of the studio and gave orders he wasn't to ever be allowed back on the lot. (Laughs)

So, he went to MGM and signed up and became famous for all those big musicals. I worked quite a bit with Buzz as a cameraman at Warners. I helped with some of the big special effects sequences -- pillars twenty feet high and three feet thick -- big columns moving around the set like dancers. Busby Berkeley became famous at Warner Bros. because he was arrogant. He would not do a number unless it cost $80,000 or more. It was a minimum; he'd plan a musical routine, then he'd have it budgeted. If it didn't come up to the minimum, he'd throw it out and start something else. (Laughs) It might be a hell of a number, he didn't care. Jesus, what an attitude. Ego versus fiscal responsibility! He expanded his original instruction to great fame; the key was his personal type of shots -- patterning swimmers in water like floral arrangements with beautiful girls -- cuts from a fan in a woman's hand to a matching giant fan, and then withdrawing the fan. Behind it was the Grand Central Station filled with women! His mentor was Larry Ceballos, Warner Bros.' head dance director at the time.

There were many stories, but as I understand it, Busby Berkeley came from New York, an obscure choreographer. He came to Warner Bros. At first he'd sit around, do some drinking, nothing much else. Ceballos took him in hand and showed him how to stage musical numbers. He did have a tremendous imagination, expanding the instructions with a real flair. He really came to flower at MGM, making BABES IN ARMS, and other big musicals.

ADAMSON: Wasn't he famous at Warner Bros.?

HASKIN: Well, yes. Famous. He did 42ND STREET, GOLD DIGGERS, and various things. Dick Powell and Ruby Keeler things. Real innovations.

ADAMSON: He must have had more money to work with at MGM.

HASKIN: Certainly. But his genius for novelty shots had been developed at Warner Bros. From there, he commanded big fees at MGM after the trial.

ADAMSON: Norman McLeod is another interesting person you knew.

HASKIN: Yes, I go back to the beginning with Norman McLeod. His first experience in movies was with Jack McDermott, previously described as a writer-director, in the old silent days.

ADAMSON: A Hollywood character.

HASKIN: Yes. As a young man he had understudied Frank Tinney, a big stage comedian of the day. Jack had gone to Notre Dame. He had a history of weird accomplishments you wouldn't believe. He knew everybody in town. He wrote scripts for Harry Carey, and so forth.

Jack met Norm during World War I. They were in the Air Force together training at the University of California in

Berkeley. I was an undergrad at the school. The campus was full of Air Force trainees studying to be flyers. Jack McDermott, among his many talents, could play a bugle, so he joined the Drum and Bugle Corps.

Norm McLeod turned up in Ground School, met Jack, who said, "Hey, you get out of all the drills in the Drum and Bugle Corps. Come on. Join up." Norm said, "But I don't know how to play a bugle." Jack said, "Aw hell, doesn't matter. Just hold it up to your mouth, imitate the other buglers. You don't need to blow it." (Laughs)

I remember, after Retreat, the Bugle Corps would march along the pathways across campus over to the barracks. They'd be in single file playing a rousing piece. Norm would be cleaning his mouthpiece. (Laughs) He couldn't blow a note.

Finally, Ground School was over, and they were sent to Texas -- Fort Dix. It was a tremendous place, with a huge parade field. There were thousands of trainees there. Norm, when he arrived, told the sergeant in charge that he'd been in the Bugle Corps at Berkeley. The guy signed him up in the Fort Dix Corps. Norm figured he'd escape all that drill.

Later on, he's wandering around and sees the camp bulletin board. On the list for the next morning at 4:30 a.m., he's assigned to blow Reveille! (Laughs) Jesus! Well, he panicked. He ought to have gone to the sergeant and made an excuse -- say he cut his lip with a razor, anything. But he was too guilty to think clearly.

At dawn, next morning, he stood in front of a megaphone six feet long, quivering. The barracks reached clear to the horizon. He put the bugle to his lips and blew. It went: "AAAGGGGHHHH." Hardly Reveille! (Laughs) Soldiers came running out, grabbed him, put him in the brig, and took away all his privileges for faking it.

Anyhow, in spite of it, Norm was pretty good during the flying instruction period. Later, he became an instructor himself. Jack, however, being a fly-by-night character with no instincts for aviation, became known as the Mexican Ace! He had wiped out three of our airplanes personally, never passing solo, and finally was crashed out.

Now, fade out, the war was over. Jack was set to direct a Christie Comedy, a one-reeler. Norm wanders into town from Seattle. Jack had always told him, "If you ever come to Hollywood, come on down and I'll see that you get a job." So there was Norman, fresh from Seattle without an ounce of knowledge, ready to accept Jack's promise! Norman said, "Here I am. Give me that job." Jack said, "Well sure. You're my assistant." (Laughs) Norm said, "Thanks."

Next day is set to shoot according to the schedule. Jack arrives, then Norman, but no actors, nobody else. After a while, the studio production manager came to Jack, asking, "Where the hell is your assistant?" He pointed to Norm sitting in a chair alongside. The production man asked Norm, "Where the hell's the cast -- where's the cameraman?" Norm had thought being the assistant was to assist McDermott to direct. So that was Norman's auspicious start in pictures.

ADAMSON: (Laughs) He was supposed to be, strictly speaking, the assistant director, and to go out and assemble everybody?

HASKIN: Yes, of course. Jack had only said, "You're my assistant. Just go over and tell the cashier." It was a very informal operation at Christies', to say the least. Norm was reclassified as a gag man, and a new crew started the film. After several months, he had the idea of illustrating the subtitles with the little hairpin figures. However, he didn't have any more technique for drawing than he'd had for the bugle. He didn't know the proportions of anything.

I helped organize his little hairpin figures -- tried to instruct him. It got so he could express certain ideas pretty well -- simple ones.

ADAMSON: Sort of a basic cartoon technique?

HASKIN: Yes. Well, I had been a cartoonist in San Francisco, so it was easy enough for me.

ADAMSON: And you drew some of these if he wasn't around?

HASKIN: Yes. There were about twenty-eight, thirty titles in each film, on black cards. I'd use white ink and draw these little hairpin figures illustrative of something the title was saying.

I think I got about twenty-five dollars which was a fortune, if you were starving. (Laughs)

I've forgotten whether Norm and I were living together when he got his first feature assignment to direct -- a film with the Marx Brothers at Paramount. He was terrified. (Laughs) Oh, God, that was something.

That was his initial picture, although in your book you referred to a couple other things he'd done previous to that.

ADAMSON: That was writing, that wasn't directing.

HASKIN: Yes. I think that those credits are apocryphal, anyhow. Believe me. He had only been a gag man for friends he knew.

ADAMSON: He supposedly had worked on SKIPPY, but Stu Heisler told me that a neighbor of his had written SKIPPY, and that it wasn't McLeod at all.

HASKIN: That's right. Norm framed up a little background resume to present to Paramount. He actually had worked with the guy in charge of production.

ADAMSON: Don Hartman?

HASKIN: Yes. Hartman and he were gag men at Paramount together. He told me later that Hartman was one of the dumbest gag men he ever knew.

ADAMSON: Norm told me that when he was set to direct at Paramount, he came home and said, "Geez, I got my assignment -- to direct the Marx Brothers."

HASKIN: He was terrified. (Laughs) Oh, God, that was something!

Chapter Five

**THE THIRTIES**


ADAMSON: When you first came back from England, you went to work for Columbia?

HASKIN: Yes, I think it was the first thing I did, the job as cameraman. I could have stayed there, but I went out to Warners, renewed my old touches. It was suggested that if I needed bread, I could take a job in the Special Effects Department.

ADAMSON: In '32?

HASKIN: Yes, as I recall. I went into the Special Effects Department as a unit cameraman, and then I went out on production from there and shot a few films -- AS THE EARTH TURNS, BLACK FURY, etc. Eventually, Fred Jackman, head of the department, quit. They gave me the job as head of the Special Effects Department.

ADAMSON: Now, that was some time in the late thirties.

HASKIN: No, that was around the mid-thirties. There were six first cameramen in the department, including John Stumeier, Kenny Peach, and Hans Koenekamp, the greatest individual trick man in the business, and the old original in my book. Jackman used to pick Kony's brains all the time. Then he'd tell the producer, "Well, I figured this shot out."

Kony never had enough gumption to expose this baloney. So eventually, Jackman quit. I took over. I decided, I'd be damned if I was going to pick Koenekamp's brains, just as a matter of personal principle. I dictated the way that all the shots should be made for the nine years I ran the department. Of course, I turned Kony loose on a lot of them, and let him take the credit. Before this, I used to watch Jackman call all the first cameramen in -- I was one of them at the time. He'd say, "We got some shots in this picture, and here's a tough one. I've got it figured out, but I want to hear how you guys would do it."

The rest of us would fumble around with it. Then Kony'd say, "I'd do it this way . . ." Jackman would say, "Exactly the way I had it." (Laughs) He couldn't have done the shot himself! He ran a paternalistic department. It was a studio within a studio. I could have made features in there that they would have known nothing about. I even had my own laboratory and sound department. That's how secretive Jackman had been in putting the department together. He came from the tradition where every studio had its own trick department behind velvet and walls. Nobody was allowed to go in there.

ADAMSON: Sounds like that laboratory in DON JUAN.

HASKIN: Yes. Yes, absolutely. Real weird security, which was enforced. This kind of thinking almost wrecked the movie business, because these things became more and more expensive, developed individually. Each studio had its own department and was running it unilaterally. Well, it just compounded the cost of production to where it was ridiculous. Finally, William Beatty, a patent attorney, worked out a patent agreement amongst all eleven or twelve major studios. They agreed to share standard procedures at least. Of course, we all kept something secret.

For instance, if Paramount was developing something, they could be asked to reveal it, on the tentative agreement that you would pay part of the cost of development for subsequent use of it. After a specified period of exclusivity. At least, this procedure became tolerable, particularly when special effects came in big. Jackman was one of the original special-effects-for-hire guys after he left Sennett. That's how he landed at Warner Bros. as head of that department. He would do a job for $3500 that cost him only a fraction. He'd jump horses over cattle; trick shots like that.

And Kony always figured them out for him. (Laughs) That was Kony's cross. When Jackman quit, I wasn't of any mind to take the damn department -- I wanted to get back to shooting features. Being confined on Stage 5 was not to my liking. Bill Koenig, production manager of Warner Bros., came to me when Jackman left and said, "I want you to take the department." I said, "Jesus, the logical man is Hans Koenekamp. He's the greatest trick man who ever lived."

Well, he didn't think much of that, because he didn't know Kony. Anyhow, I deferred my answer, went down on the stage and looked for Kony. I couldn't find him. He hid out for seven days, somewhere on the backlot. He'd leave home, and hide out around the studio. He was just too shy to handle people, and the job necessitated working with producers and directors all the time.

He was not that kind of a trick man; he would take his actor to a corner of the stage, and pull the velvets around. Two days later, he'd come out and deliver the shot of him flying over Berlin or what-have-you. You didn't know what the hell he might come up with! He once brought the <u>Lusitania</u> up the rapids below Niagara Falls! (Laughs) So I took the job, and I had it for nine years.

ADAMSON: Just because you couldn't find him for seven days.

HASKIN: Yes, yes. As I say, the Warners Special Effects Department was one of the wonders of the picture business during its time. It got so that around the lot we'd have a half dozen production companies going, on various stages, and they all knew that if anything got tough in the day's shooting -- "Oh, forget it! Let Stage 5 do it." So we were a sort of an emergency outfit -- anything that had difficulty to it was ours.

ADAMSON: Did that include rear projection?

HASKIN: Oh yes. All the rear projection. Actually, at the time I got the department, we were using traveling yellow keys, as we called them. This method was the predecessor to background projection. We had background projection, but it was pretty limited. The screens were glass, and quite dangerous to handle. A guy fell through one of them one day. He was cut to ribbons, although he survived. Eventually, we got the cellulose type of thing.

ADAMSON: Let's go through the principle of the yellow and blue keys.

HASKIN: Yes. For instance, the great Albert Einstein, with his wife, visited the studio one day. They were brought around by Warner and Zanuck and all the bigwigs of the studio to Stage 5, Special Effects. At the particular time, I had a yellow key shot of the positive print of a buggy in front of a blue screen all tested and ready. All that was visible on the set was the buggy. The background of a country town was in the camera. This "yellow key" had been loaded in the camera, and would run along with the negative, forming a traveling matte through which the foreground image lighted with yellow lamps would penetrate, while the blue backing printed simultaneously the background of the country lane on the yellow key; forming the unit of the required scene.

ADAMSON: Onto the fresh negative.

HASKIN: Yes. Lighted, the blue backing printed this positive print of the yellow key. Joined with the foreground lighted yellow to penetrate the "key," it became a composite.

ADAMSON: So, if somebody waves his hand and blots out the blue -- that's part of the background that doesn't photograph?

HASKIN: Yes. But the hand is being photographed. It's a perfect traveling matte. With a well-made yellow key print running through the camera, the yellow-lighted foreground would penetrate the color in the key, and the foreground was being exposed perfectly on the negative. The blue light from the backing striking the yellow print would make it a black-and-white image, penetrating to the negative, photographing simultaneously. Thus, the composite. . . .

Anyway, I suggested that Einstein and his wife get into the buggy. We shot them pretending to ride along. They were quite pleasant about it. After touring around the studio for a half hour, they returned. In the projection room, Einstein was astounded to see himself and his wife riding down the streets of Arroyo Grande!

(Laughs) I had staged the background some months before. He couldn't figure it out -- "Oh, oh, it's wondrous." He went off talking about it to everybody -- "Oh, oh, I never have seen such a thing!" He may have astounded me with his theory of relativity, but I astounded him with my yellow key. (Laughs)

ADAMSON: This was in the mid or late thirties?

HASKIN: I should think around '33 or '34. I came back from England in '32, and I fiddled around, did a picture or two, and finally, I took a job in the Warner Bros. Special Effects Department. It was quite fascinating for a while -- the tricks, miniatures and various other methods of effects I fiddled with.

As head of the department, I expanded it, believe me. I hired five special effects directors, including Larry Butler, Roy Davidson, Jack Cosgrove. I had about six to eight first cameramen, and eight of the top matte artists in the business headed by Paul Detlefsen, the Llarinaga Brothers, Chesley Bonestell, the greatest space artist that ever lived, and a guy named Hans Bartholovsky who could grab a brush and in ten minutes paint you a hillside full of weeds, which is an art, believe me! (Laughs)

That was one of the weirdest outfits in the department. They all sat around and painted, discussed the world affairs. Eight matte artists giving their opinion of the way the world should be run, should have been preserved for posterity! Of all the naive, childish intellects I ever ran into -- !

I had an engineer, Bill Thomas, who developed the first flexible screen for background projection. Actually, he had his mitts into everything. It was during the war. Before anybody ever heard of synthetic rubber, he had balls of stuff bouncing around the stage. I don't know what the hell was in it, but later it turned out to be synthetic rubber.

I must have had 125, 130 guys working for me. Every couple weeks, I'd have a little get-together, and warn them that if the place caught fire, not to run out into the street, but to zip to the cellar, because if Warner ever found out I had that many guys working, he'd kill me. And fire them all! (Laughs)

ADAMSON: (Laughs) Well, how were they paid if Warner didn't know?

HASKIN: Well, it wasn't a clandestine operation, but the sight of 125 guys running out of the building would have set Warner off to heights of rage.

ADAMSON: Well, he was really very tight.

HASKIN: He had a lot of freaky things he was tight about. He had come up the hard way -- in the early days the company was often without funds. He had a fetish that when you left a room, turn out the lights. If he walked by an office and the lights were on and nobody was in it, he absolutely freaked. He couldn't understand the disregard of people leaving lights on in an empty room. It'd drive him nuts. At great expense, he'd had the Art Department make signs for every light switch in the studio -- the whole First National Studio -- "Turn out the lights when you leave." Nobody paid much attention to it, but that's the way it was.

He also hated to see wasted nails. You know, studio carpenters are sloppy; they build sets quickly, practically throw them together -- BOOM, BOOM, BOOM! The floor is loaded with nails after they finish and walk away. The janitor is supposed to clean up. The whole studio is actually a bed of nails. Warner couldn't stand it, complaining -- "Why don't they put the nails in the board, instead of throwing them in the air?" So for $11,500 -- in those days this was big money -- they built a magnet machine that would go around the lot and pick up all these vagrant nails. I kid you not.

ADAMSON: How long would it take to pick up enough nails?

HASKIN: I don't know that it ever began to pay the cost of his machine, but you'd hear the poor thing grinding away all night -- RRRRRRR.

He also had a fetish about step ladders. A movie set runs on 1-step, 2-step, 5-step and higher ladders. Every time a new batch of ladders had to be made, he'd say, "What the hell happened to the old ones? Where are they? Did you take them home, you bastards?"

Those were his penchants for economy. And yet, when I was head of the Special Effects Department, I could gauge him like a book. I would develop the damndest things, for example, the traveling matte camera that became a 3-color camera, bypassing the Technicolor patents. Don't think it was made from spit! I had to get an appropriation, personally, from Warner himself. Nobody else had the right to O.K. appropriations.

So every week or so, I'd need $85,000 or $150,000 for some new knickknacks. I'd watch carefully and sniff out the atmosphere to judge when he was in the right mood. Then, I'd fall in casually alongside him on the way to the cafe or something. I'd say, "How's it going?" We'd been friends since he didn't have a dime. Finally, I'd say, "I have a -- ," naming the sum required. Halfway through he'd say, "Oh, O.K." We'd split. That's all I needed. I'd just go to the cashier and say, "He O.K.'d this." That was the end of it.

ADAMSON: He didn't have to sign anything?

HASKIN: No. And he never backed down. Along with Fred Gage, and Al Tondreau, I developed a complete color system -- 3-strip camera, with additive color printer and all that went with it. We applied for patents all the way. When he saw our first test -- he gave us no thanks at all. He held the film up to the dirty window, and said, "How can we fix it so nobody else can get this?" (Laughs) And then, "Full speed ahead." Ten days later, he cancelled the whole deal. Mr. Herbert Kalmus, of Technicolor, who had gotten wind of it, came up to see him and said, "I suppose you're going to cancel all your assignments of 3-strip Technicolor, is that it?" Warner yelled, "What are you talking about?" He said, "What about this color system you're developing?" Warner knew he was licked. Kalmus said, "If you want any of your pictures in color, junk your system."

ADAMSON: Didn't he have enough belief in it to dump Technicolor and go with what you had developed?

HASKIN: Well, he had belief, but it was a year or two away from completion. We were still testing it.

ADAMSON: I see. Meanwhile he had commitments.

HASKIN: Interim commitments. And he was the one who leaked it. We had kept it absolutely dead secret But after he saw the first test, he started bragging around town at a party. Kalmus heard of it. Immediately he was in Warner's office.

ADAMSON: What we don't have on tape is when your plan came about to change the film speed back to 16 frames a second.

HASKIN: I first had the idea in the late twenties. Both Duncan Mansfield and I worked on this plan to drop the 24 frames per second speed of the sound system, and save film. It could have been 18 to 16, 20, maybe 22. At 23, it would have saved money. However, we were heading for 16, because the problems of shutter flicker had all been ironed out into a steady picture in the silent days running films at 16 speed. Extra blades in the shutter in the open parts were developed so that the persistence of vision factor was maintained in rhythm, and sustained. You could not run at 16 with a single blade shutter. That would unbalance the rhythm of persistence of vision in the human eye. Most successful were smoked glass blades in the shutter. They would not quite cut all the light, but enough to hide the movement of the film being yanked down. A relatively simple matter.

Around the late twenties, when sound on film came out, Duncan and I were in England together. We talked about this plan, but didn't do anything. We formed what we called the "Hasman" plan from which we developed a pig-in-a-poke procedure to get the producers to sign up before revelation, so we could get money out of it. There was nothing patentable, so this was the best method of protection. In Boreham Wood in the sound department, I had tests of sound on film photographed, recorded, and printed up to 12,000 cycles.

The ear ceases to hear at about 7500 cycles. That much above audible range, we could slow the system down. Do you see the equation? Today, of course, you've got ultra-high speed, unlimited cycles -- almost like the speed of light. All the latitude in the world. But today, nobody has sense enough, particularly in the research science division of the Academy, to envision the possibilities, or the savings factor.

It would save untold billions! From the time I was in England up to today, it would have saved the cost of the Korean War, practically -- in the cost of raw stock -- let alone labor and extra shipping cost, etc. I personally spent thousands of dollars, trying to put this scheme over. Hoping, of course, to tie it to a small percentage of the demonstrable saving.

If we could ever have interested anybody enough to see what we were talking about we'd have been home free. At one-tenth of one percent participation in demonstrable savings, we'd have had it made. Nobody could trick us by a phony count; our percentages depended on the film sales. Just on raw stock footage. Eastman, or Agfa, or anybody else.

ADAMSON: Where did you try this?

HASKIN: Actually, I made thorough tests in the thirties, when I was head of Special Effects at Warner Bros. I had distributors on my stage to synchronize the units, recording apparatus, my own laboratory. A studio within a studio -- every function of filmmaking was in Stage 5. The entire sound system could be run at any speed required.

I made a test -- I think Kony photographed it -- one camera shooting 16, one 24, simultaneously. The sound recording for each one was at proper speed -- 16, 16, 24, 24, etc., compensated, as I recall, by neutral density filters, rather than stopped down to make the difference in exposure, because that would have made one sharper than the other, stopping f 5.6 on one and leaving the other at f 3.2.

I cranked out about 100 feet on the action at 24 speed and about 60 feet at the 16 speed. We ran them on matching projectors in the projection room, cutting from one to the other. Aside from a slight difference in contrast, photographically, there was no alteration of the sound or picture. Later, I made a big effort in England when I was there directing TREASURE ISLAND, a Disney film. We were shooting at the Denham studio, of the J. Arthur Rank Company. Freddie Young, my friend who I had brought up in 1919, and I would go to lunch together. I told him about the Hasman plan, and how many times I'd tried to put it across. I just told it as an interesting yarn. He said, "Well, something should be done about this." Freddie's a very serious guy and dedicated to life. He finally set up a luncheon date for me with Mr. Rank and himself in the private commissary.

We had lunch with Mr. Rank, a charming man who knew lots about milling grain, but nothing about making pictures. Although he was ignorant of the mechanics of making a film he understood what I was talking about when I explained the Hasman plan. I could tell -- he got it quickly. He said, "Oh yes, quite. I'd like to have you reveal this to my engineers."

So we set the date. I met with his technical staff and gave them comprehensive revelation of the whole idea. At the completion, before questions were asked much, a head engineer asked, "I say, wouldn't that squeak the voices?" At which I just thought to myself, Well, for chrissakes, this guy's an engineer, and this is all he knows about sound pictures! (Laughs) It was a hopeless situation. With politeness, I broke off negotiations.

ADAMSON: So it ended with "squeak the voices" in 1950?

HASKIN: Yes.

ADAMSON: But you tried it with other studios in Los Angeles?

HASKIN: The first attempt I made was early in the thirties. A friend of mine, Albert Kauffman, a member of the Producers Association, was instrumental in giving them a brochure outlining the claims of what the plan would do. Without revealing how it worked, because there was nothing patentable.

Several other members of the Association were interested, but none of them would go for a pig-in-the-poke -- or sign even a tentative agreement, without it being revealed. So that was the end of that. Many times later I tried. But so firmly entrenched is status quo in Hollywood, that nobody was willing to rock the boat. At least it was a big vision. Even in the early thirties, by statistics from weekly Variety, it could be demonstrated that many, many millions of dollars could be saved per year. Since then, production has expanded immeasurably.

ADAMSON: There was saving of raw stock for the picture and --

HASKIN: Every function you could think of. Chemicals in the laboratory, light on the set. Thirty-three and one-third percent. Less shipping cost, fewer reels, etc. It was a real solid economic plan.

ADAMSON: Your earliest special effects credit I found was for THE ROARING TWENTIES in '39; you and Edwin DuPar. Then, later you told the guy who wrote the Don Siegel book that

Siegel had done most of those montages for THE ROARING TWENTIES.

HASKIN: Siegel was my montage director at the time. On ROARING TWENTIES, he and I alternated -- there were so many to do. About six or eight major montages for the period/era changes in the story.

ADAMSON: There's some wonderful stuff. Giant tickertape machines going up and exploding . . .

HASKIN: Yes. Wall Street melting, and so on. We had some imagination going on those things.

ADAMSON: Yes. Did you ever hear of a picture called BROTHER CAN YOU SPARE A DIME? It was a compilation film of the Thirties that was made a few years ago. That's how they covered the Crash -- with that same scene of the tickertape blowing up.

HASKIN: Don and I worked together on a lot of films. MISSION TO MOSCOW, etc. One of the noteworthy jobs I did as cameraman before taking over the department was MIDSUMMER NIGHT'S DREAM, with Max Reinhardt producing. William Dieterle directed. Henry Blanke kind of wandered around as go-between. He was supposed to be translator, but he had no heart for it. He would listen to them, then walk away. He understood it, so what? On the set nothing was spoken but German. Well, I had some real tough effects to do. One I remember distinctly was the scherzo, a dance with little fairies materializing out of the grass, cavorting around a bit, then flying off over the trees. A combination of coordination and trickery that's most difficult to organize.

ADAMSON: You had to do it in one shot?

HASKIN: More or less. But the pièce de résistance was materializing these girls out of the grass in the meadow. My engineer, Bill Thomas, and I put a huge plate glass on the set, staked down in front of a test camera. We marked where every girl would be on the glass. We took the glass back to the shop and he spent a day grinding out hollow places so that the girls would appear to materialize. To say the least, it called for precision. The optical plate was thick. Thomas ground it out in channels -- indentations in the glass which became distortion lenses for each girl's area. The girls crouched down before appearing, then stood up on signal, slowly appearing through the little distortion lenses into clarity, coming to pause just above it.

There were about 100 dancers, each with her own distortion area in the glass. The set of a fairyland glade was built around the marks where the girls had to come up, and Glenn Beldt, wire man, organized his rigs up high, to be attached to the girls at a certain point during the dance. He would then lift them off on wires, flying over the trees.

Now, there is very little leeway for any changes with such a shot after it's tested. The process of directing had long been settled -- and the dance director had rehearsed his action, and placed the girls. For final testing before shooting, we needed a dress rehearsal with the girls to finalize all the marks. The whole thing was all ready, girls in costume, Glen Beldt's wire rigs, the special effects technicians.

Enter the new element of Mr. Reinhardt, Mr. Dieterle, and Mr. Blanke on the set for final approval. All speaking German. The great Mr. Reinhardt must lend his magic touch to this project. His magic touch consisted of coming on the set, talking in German to the dance director, ordering the rehearsal according to his specifications. After a long, noisy dialogue, the dance director set up the girls in position for the scherzo, but now it's <u>backwards</u>.

My camera is tied down, the optical plate glass is all in position with its lenses, the marks are there for the girls, and Mr. Reinhardt has ordered it staged as if the camera were part of the stage itself, playing to the audience out there somewhere in limbo. This is dead truth. He staged the scherzo backwards! And despite fierce objections, that's the way we shot it! A real hodgepodge. He faced them away, backs to the camera. His idea was that we were all technicians, therefore, we're the theatre performing to the audience out there somewhere beyond. I was livid! But I couldn't get through to any of these characters at all. Blanke had been my assistant when I was directing silents, but he was listening only to Reinhardt -- in German! There was so much screaming, I never did get it straightened out. Finally, I pushed the dancers around trying to fit them as best I could into the distortion lenses. Finally, we shot it. Unbelievable!

ADAMSON: Never with them facing forward?

HASKIN: No, no.

ADAMSON: How did the structure work on MIDSUMMER NIGHT'S DREAM -- did you just do special effects shots? Hal Mohr was the photographer, wasn't he?

HASKIN: Yes, but I did all the special effects shots myself. You see, Jackman did establish one good thing. He believed that a production cameraman usually has no idea what a special effect is all about. So the production man had no authority over special effects; usually stayed away when they were shot. These involved shots were planned, set up, and finally tested by the special cameraman. I had tested the scherzo. They all saw my rough rehearsal on film in the projection room, said, "Oh, great, great!" Then they went right out, and staged it backwards! Can you believe it?

Anyhow, Jackman organized it so that even a simple back projection shot was tested by our special effects cameraman. The day we'd shoot this, the production cameraman would play a little golf. The director could go into the projection room, see the test, then come out and shoot it. It was a highly efficient way of doing special effects.

ADAMSON: This is a cinematography credit that I have for you on this film. The way the credit reads is that the film was shot by Hal Mohr, Fred Jackman, H. F. Koenekamp and Byron Haskin. It's not broken down into special effects shots or sequences.

HASKIN: Yes. Well, Kony shot some backgrounds. Fred Jackman did nothing but walk around and collect money for it. I was the special effects cameraman assigned to the film. Why Kony's name was on there, I don't know -- I did the whole picture. But who cares? When I took over the department, I tried to break the pattern of the department taking screen credit for special effects camera work. It grated on me. I didn't want credit for work I didn't do. But it had become automatic in the title department. There was my name anyhow.

ADAMSON: MIDSUMMER NIGHT'S DREAM is the same year as BLACK FURY.

HASKIN: Yes, MIDSUMMER NIGHT'S DREAM was probably the end of my special effects tour as a unit cameraman. From there I went back to shooting productions. However, I believe that the film I did when I left the Special Effects Department was AS THE EARTH TURNS. Later, I did BLACK FURY, and then THE GREEN LIGHT with Errol Flynn. I photographed several pictures before Jackman quit and Koenig insisted that I take the department.

ADAMSON: Could we talk about BLACK FURY? You apparently went to Pennsylvania.

HASKIN: Yes, for pre-production shots, second unit work, and backgrounds for rear projection. We met Judge M.A. Mussmano, author of the book Black Hell, in Pittsburgh. I say, "We" -- Mike Curtiz and his staff and myself. I had my own photographic staff. I remember one small instance of the madness of Mr. Curtiz getting me in such a jam where I almost got killed. The tipples of the coal mines were about 150 feet high, housing the elevator apparatus for the miners going down to the mines. It had other functions as well -- to hoist coal up into little dump cars in the corridor at the top, to load into big railroad cars.

Curtiz, as usual, always seeking "unusual" angles, started up a little iron ladder. I kid you not -- it was no wider than eighteen inches. It had narrow steps on it, and a low hand railing on each side. This rickety contraption went on a diagonal to the top of the tipple! There was one little platform about three feet square halfway up.

The first thing I know, up goes Curtiz like a monkey, having been a circus acrobat. He yelled, "Bunnie!" I looked up, and this bum is halfway up holding up a finder. "A great shot from up here. Come on up and take a look." I said, "I can tell what it looks like from down here. It's O.K. with me." "No, you must come up and see." God, I climbed up to this damn thing, assailed by vertigo in the worst way. I almost fell off, getting up to where he was. I said, "O.K." -- I didn't even look at the shot. He was satisfied, and rushed down leaving me up there! By myself!

My head was swimming so badly that I thought, "God, the only thing to do is go up." I could do that without looking down, get into the tipple, and find the back way down. So I climbed to the top of the damned tipple, jumping inside the corridor. AHH! At last! Buildings around me instead of a spiderweb. I walked, oh, a quarter of a mile back along some rails, and I come out of this shed. I was on the top of a cliff. Far below were these little ants of the company, wandering around with Curtiz, looking for me. There was absolutely no path, no way to get off the top of this cliff. Finally, I had to go back into the tipple corridor again, and climb back down that damn spiderweb ladder. How I ever survived, I never will know. Naturally, because I'm telling it, I did. Somehow. (Laughs)


ADAMSON:   You had vertigo problems, but you never got seasick?

HASKIN:    Yes.

ADAMSON: Did you want to talk a little about the lighting in the coal mine scenes?

HASKIN: Yes. The fidelity of the opening scenes in the coal mine is due to the special kind of lighting, using the source of the little lamps on the miner's hats to light the sets. Having watched the effect in the coal mine, back in Pennsylvania, I decided to duplicate the flickering and directional light of these hat lights by putting small spotlights offstage around the perimeter of the set and manning them with electricians on ladders -- each electrician responsible for the beam of light from a particular miner's hat. He was to watch the miner's hat, and move the light in coordination with the movement of the man's head. It gave a most realistic effect. Only flawed by one thing -- the set was a bit too black.

I looked at the rushes critically, and was well pleased -- the reality transcended the flaw that it was pretty dim. There was little general light revealing where people were. Next day, word came from Mr. Hal B. Wallis, executive producer -- what the hell was I trying to do? The company spends millions for sets, and I don't show them (which is the way I would interpret what he said).

I got a message to come up and talk with him, and I did, and we got into a row about it. Then, I got into a snit and went back down to the stage and ordered in a lot of big arc lights and lit it up like Grauman's lobby. It was a shame, because if I had restrained my anger, I wouldn't have gone overboard to this extent. A bit of repainting of the set would have solved the beef. It could have been a realistic effect like actually being down in the coal mines.

The real coal mines were depressing and grim. Particularly, our participation in shooting our scenes. Almost threatening. Later, when I found out our company had put up money for the union pension fund so John L. Lewis, head of the union, would leave town during the shooting, I realized we were actually in danger of being rapped over the skull.

ADAMSON: By union people?

HASKIN: Yes. Quite obviously. I don't know what the sympathies of the thing were now. I did at the time we were back there. We all went down in the coal mine with Mussmano, and the workmen. I think that he represented a threat to the mine owners and the coal and iron police. Why Lewis left the state, I don't know. So that we wouldn't start anything, I guess.

ADAMSON: Well, the way it works out in the film is that the union is nice guys and the management is nice guys --

HASKIN: Yes, well, Mussmano did go down in the coal mines, and he wrote this book. It was highly inflammatory, and named names boldly. I remember that Warners made sure all the controversial element was tuned out. Witness the change from Black Hell to BLACK FURY. It's all right to be sympathetic to the workers, but not to show the coal and iron police as thugs. (Laughs)

ADAMSON: What they did was have the coal and iron police replaced by a gang of thugs who came in and put cop's badges on. One guy even had a line -- "It's the first time I've ever been on the right side of a cop's badge." Obviously they're just thugs that have come out of nowhere. So an unnamed agency gets all the blame. The unions, the workers, and the management all come off like real nice guys. (Laughs)

HASKIN: (Laughs) The old Hollywood shuffle. It happened every time.

ADAMSON: Did you look at any of the miners' homes?

HASKIN: Yes, we went through the villages, went through the homes. I went into this one place, so I speak first hand, not by hearsay, about the appalling conditions under which they lived. Two babies were lying on a cot on the floor in the living room, the flies just blanketing them, and a single bulb hanging from the high ceiling was the only source of light. Actually, they would unscrew this bulb and take it upstairs into the bedroom at night. They had one bulb. No indoor water -- nothing -- no sanitary facilities. It was just the most primitive thing I ever saw.

It did not surprise me too much, because I had previously seen evidence of conditions one should think didn't exist today. That was during the pre-production shooting of the Battle of Franklin, for THE BISHOP OF COTTONTOWN. It was a story of industry in the South, post-Civil War -- little children sitting there, coughing with consumption at the mills, from the dust and so forth. Jesus, we went down there, in the late twenties, and in spinning mills back in the woods were little children sitting there coughing and the dust flying around! (Laughs) Today, I'll guarantee you, it's the only part of the United States the unions haven't been able to lick yet, because the conditions are advantageous to manufacture down there. But I was in factories in the South, location hunting for BISHOP OF COTTONTOWN, where it's still exactly the same as described in the book, immediately after the Civil War.

ADAMSON: Did you film this?

HASKIN: No. But little kids were sitting in rows at these treadles and mills -- the mill was located clandestinely, in a hidden valley, with deep woods around. So the impoverished state of the coal miners of Pennsylvania I knew was not unique. Capped by the fact that, at the time, there was little work and wages were low. It was a bad scene.

ADAMSON: Where did they get their water?

HASKIN: In the little plaza in the center of the village. There'd be fifty-five or sixty huts around, and one faucet in the middle of the village. They'd carry it in buckets back to the houses.

ADAMSON: Did the mining companies set up these villages and kind of stick them there?

HASKIN: Yes. Mining towns -- part of the pay was scrip in the company store. It was that way in Mississippi, too, in that film we made with Richard Barthelmess, CABIN IN THE COTTON. We went down to Stovall, Mississippi, to an 1100-acre plantation with a company store in a company village. Two hundred and fifty blacks lived there on the edge of the swamp in huts.

ADAMSON: Didn't they get a break at the company store?

HASKIN: They could only buy stuff with scrip. The scrip was worth half.

ADAMSON: In other words, they were getting robbed again?

HASKIN: Yes. Poor sharecroppers. They could never leave, because they were always in debt to the company store. The store'd just carry them along on credit, then when they'd get paid, they'd get the debt almost paid off, only to run into debt again. Each year they would chop cedar from the swamp for fences -- spring was the time to put fencing around some of these huts. Come winter, they'd burn the fence to survive the cold. The windows were covered with greased newspaper. Appalling!

ADAMSON: This is Mississippi?

HASKIN: Yes. We almost got tarred and feathered there. This was during my period as a unit special effects cameraman. I was assigned to many locations. On CABIN IN THE COTTON, I went down to Mississippi with the location manager, Bill Guthrie, and a crew. We were sworn to secrecy about what we were making, because the author had left the state in a very rapid fashion, pursued by guys with bloodhounds and clubs.

We didn't announce what we were doing. Guthrie arranged with a plantation owner, Mr. Stovall, to use this plantation. We stayed in a hotel in town, and drove quietly out there during the day to photograph backgrounds and various scenes for the second unit work. Guthrie was sort of a politician, who had been in the Secret Service at one time, one of the presidential guards. He still had a lot of political connections. He made friends with the local postmaster, one of the few Republican officials in the South.

This guy was something of a lush, and he used to have drinks with us at the hotel. He invited us out to a barbecue in his shack on the bank of the Mississippi River running through there.

That evening after work, we got into a couple of company cars, and drove out there toward sundown, into these willow, sort of canebrake roads. He'd given us directions, and said he'd meet us out there with the steaks on the fire and some booze, and we'd sing and look at the river and have fun.

Somehow, we arrived a little early. The tiny shanty was up on stilts. We hollered. There's only one old guy at this shanty, so old he could hardly wobble. There was no fire, no steaks, nothing. It suddenly occurred to us that maybe all was not kosher in Denmark.

I said, "Get in the cars quick, and let's get the hell out of here!"

We'd gone 150 yards back through these willows, when here comes a posse with a big kettle of boiling tar, poles and bags of feathers. They had found out what we were shooting, and were going to give us a little ride. We'd probably have ended up in the Mississippi River trying to swim to Arkansas. (Laughs) It was about a mile wide at this point. Well, we scooted through the willows, and gunned the cars out of there. The last I saw of them, they were trying to turn around and come after us.

ADAMSON: Were they in a truck?

HASKIN: No, they were in a big open car.

1. On location for The Bishop of Cottontown (1923), never completed due to the death of Producer-Director Alan Holubar. Left to right: Haskin, H. Lyman Broening (cinematographer), Roy Musgrave (stills). See pages 46-51.

2. The case and crew of The Sea Beast on location (1925). John Barrymore is bare-chested in the foreground. To his left, the director, Millard Webb. Byron Haskin is directly behind Webb in pith helmet. See pages 59–62.

3. The cast and crew of When a Man Loves on location (1926). John Barrymore is reading newspaper, lower left. To his left, the director, Alan Crosland. Haskin in suit standing to right of cameras.

4. The cast and crew of Matinee Ladies (1927), Haskin's first directorial credit. See pages 74-75.

5. With cinematographer Winton C. Hoch on Captains of the Clouds (1937), Haskin was second-unit director. See page 96.

6. In England on <u>Treasure Island</u> (1949). Left to right: Bobby Driscoll, Walt Disney, Byron Haskin, unidentified, Skeets Kelly, cinematographer Freddy Young. See pages 169-184.

7. Byron Haskin (seated on raft) directs Robert Newton as Long John Silver. <u>Treasure Island</u>.

8. In production on <u>Warpath</u> (1951). Byron Haskin, Jim Paisley, Edmond O'Brien. See pages 184-196.

9. Miniature work on The War of the Worlds (1952). See pages 199-208.

10. Mr. and Mrs. Byron Haskin in Tokyo, 1954.

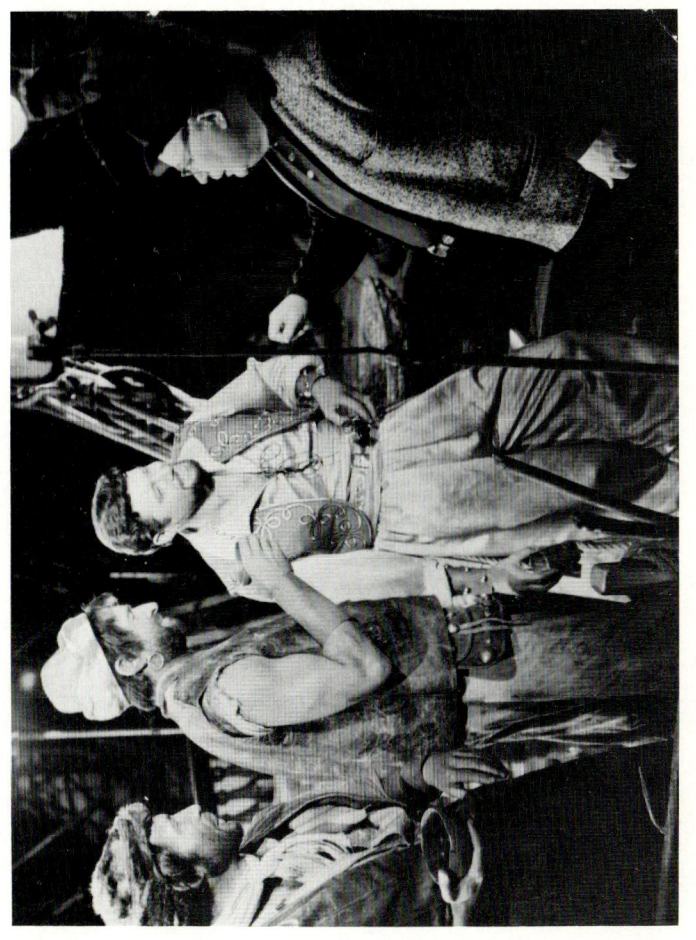

11. Directing Guy Williams in Captain Sinbad (1963). See pages 246–257.

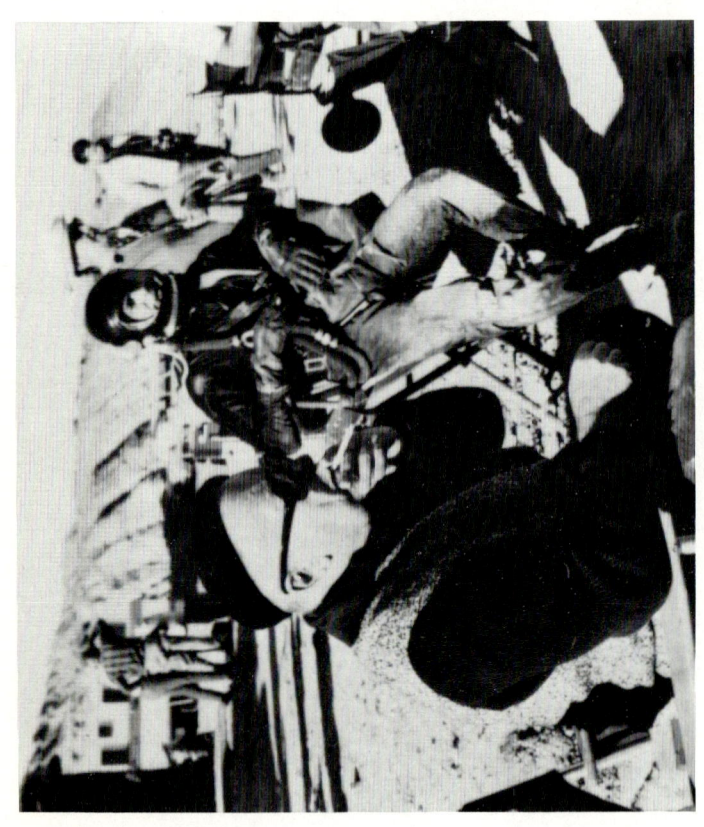

12. On the set of Robinson Crusoe on Mars (1964). See pages 257-268.

ADAMSON: So was that the end of your shooting?

HASKIN: We wound up the necessary stuff the next day and got the hell out of there that night.

ADAMSON: (Laughs) That's great. So that was during the thirties? Were you at Warner Bros.?

HASKIN: Yes. That was CABIN IN THE COTTON. Richard Barthelmess starred. Directed by Mike Curtiz, of course. What the hell did he know about the South? Right out of the mountains of Hungary. (Laughs) Oh boy! All the Warner Civil War pictures were assigned to Mike Curtiz.

He had a weird technique. Gunfights, whether in the Civil War, or among cattle rustlers, he regarded as a contest with whips.

"All right, these boys, shoot! Drive 'em back!"

The fact that a bullet knocks a guy dead never entered his mind. A fight between the Rebs and the Union was only: guys charge and drive other guys back, then the other guys summon courage, and they drive the first attackers back! Nobody's dead on the scene of battle. (Laughs) It's like they were fighting with bullwhips.

Historically, the renowned Battle of Harper's Ferry was with a few troops and a couple of Navy guys getting in trouble on foot.

Not with Curtiz! With him it was the Cavalry. Hundreds of horses tearing along the road to the fight. Jesus! No respect for history -- in fact, he never heard of it, I guess.

ADAMSON: We didn't talk about CAPTAIN BLOOD, which was directed by Curtiz. You have a second unit credit on that . . .

HASKIN: Well, many actors portray characters; a lot are personalities, like Errol Flynn.

In the beginning, I made tests for CAPTAIN BLOOD. Flynn attempted, in a conventional sense, to <u>act</u> the role of Captain Blood. Well, his efforts were the most amateurish performances ever shot.

When he saw those rushes, he realized his own limitations. He swore a bloody oath never to <u>act</u> again. He never did. He played a personality from then on, with the little quirks of his cheek, and sly glances. He became an "attitudinizer." He never was an actor after that, because he knew he was so amateurish as to be laughable. (Laughs)

ADAMSON: Well, wasn't what he was doing sort of Fairbanksian?

HASKIN: Yes. In spirit anyway. He was an ebullient personality, an extension of the charming male. Oh, the greatest star of the early days to me was Doug Fairbanks, Senior.

If I were to do it over again, I would go to an acting school to condition myself to direct. I found out many things from my wife, Terry, attending acting workshops. She is a fine actress -- among a thousand other things! One of the finest actresses ever in movies, never playing the big roles; only occasional supporting parts. She was a member of the famous Bob Gist Group. Gist was a genius at teaching the art of acting. She'd come home and discuss techniques. I picked up hints about the finesse of acting, and what it means. How to get actors into their roles.

ADAMSON: I noticed that in COLLEEN, which you did some of, and I MARRIED A DOCTOR, the lighting is distinctly different from, say, BLACK FURY.

HASKIN: Yes.

ADAMSON: How was that arrived at?

HASKIN: Oh, I always had a feel for the type of film I was shooting. Lubitsch demanded this of his cameraman. Lubitsch was one of the few real "auteur" directors. He had a journeyman cameraman named Charles Van Enger. Lubitsch liked soft, flat light -- because his stuff needed the fairy tale quality of high comedy like THE MERRY WIDOW. He loved to shoot around windows with drapes, lacy and light and airy, reflections of his people in the glass. Charlie Van Enger was particularly adept at this style, because he was no Seitz who specialized in studied definition with light. The laboratory had a great deal to do with Van Enger's success because of Fred Gage's expertise. The combination of Charlie Van Enger, Ernst Lubitsch and Fred Gage made these films memorable.

ADAMSON: Did you ever work with Lubitsch?

HASKIN: A few times. I approximated the style that he wanted, although I hadn't the basic flair for it that Van Enger had. After Lubitsch left Warners, he changed entirely. He left style up to cameramen after that. His later films were conventionally conceived.

But the original Lubitsch style was something to remember. You'd know exactly who made it, and where it came from.

Lubitsch was a master technician on his silent films. Every tiny detail was in the script exactly as he intended to shoot it. It was amazing. He prepared the scripts himself. He was an absolute master of the shooting continuity, which is the primary responsibility of a director.

## Chapter Six

## THE FORTIES

ADAMSON: I'd like to talk a little about ACTION IN THE NORTH ATLANTIC.

HASKIN: I was in charge of the Special Effects Department then.

Lloyd Bacon had been a long-time director for Warners. On sort of middle-range kinds of pictures. Nothing very important, however. By passage of time, his next option called for quite a healthy boost, in terms of money.

It was general practice at Warner Bros., when an option was due, to launch the poormouth bit, you know -- "Times are bad . . . We're lucky to be able to pick you up at all, at any price . . . We can't carry you with any raise" -- that sort of thing. I had been a victim of it many times. So had everybody else on long term contract. But along with the passing of time, Bacon had also achieved a large enough ego, he wouldn't stand for the con job. He thought he was very important in the business, so he said no.

They said, "All right, you're a free agent as soon as this period of your contract is up." Which was not too many weeks away.

He was assigned a picture called ACTION IN THE NORTH ATLANTIC. It was a modest-budget story of a convoy crossing the Atlantic from Halifax to Murmansk, with the tribulations of the crew under submarine attack.

The prologue was an incident of a freighter being torpedoed and sunk in flames. It had nothing to do with the main story line; just a piece of melodrama hooked on the beginning to show how brave merchant sailors were during the war when they hired out to go to sea.

I fell heir to staging the special effects of this prologue. I remember having seen a particular shot in *Life* Magazine, of a lifeboat being lowered from a merchant vessel just at the moment a shell hit -- POW -- ! All the guys flying in the air, and the lifeboat disintegrating.

So I duplicated this action on my stage, with a ship set, stuntmen on wires playing the sailors. The funny part was, on the first take, everything went off but the powder charge, so the stunt guys all flew in the air without any visible motivation. (Laughs)

Meanwhile, Bacon, in a retaliatory mood against the studio, had the art director make a very detailed entire top deck of a freighter to shoot the prologue of the picture.

Actually, if you'd dropped the whole prologue, nothing would have been lost from the story. It only led up to the union hiring hall where the sailors come in and sign on for another trip -- showing bravery.

Anyhow, Bacon spent the entire budget for the whole picture on this prologue. The fire he staged damn near burned down Stage 22, the biggest stage in town. No money left in the coffers to complete the movie! Jerry Wald, producer, was a friend of mine. He fell on my neck and said, "My God, you've got to help me out!"

The next disaster: Bacon up and quit. Walked off and left the picture, about half shot.

Bogart was in it, along with the standard Warner Bros. stock company.

Jerry said, "You'll have to help. Take it over." I did. Shooting miniatures and projection process. George Amy, the editor, and I would cut some sequence to see what we needed and then go out and shoot it. The next day we'd see the rushes and put it in. It was real down-to-earth, grassroots picture-making, I assure you. (Laughs) Jerry convinced Warner to continue financing it, and we went ahead.

Added disaster: The Mexican cutter, previously assigned, name of Tommy Pratt, who'd been Bacon's man, came in at night, took all the baskets of trims, cut them into 2-, 3- frame bits -- just chopped the whole thing to pieces with his scissors! Warner wouldn't O.K. reprinting. (Laughs)

So Amy had to start over with his assistant cutter, Chris Nyby, who later became a director. Chris worked day and night fishing pieces out of the basket, matching them up and pasting them together. These were the scenes we cut. Gad!

I was responsible for a big percentage of the direction of this film. Finally, when we got it together, it was released, and made some money.

I remember creating the port of Murmansk, never having seen it. We had the ships win through to Murmansk, despite bombing and torpedoing. I actually made shots showing a whole wolfpack of submarines beneath the surface. Paul Detlefsen, matte artist, combined painting with miniatures. It looked tremendous -- this entire wolfpack of submarines heading for the convoy.

ADAMSON: You used Jack Cosgrove on this, right?

HASKIN: Yes. I had a full convoy of merchant ships with submarines, in Santa Barbara harbor, using Stearn's Wharf as base. Wires were strung across to the shore at the yacht club. The convoy was under attack by wolfpacks, and coastal bombing planes.

There were nearly 450 units of miniatures in the shot. All at one-inch to the foot scale.

We had guys in the ships, turning the small inboard motors. The controls for explosions and other effects were wired to the keyboard in front of the operator. Shooting out to sea, showing the horizon. In Santa Barbara, the waves in the harbor are in reduced scale naturally. Just about right for open sea in miniature.

I don't think Cosgrove ever knew what he was doing up here. I'd go up weekends from Hollywood, order certain shots made. The rest of the stuff was just hit and miss spectacle which didn't tell any story. To mean anything, miniatures have to tell story. They're not just cut in to amuse the public.

I learned much about full scale action from that assignment -- like a torpedo going off and wrecking a battleship -- it requires an absolutely meticulous detailing of every phase of the operation.

For instance, firing depth charges. A sailor-lookout sights the enemy, so you've got to have a shot of him sighting them, then he yells into his phone, necessitating another shot of the guy with the big helmet and the earphones hearing the news -- then this guy yells at the captain; another shot showing the captain pick up the phone, give orders to the exec -- "This is the captain," etc. Another shot: The exec getting the message. He yells into his phone. Cut to another shot: the guy receiving the message on the fantail; cut to another shot: the guys at the depth charge racks and so forth. They say, "Fire," "Fire," "Fire," "Fire," "Fire!"

How the hell they ever hit anything in the Navy, I never will know. You have to go through so many guys yelling, "Fire one!" that by the time the projectile is fired, everybody can grow a beard!

Anyhow, crap goes flying in the air and drops onto the surface of the sea. Then you cut below, seeing the depth charge coming down and down under the sea. Next, shots in the submarines -- all this detailing is absolutely necessary. You can't skip any part of it for the sake of tempo. It sets the tempo, because it becomes a credible thing to the eye. No shortcutting the routine -- the more shortcut, the less sense it makes and the weaker the effect. And slower the tempo.

I passed this information along later to Don Siegel. He never forgot it, and he became a good action director -- did good melodrama fights, and so forth. Every little bit of a fight in a Siegel film is there -- the guy doubling his fist -- BOOM! POW! -- he goes halfway out the window and they grab his feet, then a shot of the traffic below, where he would fall if they'd let go of his feet. (Laughs) All these tender moments.

ADAMSON: (Laughs) How do you mean Bacon almost burned down the stage?

HASKIN: Well, staging a fire in the movies involves torches from gas tanks. Blazes are placed at doorways and other cracks and holes. They're hot fire. The grids of the sound stage above are full of trash, as well as lamps and men. The flames leaped up there. The trash caught on fire. The Fire Department rushed over and put them out. The stage needed extensive repair.

I did the same thing at Paramount directing WAR OF THE WORLDS, when Martians first landed with their disintegration rays and their flame rays. The Army camp was to be set on fire -- when the guy who has burning napalm on him runs through the foreground.

Making this shot, I thought, That old stage needs a little dusting out up there. I'll let them go for a while. I held the button to stop it in my hand. (Laughs) I let it go for a while. God, the guys were running around yelling -- "Hey, hey, hey!" Georgie Barnes, cameraman, was pale. I finally shut it off.

That's enough about ACTION ON THE NORTH ATLANTIC. There were solid things I learned, that stood me in good stead when I finally got to directing features. . . .

The business of my directing might be called ill-starred in certain ways. Maybe, temperamentally, I wasn't oriented to directing as much as I was to cinematography. Analyzing my directing, I must consider in retrospect that I was a doer, more than a discusser, or a talker-about-things. I *did* things.

On the camera, I was independent. If I visualized a coal mine a certain way, I ordered little spotlight units and made it look like that. There was nobody to say nay, as long as they could see the actor and hear the dialogue. I had great independence as a cameraman, and great creativity. It was completely fulfilling for me, personally.  Naturally, at times there were problems -- such as Hal Wallis chewing me out. But in directing I had to attack a new angle completely.  I used to wonder at myself -- what the hell I'd been doing back then, photographing pictures with good directors, and watching them stage action. Why hadn't I really collected a lot of keys to this kind of endeavor?

I hadn't. I had been too dedicated to my photography. I didn't give a damn what the director was doing, as long as the actors knew when to turn left a little, and so forth. It isn't that I was insensitive to drama -- I appreciated a lot of the scenes -- but it didn't appeal to me at a gut level.

So that when I finally made the change, I realized I was in trouble if I didn't learn the basics. It was high time; I was not a kid anymore.

ADAMSON:   When you made the change the second time?

HASKIN:   Yes. I was motivated by, I think, the imaginary social inferiority of cameramen at that time. There's a heavy caste system in movies. Socially, the A parties, the B parties, and then on to the bums.  Along about X, Y, Z is the cameraman's party.

An A party may consist of all the cocaine-fiend stars -- people featured on the front page of <u>The Star</u> in the supermarket. Pretty high and mighty.

My first wife felt I was demeaned by not mixing socially with super-stars. It was, to state it plainly, too high an echelon for cinematographers.

In retrospect, I honestly never felt that I had something special to tell the world. A lot of directors maintain they've got this deathless message -- which I question.

However, the big money was there: big fees for directing a picture, particularly if you get a hit or a semi-hit, good at the box office.

The reasons for becoming a director were comparatively unimportant, as far as I was concerned.  There was no artistic urge to deliver my particular kind of art as a director, I was showing what I could do with the camera. In certain pictures I directed, I did achieve some fulfillment through effects I worked out, along with a bit of pride. Actually, in my training in the University of California -- I studied art -- I had aimed to become an editorial cartoonist. That was to be my future -- until I wandered off to Hollywood. With all that training, I just dropped art, although I was a natural cameraman because of it. I still paint pretty well, even today, though I've forgotten most of the technique.

I liked shooting with the camera. I liked the challenges, and I liked the responsibiity that was mine alone, to solve problems. None of which occurred much as a director, because there was always so much interference from every quarter. There wasn't a soul in the higher echelons above directing -- producers and supernumeraries -- who didn't feel he was a better director than any director.

Wallis fancied himself a great director. In fact, when he would lend out Lizabeth Scott, he would rehearse her for hours in his office in the way he thought she should play the scene. The upshot was that seldom did anybody hire her. He was close to being the worst director in the world. (Laughs)

No flair, or touch for it at all.  No simplicity, no consistency to his technique. Yet, he was quick to note the lack of these qualities in any other director.

A lot of these things I picked up, and about the time I quit being a director, which was after THE POWER at MGM, I took a survey of my abilities, and found that at that time I was perhaps one of the best directors in the business. I had seasoned my techniques. I had matured. My reluctant talents had finally blossomed; about that time I quit.

I was glad to get out of it. It had become a tension-ridden kind of a job. There was little fulfillment. Toward the end of a day of shooting just to meet the schedule, you found you were shooting the schedule instead of the script.

ADAMSON: You had a chance to direct four silent pictures, then you were a cameraman again.

HASKIN: That's right. They were all lousy. No story I could believe, or anything else. I was assigned to them, directed them, and they stank. Eventually, I quit and went to England. But I still had high hopes.

Several years later, I broke Warner down, and he said, "All right, find yourself a producer and get a story together, and we'll put it on the schedule. You can direct it."

I got with Jerry Wald, and he and I started searching around for a story.

Interestingly enough, I ran into one at my agent's place. Frank Orsatti was handling me at the time. He had bookshelves on each side of his desk, not that he ever read a book. He was a real gangster. He used to point to the shelves and say, "Hey, there's a lot of stuff in them books, you know that?"

One day, he picked one, handed it to me. I looked it over. It was written by a guy named Traven. Treasure of the Sierra Madre.

I took it home and read it. Jesus, I went wild about it. Next day, I gave it to Jerry Wald and told him I wanted to make it. He said, "Hey, we own that." (Laughs)

Warner Bros. owned it! My agent didn't even know it! Such is the way of fate that possibly we could have gotten this out of the vault and started writing a screenplay, except that Steve Trilling, exec in charge of production (under Warner) phoned me and said, "Hey, the boss is in Hot Springs, Arkansas. Before he left, he told me to talk to you."

I was on contract, still with eighteen months to go, as head of the Special Effects Department. Instinctively, from long experience, I knew what it was. I girded my loins for the battle. I went to his office. He said, "The boss wants you to sign a contract."

I said, "I'm on a contract."

He said, "No, he wants a new contract."

It quickly came out: The money that Warner was offering was so little that at the end of seven years, I would just be getting what my existing contract was paying!

Now, I was a twenty-year alumnus of this "snake farm" -- I couldn't even remember how many times they had "shiggered" me into dropping a contractual raise at option time, under a plea of poverty and bad times. It was standard procedure for them.

I blew up. I thought it was a piss-poor price to pay for twenty-odd years loyal service to this company. Often waiting on checks or sometimes never getting paid at all. The first guy to the bank was the one who got his pay. But gratitude is a commodity little known in movies. It's just a part of the mythology.

A worker may tell himself, "I'll work like hell, and they'll be grateful." Nothing could be further from the truth.

ADAMSON: You would gradually have worked your way back to where you already were?

HASKIN: Yes, every year the option called for a little more money. By the time seven years had passed, I would be up to my current rate of pay, without even the raise at option time I had coming to my existing contract.

ADAMSON: This was as a director?

HASKIN: Yes. So, I blew my stack.

In retrospect, it was one of the big mistakes of my life. I should have said, "O.K.," signed it quick, and started developing the story. I would have made thirty pictures in the next two years, and had the movie business by the keester.

Instead, I chose to play the wounded tennis player. I sent Warner a telegram four pages long in Hot Springs, Arkansas, telling him what an ingrate he was, et al.

Well, friendship ceased. I tried to get a release. They wouldn't let me out of the studio. I had eight months left on my current option -- and eighteen months total, I think.

The next thing I knew, TREASURE OF THE SIERRA MADRE was on Henry Blanke's schedule, with John Huston assigned to make it! (Laughs) And he did, as you know. So, that's what a person's judgment amounts to in this business.

I should have said "Great, I'll work for nothing," to get some good films on my record. But that's hindsight!

ADAMSON: And then you could have gone somewhere else.

HASKIN: Yes. I could have renegotiated after any kind of a hit, but I was too dumb, and my agent was worse. Frank Orsatti was a go-for for Louis Mayer.

In other words, I blew the chance of a lifetime. After eight months had passed, a friend of mine was in the office when Warner was working his daily evil, and at this point, some new options to be picked up dropped onto his desk from the Legal Department -- among them, mine, on my Special Effects contract. Warner looked at it and said "Here, this guy Haskin, what'll I do with him?"

Tenny Wright, the production manager -- my friend -- said, "J.L., why don't you let him go?"

Warner said, "O.K."

That was it. I got out of the last term at Warners. Reprieve . . . !

Now that I was free, I began planning a career as director. James Cagney, meanwhile, had left the studio and had formed his own company, he and his brother, Bill. Hal Wallis had also left. He'd had his own unit at Warners but they stole him blind, so he formed his own company, migrated to Paramount.

So I went to see Jimmy Cagney. We had been good friends. He had me talk with Bill -- he deferred to Bill -- and they offered me a deal that was fantastic.

I said, "Well, I gotta look around, Jimmy, you know, in fairness to myself and to the opportunities that might arise." Another sign of my abysmal stupidity! He said, "All right, I'll tell you what -- go, look the whole business over -- everybody that will give you the time of day -- come back here and I'll match the deal." Well, what could I ask for that was better?

Naturally, in eight weeks I had signed with Hal Wallis! (Laughs) So I had no more integrity than any of them! It was a good contract. In addition to my friendship, I had professional respect for him. He had tremendous impact as a producer. That probably swayed me.

However, with any decency at all, I should have gone back to Cagney, and joined him. As it subsequently proved, I would have been much better off. All the Cagney outfit needed was a good journeyman guy who knew the score, and they would have made some top films. Bill was no filmmaker at all. Bill got a film together; it was a bomb. Time after time.

I'd been picture doctor for Warners for several years, with Hal Wallis, executive producer. He'd start to throw a story in the ash barrel, and then he'd say, "Well, no, have Bun look at this, and see what he can do with it." I'd figure out the best method to make it. Some biggies, too. For instance, one of them had already been scheduled to go on location, to the Aleutian Islands. The company was scheduled to leave from Eureka in whaling boats and sail to the Aleutians for the shooting, actors and all!

Christ! The first thing I did was call the Weather Bureau and ask, "How many days of sunlight a year do they get in the Aleutians?" The guy had a tough time finding three days a year! (Laughs) So I told Wallis, "We'll make it on the water stage -- forget the Aleutians." It was with John Garfield and Eddie Robinson -- THE SEA WOLF. And it turned out all right. Shot right on the stage. (Laughs)

Geez! Can you imagine Eddie Robinson and those actors in the Aleutians, trying to play scenes? With fog, and snow and ice? Impossible!

I would have been the ingredient the Cagneys needed to make the thing work. Furthermore, in those long hiatuses they often had, he could have loaned me out to MGM and a few prestigious studios. Again, I listened to the wrong party -- myself. I signed with Wallis. As to my career with him, I put in every trick I could think of to force him to let me shoot a film. For instance in my contract, if at the end of the first year, I had not done a feature, the whole deal was void. He was a tough customer, and I knew it.

Well, the first year passed, and no film. He would let anybody turn me down -- Loretta Young refused me. Who the hell was she to have artistic control?

Finally, three months after the contract was legally void, he had to go to England. Before he left, he assigned me to a story. It was a play that had bombed on Broadway -- eighteen nights, and back to the warehouse, one of those things. Luther Adler had starred in it. A conversation piece about old-time gangsters.

I fooled around with that while Wallis was preparing to leave, and got a script together. The story was difficult to develop and dramatize. Finally, Wallis assigned a writer, Charlie Schnee. He was a "switch" writer -- the beginning of every scene was at the end and the end was at the beginning. This I found out later, when I began to shoot his stuff. (Laughs) Burt Lancaster, Kirk Douglas, Wendell Corey, Liz Scott, George Rigaud, Marc Lawrence, all these young guys -- it was their first feature together -- were cast in the film. Then Wallis left.

Every morning I'd come onto the stage, passing dressing room row. The principal actors would all be sitting in their dressing rooms, brows clouded, studying their scripts. As I'd pass, they'd yell, "Hey, Bunnie!"

I'd accelerate and say, "Wait a minute, I'll fix it." I rewrote the thing every day. Then I'd give them the new scenes, and we'd stage it.

Eventually, it played, and was a big grosser. However oversimplified, the audiences really liked it at the time.

ADAMSON: Yes. It's a good picture. It's still got a good reputation.

HASKIN: Anyhow, Wallis came back, toward the end of shooting the picture. I began to get the pink notes. I existed throughout the rest of that film under a barrage of pink notes, because I had dared to take the bit in my own teeth. It was my first -- I had to. I was going to rise or fall on my own efforts.

He'd send me a note: "See me after work." I'd go up to his office at day's end, and the first thing he'd say was, "When do you think the function of a producer begins on this film?" (Laughs) Well, I always had the answer on the tip of my tongue, but at least I had judgment enough not to say it -- that I'd been in the business fifty years and never found out it _when_ it was! (Laughs) It would not have endeared me to him.

Unfortunately, I had a careless cutter. He put the film together any old way. When I saw his first cut, I didn't know what the hell I was looking at.

I had to take it over and recut it myself the way it was shot. Finally, Wallis saw it, and grudgingly gave his okay. No opinion -- good or bad -- one way or the other. I tell you, I put in more effort on that than Ingram did on THE FOUR HORSEMEN OF THE APOCALYPSE, or any Academy Award film. Believe me. Just pure tearing you to pieces -- night and day. I'd sit up all night writing the damn thing.

The way Schnee had written the screenplay, if I'd shot it that way, you couldn't have told what the story was.

At least I learned that there were definite things about directing that I had better find out, quick! One was handling the actors. Strangely, I'd never really gotten close to actors before, except to photograph them. I was uncertain. Going overboard in certain cases.

I tried out too many things with Kirk Douglas, telling him that the guy he was playing was a real freak, a man without fear. Kirk was so in love with this concept, he wrote me a fan letter, wanting me to direct all of his future films, because I gave him such a lift with this crap.

Well, came the scene when Burt has to grab him and threaten to hang him on a meathook in the freezer if he doesn't give up half ownership of the cafe. Kirk played it just twiddling his thumbs.

I said, "Wait a minute. What are you doing?"

He said, "Well, I have no fear. I don't know what fear is." (Laughs) I was hoist by my own petard -- I had to modify the concept, and I did a fairly creditable job.

Then, of course, with the trials and tribulations I had with the screenplay, I had to say to myself, Well, there is such a thing as dramatization, and this I don't know much about! (Laughs) So I began a steady, step-by-step course of the study of dramatization. . . .

One of the big things I found out in the crucible of I WALK ALONE was my uncertainty in handling actors. I had a hell of a time with Marc Lawrence. He was the archetypal gangster type. It was very difficult, because he tended to come on double-George Arliss right off the bat -- he gave you everything plus. He overacted till the scenery was jumping out of the way. Not from the school of the terse, no-movement-no-blink, style of Bogie. Marc Lawrence gives everything, plays all the parts and every nuance in the story, plus what-have-you? I didn't know how, within the framework of politeness, to tell him to cool it, which of course, I learned later. He was the biggest problem to me, because I can spot a phony performance immediately, and I knew that he was overboard. He would hate himself, I would hate him, and the producer would hate both of us!

At that time, Burt Lancaster was not yet an actor but a "poseur"; you know -- he hit postures with tremendous force. I let him go with that, because at least he had impact and power. It became his style in his early years of acting.

Kirk was the typical guy in the acting class who, if they said, "let it all hang out," would be the wildest. He was an interesting actor, though, not in the sense of overacting like Marc Lawrence. Marc Lawrence just overdid things. Kirk's dramatic training had been very thorough, but sometimes he overlooked the reality in a scene. In a movie you have to maintain credibility of human behavior or the audience doesn't believe you. For instance, we had a scene located out on Long Island; Kirk was wealthy, Burt kind of broken down. Burt was trying to get his own back from Kirk --

ADAMSON: After he's just gotten out of jail.

HASKIN: Yes. He went out there in a taxicab with the girl to confront Kirk. The fight ensued.

Well, as they came in, Kirk pulls a gun on Frankie, and there's a confrontation, see. In rehearsal, he's supercilious about it because of this crap I'd been telling him about fearlessness. He believed that he was the bravest man on earth.

ADAMSON: Without fear.

HASKIN: Yes. So he walked by Burt nonchalantly.

I jumped in and said, "Wait a minute, wait a minute. For chrissake, this guy is built like a panther. If you got that close to him, he'd spring on you, take the pistol away from you, and shove it!" (Laughs) He was able to see the reality, agreed to modify his carelessness. At least I could reason with Kirk, bring him around to some understandable kind of human behavior.

Liz Scott was the unknown quantity. I did a couple of other pictures with her, one with Dan Duryea, TOO LATE FOR TEARS. From my career as a cameraman, I had some plusses: I could tell immediately if an actor was into a scene. Liz was then an unskilled actress. She had a habit that she'd look at everything but the other actor's eyes. She didn't know how to play eye contact. This is vital to any conviction in a scene. It has nothing to do with finesse of acting, it's just a visual thing: to be convincing, make contact, eye-to-eye, and the scene comes to life.

She would fish around, looking at his necktie, his lapels, the top of his head, his ears. Everything but his eyes. She also had a habit of leaning her head to one side, Burt also. Usually, he'd lean the opposite way. Now the two of them were making an X on screen.

ADAMSON: Yes, didn't you have some kind of difficulty working with Burt?

HASKIN: I didn't have any clash with him, if that's what you mean. However, Burt was so full of energy, he was a difficult man to harness. Both Douglas and Lancaster were acrobats. The minute I turned my back, they'd be going over the top of the set. Sheer exuberance.

Burt was not an actor at that time, although, as his career has progressed, he learned the craft, and has given many fine performances.

In I WALK ALONE I had the laborious task of finding out why a script would read beautifully and still not play. The town is still full of screenplays that don't play. They read beautifully, but ignore the fact that filmmaking is an entirely unique and different way of telling a story. You don't do it with a pen, you don't do it with a typewriter, you don't do it with a Xerox or printing press, or yodeling, or playing a guitar and singing -- it is done with pictures that move, still pictures that move, accompanied by the sounds thereof. It's something entirely novel. It's a medium that never existed before the advent of moviemaking.

ADAMSON: Well, when you say they read beautifully, but don't play, you mean there isn't enough action, or nothing to look at -- ?

HASKIN: The scenes are not constructed suitably for the medium. Don Siegel, a protégé of mine, was making his second film; in spirit, something like KEY LARGO -- it had overtones of that. The screenplay was written by Philip Wylie. It was a very, very literate job, and the dialogue was just crackling, but the damn thing was the dullest thing ever made. It just about wrecked Siegel's career.

ADAMSON: The film itself.

HASKIN: Yes. His first job had been a little exercise in the London fog -- Sherlock Holmes-time. He did pretty well with that.

The second one with a big Philip Wylie script and important players damn near did him in. (Laughs) He just managed to squeak by, and continue as a director. I had read and believed this beautiful prose, and it was a shock to me at the time. I realized why -- because it was just static, and it lacked the conflict of dramatization. It was a slick group of scenes that got nowhere, really, because they were not related to the central theme of the story. . . .

Oversimplifying the case, let me illustrate: Shakespeare's Romeo and Juliet is the standard upon which to base classic dramatization. It has what's necessary at the beginning of any story, a provocative situation that says, We are telling this story because this day such-and-such was going on.

So in Romeo and Juliet, there is a provocative situation. The reason you tell that particular story is that there's a hell of a fight going on in the streets of Verona between two families -- the Montagues and Capulets.

ADAMSON: And right away, you've got a conflict.

HASKIN: Yes, and it is a conflict to the death. Important; this was a real fight -- enmity, hatred, bigotry, and all the things that go with it. Demanding audience attention.

Now, that's a worthy reason to begin a story. As it continues, a boy from the neighborhood falls in love with a girl from the neighborhood. The audience is aware before anyone else that he is a Montague, she is a Capulet. The characters don't know. They are the children of the dramatization. That's why they must not know it.

The next thing, boy and girl discover that one is a Capulet, the other a Montague. This knowledge provokes the first big dilemma of the story.

What is Romeo, whom we call our protagonist, going to do about it? He's in love with this beautiful young girl from the enemy family, with full understanding of consequences. It's up to him. He's faced with making a willful decision.

What to do? Go to Abyssinia and become a monk? Or do something about this lovely girl?

There follows an immediate series of events, all ominous. All suspenseful.

Romeo opts to marry Juliet. (Laughs) This simple willful decision brings on all the trouble. So, the full thrust of dramatization is begun.


ADAMSON: How does Romeo and Juliet come into play when you look at a script?


HASKIN: Well, it's a blueprint of the steps of proper dramatization. Of course, there's more to dramatization than the little thumbnail pattern we've cited of Romeo and Juliet.

Suffice that I started assembling a shelf of reference books. In this effort, I found that there was nothing valid existing about the mechanics of directing movies. I collected a working library of reference books about the art of dramatization. An art, incidentally, which has never been held in very high repute in movie circles. In fact, we are just emerging from an era during which it was ignored completely. You know, the Italian influence: one-man's-opinion-of-the-scenes and the hell with plot and all that stuff. A series of films -- avant garde things, about the time EASY RIDER came out. It was a very destructive wave of thought about what it takes to make a motion picture. Luckily, it's come back to dramatization to a certain degree recently. Not all the way, but I hope it will. . . .

Anyway, I just had to apply myself completely to learning. I had to know to get a grasp on the art of directing.

ADAMSON: Now, this is around the time of I WALK ALONE?

HASKIN: Yes, right around then. When I began my whole career over again.

Actually, I found a book that is out of print by an old writer named Krows, called <u>Playwriting for Profit</u>. It has the whole story of dramatization in it. I studied it assiduously.

In undertaking my own book, <u>How I Learned to Direct Movies</u> (working title), I was horrified to learn that nothing definitive has ever been written about how to direct a movie, or even how to direct scenes, with any professional validity. As I delved deeper into it, I saw why. It's very difficult to describe this unique process. But I'm giving it the old college try, and I'm going to do my damndest to produce a worthwhile textbook.

ADAMSON: Why do you think it's so tough to describe?

HASKIN: Well, it's such an elusive art, with a myriad of methods and as many practitioners. I am amazed that nothing valid has been written in all the years movies have been around. Most of the material about directors and their work is biographical, or autobiographical; or listing various directors and what they've done, as kind of guidebooks. Nothing about the techniques of filmmaking. What it entails. Its mystique. The seeming absence of rules. A very complex subject. One even learns that what's a rule today is not a rule tomorrow.

I finally evolved a directing style of my own -- not that I ever had too many chances to demonstrate it very aptly in the films I've made. The major responsibility of the movie director is to formulate the shooting continuity. It is the one thing he is wholly responsible for. I've known directors who ignored this responsibility, leaving it to the cameramen, or sometimes the editor. But the one thing which distinguishes one director from another is his grasp of what the set-ups shall be, what they mean, and how they can be cut together.

The basic philosophy of directing is <u>telling</u> a story by means of his personal techniques. The director is the <u>storyteller</u>, not the story <u>writer</u>, nor the author. He's not the star, or anything else -- nothing but the story <u>teller</u>. Classically, a well-told film does not dwell on the identity of the storyteller. That is a kind of egoistic exhibitionism too often indulged in.

ADAMSON: Like who, specificallly?

HASKIN: Many. One leaps to mind: Sidney Furie. He seizes every chance to exhibit himself. He will pick a weird angle foretelling things that he does not mean to foretell just for the sake of cleverness. He's hampered himself as a craftsman. He had a hell of a good show in THE IPCRESS FILE, yet he kept overstressing weird angles to shock the eye rather than telling his story unobtrusively.

There was one angle I never could analyze. It was a scene in the basement of the garage where there's a sudden chase and a gunfight. The villains dash away on foot. Then, this puzzling cut. There was a blur in the foreground as the men ran away. I couldn't figure out what it was supposed to be.

When I was preparing THE POWER at MGM -- we were running several films similar in type, including THE IPCRESS FILE. By God, I said to myself, I'm going to solve the mystery. So I went down five feet from the screen when we ran the picture, put on dark glasses, waited. When the shot came on,

I saw what it was for the first time ever. During the action, somebody had dropped a pistol. It had fallen to the floor of the garage. Furie had framed his shot through the trigger guard of the pistol lying on the floor! Imagine! A tiny little trigger guard. Bound to be out of focus, a big blur. The fuzzy trigger stuck up in the middle of the shot, further confusing things!

This sounds like a minor infraction until you start to ask how he must have proceeded to shoot this angle. On the cement floor of the garage, it must have taken a jackhammer to dig a hole in order to place the camera low enough to shoot through the pistol in the foreground!

Well, a director wasting all that time to satisfy his own ego must be nuts; it surely must have taken half a day. An exercise in absurdity. Particularly in that it is also meaningless.

He had another one in the same film. The protagonist is going up to an apartment for an assignation with the girl; a normal kind of a sequence, featuring romance.

After leading the audience to anticipate some polite screwing, there is a shot in the apartment hallway, shooting down through the chandelier, showing the top of the boy's head, as he opens the door, closes it, turns, pauses a second, then enters the apartment.

I thought, My God, there's a maniac up in the attic ready to jump down and stab him with a knife! The ego of certain directors in handling a medium of telling a story is unbelievable!

Michael Curtiz was an exhibitionist, too, but he did realize he was the storyteller, and he controlled his ego. Some of his dolly shots were quite bizarre, but they always had purpose, not sheer exhibitionism.

As the storyteller, the director is obliged to keep himself out of the way. His basic obligation is guiding the shooting continuity; therein lies the key of success in this weird medium. The director must pick a succession of set-ups, shoot one after the other, with such skill and cunning as to conceal the fact that most individual set-ups were as expensive to make as buying a mansion in Beverly Hills! They are a mosaic which, laid together, becomes the smoothly told story.

Now, therein lies the art of directing. Right there. In judging a director's expertise, from that point one measures how well he accomplishes his storytelling. Not the least difficult, unfortunately, is that he's not working with cartoons or Puppetoons -- he's got live actors to cope with, and they're something . . . !

It is the director only who devises the way the story will be told in this well-nigh-indescribable medium. Then, you can't even describe a movie as merely a product for telling a story; there's added complexity: too many people involved, down to the little guys on the developing tank at night, watching your film.

The pure storyteller is the guy who sings it, out past his tonsils; or he writes it with a quill pen -- it comes from the pen right out of his mind to his fingers.

But visualize the storyteller of a movie. It originates in his mind. Generally his shooting continuity is written, springing from a sort of an ad-lib factor as he works out scenes.

He tells his cameraman, "All right, put it here. . . . Then, move into this player, then come to a close-up, then swing to this other guy," and so forth. It may seem all hit and miss.

Very few, outside of a Hitchcock or a Lubitsch, ever have solidly fixed shooting continuities. Number one, it doesn't tend to help the spontaneity of the continuity to peg it beforehand, to sketch it out. A sketch continuity almost assures loss of a fluid technique.

ADAMSON: Why?

HASKIN: It's a succession of static impressions, not the continuous movement of live action. A key to modern technique of directing is contained in the way Curtiz would say, "Bunnie, I visualize."

He was visualizing the scene completing itself in living terms. He might visualize you right out of business, if you didn't watch him, but nevertheless, that's where he was creating his shooting continuity. He'd see the whole thing happening as he walked about the set. You'd put a mark, and start the dolly track. As I said, you'd put phony tracks first, because he would probably change.

But that's neither here nor there. He visualized a shot. "I poosh my extras across here, and I do this . . . " He was a kind of Buzz Berkeley of the drama -- he created these weird technical effects of just happening that gave a verisimilitude of life, making his scenes flow, and engrossed his audience. That's a <u>shooting continuity</u>, rather than a sketch continuity. True spontaneity.

ADAMSON: Acted out or worked out right there, rather than determined and drawn ahead of time.

HASKIN: That's right. If a sketch artist sits down with a script to make a shooting continuity, you immediately have blockades of flow affecting your show. It's always turned out that way. A William Cameron Menzies production design of sketches often gave some very startling vistas, but the movement of verisimilitude to life was always inhibited. It couldn't escape that fact.

ADAMSON: Well, the actors don't feel free.

HASKIN: No, no. W. Duncan Mansfield, who was Thomas Ince's cutter for all the big C. Gardner Sullivan epics, then Harold Lloyd's with GRANDMA'S BOY, and all the rest, was a student of technique throughout the years. He and I became buddies. Between us, we theorized about the ultimate technique of a shooting continuity, discarding most of the standard procedures, substituting for them a "cutaway technique." This method was based on a simple principle: "Cut away from anybody onstage to the subsequent cut." Thus if I am shooting "X," the next cut must be without anything of "X" in it.

Take a shot of two guys nose to nose, quarreling. There is an important line in the crux of the scene demanding a big close-up of the first guy, for his reaction. Standard method would simply be to cut from the two-shot to the close-up when needed. Cutaway technique called for inventing a reason that the second guy move away in high dudgeon, or whatever motivation -- it doesn't matter. Camera follows him, eliminating Guy No. 1 from the shot, so, timed properly, cut away from Guy No. 2 to Guy No. 1 for the close-up! Well, following a thorough philosophy of "never cut to anything in the action of a scene," the director has to stage his action so that he cuts away at the highest point of interest, mounting the drama to increase tension. The director has to analyze the content of the scene -- immediately enabling him to tell if the beginning is at the beginning and if the end is at the end, or if the scene is "becocked," as the whole script was in I WALK ALONE.

I got hip to the trick finally. In I WALK ALONE, Charlie Schnee would take the climax of a scene and place it at the beginning, like a "teaser." The rest of the scene just noodled away to fill in the time. Jesus.

When I'd come in in the morning, I got so that I would take my script and put the end of the scene at the beginning, and then take the beginning and put it at the end! Voilà!

Anyhow, to get back to the technique that Dunc and I evolved -- It's not something that you could go to the U.S. Patent Office and get a patent on. Many directors have realized the value of analyzing a scene and establishing a cutaway shooting continuity for it.

Cutaway technique demands much of a director. He must keep particularly foremost in his mind that he is telling a story -- particularly, that an audience does not want to be reminded of cutting from one scene to another. They prefer to immerse themselves in the story, and believe that actors make it up on the set as they go along. To them, that is perfect direction. All the director's cunning should be applied to make them believe that.

The film in which I came closest to shooting pure cutaway technique was THE NAKED JUNGLE. I almost succeeded

At the time, I thought I had shot it without a single cut-to; that it was all cutaway.

Actually, at points, although the scenes are staged with cutaway in mind, there are many exceptions. However, in the early scene, where they are having dinner on the plantation, and she gets up to go and play the piano, I succeeded in making it all in cutaway technique. Purely. It just plays smoothly, enhancing the content of the scene as expected.

In I WALK ALONE I featured cutaway technique. For instance, when Kirk Douglas' office was first shown, with the bar, at no time did I figuratively say, Look at this splendid nightclub. No long shot establishing. The sequence of the shots was planned with the set as background. Before even the first exchanges of dialogue were over, the audience had seen everything -- that corner, this corner, all the walls, the carpet, everything in between. It did not arrest the flow of the story, it just embellished it. It was a grace note for the action, and yet the viewer was familiar with where everything was from then on. If there was a cutaway from one guy to another, you'd know where he was because you knew the whole set, with its geography.

ADAMSON: When did you develop this?

HASKIN: In discussions with Duncan Mansfield. Duncan was one of the old-time original editors, with years of experience. In the early days of Tom Ince, and Griffith, and later, Chaplin and Lloyd, he was tops. He had made a study of how to achieve dramatic effects with action, with cutting, with camera placement. Perhaps the whole thread of discovery came from Duncan. We talked about it and developed the idea. I began to see how it demanded a basic movement in the action. To accomplish cutaway technique, you've got to move.

Were I to show this whole room first, with the guy walking over there, cut closer to him, then cut to another guy with him in a two-shot, it would be James Cruze in 1924. (Laughs)

Cruze used to start at the back of the set, walk three paces, spit, say to the cameraman, "Put it here," then walk three more paces forward, spit again for his medium shot. Finally, he was done for the day. That is not making movies, its a series of still pictures, with occasional titles between them.

ADAMSON: I notice your coverage in I WALK ALONE was really, I don't mean to say intricate, but you had a great number of different angles of shots.

HASKIN: Yes, I was under the influence at that time, of Carol Reed and THE THIRD MAN. To every cutaway he had a new angle. . . . He kept changing every set-up, which I found interesting.

Anyhow, with I WALK ALONE, I had plenty of time for preparation -- a year and a half to analyze what I was going to do with it, in the way of shooting continuity. Finally, I got the assignment because all the cast were newcomers -- they didn't know enough to have any objections to me.

I thought, This is a story of intrigue -- a gangster feeling . . . therefore I am going to show it as if the audience is looking through keyholes. Intimately and closely, but secretly, at all the things that are happening. So, with over-the-shoulder shots, I'd tighten up -- at times one head would even block part of the other, that sort of thing.

This contrasted with a film I did not too long afterward, TREASURE ISLAND, in England. TREASURE ISLAND is a classic, it's scenery, the ships, and sea, and tropical islands, with inns and winding streets and waterfronts, this kind of thing -- like a series of postcards. So instead of being tight in two-shots, I would open up. There wasn't the necessity for seeing both eyes, so as to probe into the most secret desires of the actors.

ADAMSON: What did you do following I WALK ALONE?

HASKIN: Following I WALK ALONE, there were no more assignments I could corral from Wallis. I went on a loan-out to

Frank P. Rosenberg and Monty Schaff, making a film for Universal release.

ADAMSON: You were under contract to Wallis, not Paramount?

HASKIN: I was under contract to Hal B. Wallis. He loaned me out to these people to direct MANEATER OF KUMAON.

It was taken from a book that was written by a great white hunter who had slain a lot of tigers. There was no personal story in it at all, not even rudimentary. So we had to create a story out of whole cloth, laying the action in India, with tigers eating people -- MANEATER OF KUMAON, Kumaon, India, which was a district back in the hills.

We operated at General Service Studios. A writer was assigned: Lew Meltzer. He and I kicked some ideas around, got a nucleus, and began to write a pretty good story. It had the general feel of RAZOR'S EDGE.

I think it could have been an outstanding film with the treatment we finally ended up with. We had fashioned a story of a beautiful, cultivated Indian woman, educated to be a doctor in New York, going back to her home village in the hills of India. There, she meets a white hunter looking for tigers. Wendell Corey was to play this guy. He falls in love with her, she with him, and the first thing he expects her to do is leave her village and come with him. But ties have been renewed between the woman and her father and the village people, delaying her decision.

There is the danger from the tigers; the village has no doctor. The villagers look to her for medical aid.

So she comes to the choice between her love for this white man, and love for her family and the village. It made a pretty interesting kind of a story with good possibilities.

We were preparing to start to shoot, and Schaff and Rosenberg got low on money. They called in an old-time producer, whom I knew quite well from Warner Bros., Sam

Bischoff, to help get financing. In other words, Sam, through his clout, could get the bank to put up some more money. (Laughs)

Sam immediately took over much of the function of producing. He said, "Hey, about this story, what will they think in Memphis of a white man falling in love with a dark woman?"

How bigoted can you get! One day, while we were interviewing, an actress came into the producer's office, half Japanese-half white girl, Sono Osata, a lovely person. You never saw a finer looking girl in your life.

Bischoff turned to her. "What would you think, Sono? You're a black girl . . . falling in love with this white man?"

Quickly I said, "Good-bye, Sono. Forget it."

The upshot was that the resolution of the story, whereby Wendell and the girl marry, and she makes the sacrifice and leaves with him -- all that had to be cut out, by order of Bischoff. To clinch the validity of his judgment, he flung open his top drawer. In it was one million dollars worth of bonds.

He said, "There it is. I know what I'm talking about." Boom -- he closed the drawer.

Well, what can you say to a guy like that? We ripped the story to pieces.

The starting date was right on us. I began shooting with no story -- and you wonder why pictures don't have any particular punch! Well, things like this happen. It's why a lot of movies don't make any sense.

First day, Lew Meltzer in a panic hung around me on the set trying to write something. I tried to find time to confer with him.

Under those stressful circumstances, we got a yarn together. Lew and I used to call it: "From here to there with Wendell in the jungle."

Wendell was a very sharp cat, and after about ten days of wandering around in jungles looking mournful, he called me to one side and said, "What the hell am I playing in this picture? What is the scene? Who am I?" (Laughs) I said, "Don't worry, we'll get a story together somehow."

We did. It was an innocuous little story that somehow played. In it, Sabu and Joy Warner (J. L.'s daughter) married, and there was a romantic feeling between Sabu's wife and Wendell. I don't know what the hell it was all about myself! But we had some good tiger stuff in it. Jack Ford saw it once, thought it was a hell of a good film.

ADAMSON: Where was it shot?

HASKIN: Mostly Corrigan's ranch.

ADAMSON: Near L.A.

HASKIN: Yes. Chatsworth. We used Mabel Stark's big Bengal tigers. They'd happily kill you on sight. Then we also had Mel Coontz's Satan, a toothless old cat, for close work.

Harrison Carroll, the gossip columnist, came on the set one day, and I tipped Mel Coontz to put on a show. He led Satan behind Harrison, had the tiger lay his head in the writer's lap. (Laughs) Harmless as Satan was, Harrison took off!

We had a bit of fun with Mabel Stark's Bengals. They were real killers, you know. One day in the scene, the tigers were supposed to charge the camera. They came full tilt at the camera, hitting the protective screens. These gave way. Suddenly the stage was full of tigers! Wendell Corey went up a twenty-foot platform hand over hand, to the top, failing to remember that tigers can climb too. Terry, production secretary and subsequently my wife, ran inside a flimsy canvas dressing room and slammed the door.

Eventually, Mabel got chairs and guns, and herded all the cats back into a cage.

This point of view has to involve a comment on the myths of directing. You see, I was no spring chicken when this all happened. I'd had years on the camera; I'd directed silent films back when I didn't have sense enough to come in out of the rain, and allowed myself to be plowed under.

Here I was, on my second film, forgetting the lesson of the first one: I WALK ALONE with its script backwards, re-writing it myself, fighting with Wallis. Even though finally it had come out as a picture that played, no prestige had accompanied it, except for the slick shooting continuity, and a beautiful job of photography by Leo Tover.

Here I was on my second effort, and Jesus, the story thrown into the ash barrel the night before we started shooting.

Well, one can only say, there's a lot more to directing than directing. I should have been a sonuvabitch, really.

These kinds of things kill your career; they kill momentum.

I must remark this, that the poor bastard who starts out to direct films and believes that he's going to rise or fall on his own merits, is a fool. God, he can be chopped liver, in no time.

I went on from MANEATER OF KUMAON to another loan-out, produced by Hunt Stromberg. He had made some box office pictures but nothing with much prestige. This was TOO LATE FOR TEARS. I put every effort I possibly could into the cheap little story by Roy Huggins, with a fairly good cast -- the amiable Liz Scott, and Dan Duryea. I loved him -- he had great style and gave a dimension it's difficult to describe, let alone direct. So much more than you ever asked for. He's one of the pleasures of my early directing career.

The film made money. It was a pleasing picture. In fact, Wallis wryly said, "All your pictures make money. I don't understand it." (Laughs) Jesus, I don't know why, either, but they did.

On TOO LATE FOR TEARS, I had Bill Mellor photographing for me, as he'd done on MANEATER OF KUMAON. Bill was such a pleasure to work with. I'd known him for years. He was George Stevens' cameraman. We just thought along the same lines: we went onstage to the big set of the entire city, where they were starting to hang a backing on the stage wall.

Bill said, "Put the backing back in the bin. I just won't put any light on the wall. . . . "

The producer was in a panic. But I knew and Bill knew: what you don't light, you don't photograph. (Laughs) It was beautiful.

Then I had a nice guy named Lou Rosso, who worked for Herbert Yates, as a production manager. I made a deal with him: I'd cut out enough money from the sets so he could buy Dan Duryea for a leading role in the picture. He and I went around to the sets and cut enough non-essentials to save $40,000 in no time, which was plenty to make up the difference in what they were going to pay, and what Dan Duryea was asking.

ADAMSON: When was it that you were next door to George Stevens?

HASKIN: Oh, way back, years previous -- I was an assistant cameraman, as George was at the time. I was working with Marshall Neilan, for cameraman Lyman Broening.

Later, I worked for Dave Abel, and several other cameramen, even Sol Polito, whom I got to know well later.

George Stevens and I had remained friends without seeing each other for years. When we'd meet, we'd pick up where we left off. Common enough in Hollywood.

Well, Bill Mellor finally dropped dead while shooting Stevens' THE GREATEST STORY EVER TOLD. Tragic thing, because Bill was a fine man, as well as a great photographer. You know, just a regular guy -- there are the regulars and there are the finks in this business (laughs) and needless to say, one class is the vast majority and one is the small minority. I like people you can depend on.

But to get back to this conclusion about directing -- he who would be a successful director had better get pretty tough about it early on. When he has dilemmas about what he should do and it's a matter of being a decent guy or bettering himself, he has to weigh the good impulse pretty sharply. He has to cancel personal weaknesses to get anywhere as important as a director's chair. Being a good guy and two bits will get you a cup of coffee. . . . I had had a psychological background of complete independence as a cameraman. When I wanted to create an effect, it was up to me to dream it up and do it. From such freedom, I went into the world of directing, where, as Bob Rossen told me, I could never make it. My teeth weren't long enough, he said. Well, the fact that he was a Marxist sympathizer and a pal of all the known Commies in town didn't alter the truth of what he said.

Then Jimmy Cagney told me -- one night we were sitting out on the backlot street doing a scene with Harvey Parry, stuntman, driving around the corner into a drugstore window with a big car -- CRASH! Harvey forgot to tie his head back and got a bloody nose on the wheel for the oversight.

Jimmy was watching me operate at that time, and he said, "Kid, you're never going to make it in pictures. You've got too much common sense." It's a fact. "Common sense" is the reverse of "charisma," that magic which commands the big bucks in movies.

It's the difference between what I earned, and what Anatole Litvak did, with his tremendous fanfare and hype.

I was on his set one day -- a 100-foot-long room, with spectators listening to a speech. It was a long shot. He was at the back in the chair, alongside the camera.

So distant she looked like a speck, was Bette Davis, sitting on the dais.

All Litvak was saying after each take was, "We take it again."

The lights go on. The 100 extras are ready -- "Ready! All right, roll the camera. Action!" Silence. Fifteen seconds. "Cut. We take it again." Forty-eight times.

I was standing, waiting to discuss something with him. I walked over, and said, "Tola, what the hell are you doing? You don't even walk down there and tell Bette what's wrong." He looked around; we were alone, and he said, "I tell you why. I take it once, I print it, I am Breezy Eason (B. Reeves Eason). I take it forty-eight times -- I am Anatole Litvak." (Laughs) Well, this was his code; his credo of integrity! He was Anatole Litvak! Period. Screw the budget. . . .

These things are hard facts of life, but they must be included in the personality of one who thinks he's going to become a successful director. It's a tough world, because an accomplished director should be cherished like a rare jewel. Of all the goddamn complex arts, he has at his fingertips the ability to put dramatic elements together to create an illusion that will sell enough tickets at a box office to entitle him to canonization!

Instead, he is usually hamstrung, beaten down, reviled, compromised, God knows what else -- all the way through, until he finally becomes a Frankenstein's monster, or a Frankenheimer, you know, ignoring the needs of everybody else on the set. "This is a Frankenheimer film!" Period.

ADAMSON: Yes. I understand somebody saying that you're too decent a guy or you're too nice a guy and you won't get anywhere, but I'm not sure I understand the "common sense" remark. It just means, it makes more sense to be colorful than to be sensible?

HASKIN: The way I operated, for instance, shooting a montage with Cagney. When he came on stage, I'd be all ready and set up. Say the scene called for Jimmy to rush to the phone, mutter something, hang up and rush off.

Now, why the hell do you need to tell him where he came from and who his mother was in the pre-life and after-life of this scene?

I said, "Jimmy, watch this rehearsal with the stand-in." He'd look through the camera. The guy runs in, mutters into the phone, runs off. On the way back to his own set, Cagney'd laugh, "What the hell, this guy Haskin has got too much common sense. He's not giving me all this chi-chi-shit. He'll get nowhere in pictures!"

ADAMSON: I understand that you had common sense, but why is it better to work without it?

HASKIN: Well, because Jimmy's cynical viewpoint of the directors he had worked with during his career -- and he was a top star at the time -- was that most of the instructions he received were drivel. It didn't have even common sense to it. He would have to counteract this baloney and give a credible performance out of his own unit. He was getting no help. Really. That's what his meaning was, that the general level of directing is phony, really.

Eddie Goulding's dead and he did some important films, but the guy didn't direct scenes. He'd be in there and talk with the actors for a while, and you'd see him acting his brains out and the staff walking around and standing. At 20th he had several opportunities to become a director, but he refused. Anyhow, Eddie was a good actor's director. He would get performances out of them in a rehearsal, all in a group. They might as well have been sitting at a table in the dressing room for all the movements he gave them -- he didn't know what the hell to do with them. He'd get the scene all set and act it himself -- he was a ham -- and then he'd turn to the current cameraman and say, "All right, that's it. Tell me when you're ready."

The cameraman, with the operating cameraman and assistant director, had to break it all up into scenes, actually directing the action. That was usually Ernie Haller, or Leon Shamroy, who should have been a director -- Leon was one of the masters of shooting continuity. But Leon didn't want to get into the racket. Eddie Goulding hadn't the foggiest notion of how to put a shooting continuity together, and that is the one thing that distinguishes a director from the lower primates. (Laughs)

He is responsible for a shooting continuity -- each set-up it takes to tell what the scene is all about.

Tony Gaudio, old-time cameraman, was given a chance to direct once, and he said, "Well, with my sharp lighting, I'll just sit back and take nothing but long shots."

He lasted about halfway through the picture. Somebody else went in and shot the necessary breakup continuity.

The fact that you're on the camera and privy to all this breaking up of scenes and so forth, means nothing, because you've got so damn many things to do yourself with the photography -- the 101 very demanding things that a cameraman has to cope with -- that you haven't time to be observant or understanding. Matter of fact, you don't give a damn what the director's up to. So, cinematography is no school for directors.

ADAMSON: The basic problem is, I guess, when you're a cameraman, all you're concerned about is the shot. You can't think about how they go together.

HASKIN: Well, part of the business of how they go together smoothly without a jump is your business, because if you're inconsistent in your lightings and general photography, you don't last long. That was the toughest thing I had to learn as a cameraman: I could shoot a great individual scene, but the breakup and the scenes that led into it had to be in the same style of photography. Exactly. Consistency is one of the measures of a good cameraman.

I was a highly consistent cameraman. DON JUAN printed almost entirely within a range of two or three printing lights. Shadows and highlights had the same density. This is professional excellence, and it was accomplished without a light meter. It had not come in yet.

In the morning I used to take a little white flat and put two floodlight broads on it at six feet distance and study it a minute. That was the basic memory pattern of density from which I would light.

I'm going to use some of this material that I've just talked to you about, in my book. The extra-curricular life needed to bring success as a director. Unless you are a guy who can walk into a Las Vegas casino and hit the jackpot for eight straight sevens at the crap table and (laughs) hit the roulette double zero three times, you've got to be in trouble as a director. Unless, of course, you're a hardboiled sonuvabitch. . . .

Chapter Seven

# THE FIFTIES

ADAMSON: Let's see, I guess we're up to TREASURE ISLAND now. How did that come about?

HASKIN: Well, it was part of a general Alice-in-Wonderland operation that was known as the Walt Disney Studio. Any resemblance between Walt Disney Studios and a movie lot was purely coincidental. And still is.

You could go on the lot at that time and you couldn't understand what was going on. Guys were playing baseball, other recreational games. Any time you wanted to talk to Walt, go into the toilet -- he's usually hanging out in there. Or in the precision machine shop. He might be flashing a headlight for the miniature railroad he was building in his back yard at home. I wondered if Walt knew much about what was going on. It's still a question, with him long gone.

Let me tell you how the Walt Disney Company became possessor of TREASURE ISLAND, which is a story in itself.

Larry Watkin, screenplay writer, novelist, Professor of English, was a very fine writer. He wrote the novel, On Borrowed Time, later made it into a hit play. He gave me the whole background of Disney acquiring TREASURE ISLAND.

First, let me tell you how Larry got connected with Disney -- this is worth knowing.

Disney took all the proceeds of SNOW WHITE, and built the studio in Burbank. It was their practice to be on the lookout for interesting subjects floating around.

One of the "Scouts" located reels and reels of seals in the Pribilof Islands, shot by some scientists.

Walt looked at it and with his affinity for weird looking animals said, "Let's buy this thing. Get it cheap." The deal was almost for nothing. These guys had frozen their toes off up there in the Arctic to get all this film.

Disney Company bought it for a song, and I suppose the guys ate for a few days out of the proceeds.

Now, Walt possessed all this stuff, and nobody knew what to do with it. So, he said, in a flash of genius, "Well, I tell you what -- we ought to get a real literate writer, not one of these damn Hollywood screenplay guys, but a novelist or something, and let him see it, look the material over, and write a documentary about seals -- something with dignity."

Into the hopper dropped the name Lawrence W. Watkin, Professor Emeritus of a Virginia University, with a lot of degrees after his name. "Yeah, yeah," said Walt, "this must be the guy. Get hold of him."

Well, where was he? Nobody knew. Finally, looking through Who's Who, they found the name of Larry Watkin. He was in Hollywood writing screenplays. Even had an agent. (Laughs) But they never tried that -- it was too simple!

So Larry made a deal. He looked at all the reels, got an idea, and wrote a voice-over type of thing.

Then, with an editor and a story line they put scenes together that were relevant to each other, and came out eventually with a documentary. It became SEAL ISLAND, for which Walt received an Academy Award.

Walt's contribution? Well, you've just heard how big that was!

After the seal film produced an Oscar for Walt, Watkin was uneasy. He was just wandering around with no assignment. That's a bad place to be, so he elected to hide out.

He located the story department vaults, decided they were off the beaten track, and found, of all things, a story Disney owned called Treasure Island.

To keep busy, he wrote a sixty-page treatment, eliminating the bugs that Stevenson had left. Stevenson never knew what kind of a ship he was writing about. It took a whole crew of pirates to sail it out to the Island. Then, for the sake of convenience, he had the boy sail it around the Island for days alone, with Israel Hands sitting in the scuppers, ready to do him in at first opportunity. Watkin took care of that inconsistency.

Walt read the treatment, was very interested. He ordered a sketch continuity, had it pasted up on the wall in the big office, from beginning to end, with the idea of perhaps making it as a cartoon.

Larry found out how he got possession of it. Walt had always been in love with Mark Twain's Tom Sawyer. There was an agreement among major producers, for story material in public domain. If a company was first in line with a claim, they were given priority. Each year they must maintain a certain amount of expense for story development, securing the rights. It was an agreement among the major producers. Walt had always wanted Tom Sawyer in the worst way. David Selznick had prior rights as producer for MGM. MGM also had the rights to Treasure Island, as well as a lot of other things. Walt put in a kind of shotgun claim for all material not claimed, or delinquent. MGM carefully maintained rights to Tom Sawyer, but one year they slipped and didn't develop Treasure Island. Suddenly Disney becomes the possessor. (Laughs)

"What the hell do I do with this?" he asked. "I want Tom Sawyer, not Treasure Island!" They threw it in the vault.

So, jumping ahead, Watkin had found it and written a sixty-page treatment.

Now coincidence became involved. At this point in Walt's career, the Mickey Mouse shorts had begun to cost too much. His bread and butter! He'd lost a labor dispute with the cartoonists and grew to hate them like poison. (Laughs)

The bankers came to Walt and his brother Roy and said, "If you go on at this pace, we're going to have to close you down."

They held the mortgages on the studio, and were putting up the money to make the Mickey Mouses, which had run up to $78,000 for half a reel -- terribly expensive stuff.

Then, there was capital outlay -- for multi-plane cameras and all that chi-chi embroidery.

So, there was a big powwow. The bankers suggested that Disney go into a program of live action, in order to salvage the studio.

ADAMSON: It was their idea?

HASKIN: Well whose idea it was, I don't know, but it was brought up in the discussion of how to salvage the Disney operation.

Abroad, in countries like England, there were regulations against exchanging currency at the time. Sale of Disney products had piled up all kinds of pounds, which were just sitting there untouchable.

"I'll tell you what we'll do," said Roy Disney. "We've got a subject almost prepared, with a sixty-page treatment. Put Watkin on a screenplay. Do it in England, with those frozen pounds in our company over there, Mickey Mouse, Limited. We should do it there, with all those fine actors, and the British scenery." So TREASURE ISLAND got underway.

Walt said, "Let's not get one of these ordinary directors around town costing $100,000." That was the main thing. "Get some guy not so well known...."

He equated TREASURE ISLAND with a kind of gangster movie. By some quirk of fate, he'd recently seen my latest film, TOO LATE FOR TEARS. He liked the action and aura of gangsters. He said, "That's the kind of stuff we need for TREASURE ISLAND" -- which only Disney could put together. "Who the hell is this director?"

"Some guy named Haskin."

"Never heard of him. O.K., get him out here and see what we can do."

I needed a film at the time I talked with Walt, and sure, I'd do TREASURE ISLAND in England. Who wouldn't? Of course, the deal was for peanuts. Total fee was $25,000.

As it turned out we were nine months on the stage with this thing. Me and the gateman were getting about the same wages. And I was there several additional months after. However, I wasn't getting any more money.

The Disney Company was renowned as the most chintzy outfit in movies. SEAL ISLAND cost next to nothing; they got me for peanuts, likewise Watkin. The whole deal was a steal.

Well, on the Queen Mary, I sailed for England. And I was accompanied by one of the great characters of movies as unit producer, a guy named Perce Pearce. He was of English descent, from back a generation or two. Perce Pearce could start an anecdote of no interest at Hyde Park corner, and we would have to wait in front of the Denham studio for him to finish it. Back in the Burbank studio, Larry Watkin timed him one day. Perce came into his office, and said, "Hey Larry, I want to talk to you." Larry said, "O.K. Shoot, Perce." Just for fun, he began to time the visit -- looked at his watch.

Perce looked out the window. It was spring, and there were bugs flying around outside, buzzing in staccato, and lots of bees.

Larry waited eleven minutes, Perce was still looking out the window with his mouth open.

Finally, Larry said, "You were saying, Perce?"

Perce looked at him. "Well, I've been thinkin'!" He was the producer. He had been the producer, at least got credit for it, on FANTASIA. What FANTASIA had to do with TREASURE ISLAND, I don't know.

You couldn't believe him! When we crossed, evenings were black tie aboard the Queen Mary. But Perce had this big wide brim brown felt hat. It wasn't a cowboy type hat, just a hat whose brim was too wide. It snapped down in front. There was a big bullet hole through the middle of the crown. In one side, out the other. Somebody had shot at it on the hatrack, I guess. I hope.

Walt would look at him with that hat on, and slap his leg and laugh. A regular guffaw. That was Perce's function at the studio, to wander by with the hat on when Walt was in low spirits. Walt would always come out of it and laugh.

What a place! Really nuts! Walt didn't even know they were making CINDERELLA at the time! I underwent a gradual disillusionment with Walt Disney. In the beginning I was expectant, and very eager to receive the magic from the Master. This is true.

I would have signed up for ten cents to do this film because I thought, "Jesus, along the line I'll get a touch of the Disney magic, and I'll go over like gangbusters, for the association. He's taken all these Oscars, and he's the only true genius in the movie business."

Before we sailed, I had been waiting impatiently for him to call me in and give me the magic, the aura I should invest the film with. It would be a Disney classic.

Nothing.

Up in his office a couple of times, he had opened the book and read some stuff Larry had already cut out, some longwinded dialogue of pirates philosophizing and murmur, "... Great stuff ... "

Then we'd have a belt of flit, and end the conference. Where was the magic?

In England, Perce and I saw eighteen stage plays in eighteen nights for casting purposes. There were thirty-two speaking parts in the script.

During this time, Perce was somewhat of a thorn in the side. We'd get dressed in dinner jackets to go to the theatre, then Perce'd slap on the old brown hat.

One night, leaving the Savoy, I said, "For God sakes, Perce, leave that lousy hat home. It's silly wearing it with dress clothes."

"Oh, you think I need a new hat, huh?"

I said, "Yes, emphatically."

An evening later I was leaving the hotel. I paused, and looked across the street. On the Strand, the shops are pretty lowbeat. There is Perce looking in a window. I could tell his back by the weird posture.

I sneaked across through the traffic, came up behind him. I blurted, "What are you doing?" He was looking in a fifty-shilling suit joint, a purveyor of hand-me-down type suits and hats. He whirled guiltily.

I said, "Ahhhh. You're not going in there. Come with me." I waved for a taxi and said, "One, Old Bond Street."

We drove to Scott's Hatters. I had been there in 1929. Then, it was private, like a club. One needed a reference. You went and were measured for hats. It was an establishment for the gentry. . . .

With the passage of time, it had become an open store. I dragged Perce in. The hats were still beautiful, of course.

I was attracted to a showcase at one side. Under a subdued spotlight, there was a midnight blue Homburg in a case, the most beautiful hat ever made. I said to myself, That's what I'll get on Perce's head, and make him look like a king!

I turned around. He had the clerk digging stuff out of the basement. He was trying on cloth hats! (Laughs) I went over and wrenched them away from him, and said to the clerk, "Get that hat out of the case there."

It was his size, a perfect fit. With it on his head, I tell you, the transformation was miraculous. You would never know the man. He had changed -- dignity, manhood, intelligence -- all the things he lacked! (Laughs) God!

We went to the final four or five plays, and he wore the Homburg; he began to enjoy it, and began psychologically to come up to the hat -- improving as a person because of that hat.

Well, the final night came, and bejesus, here he came out of his room with the old brown hat in his hand. He flapped it on to his head. What the hell was happening?

Brief questioning brought out that Walt was arriving by air tomorrow morning. Perce had got the old hat out, to become the clown for Walt again.

Well this is all apropos of Disney's contribution to TREASURE ISLAND.

So Walt came in next day and renewed acquaintance with some toffs and swells around town -- Air Marshal Tedder and other great ones. He was booked to leave soon for a tour on the continent with his wife. I was still waiting for the magic. For the only acknowledged genius in movies to sit down with the director and the producer and give us his feeling about how to shoot TREASURE ISLAND.

By the time he boarded the train at Waterloo to go on his trip, I had had eighteen minutes with Walt Disney. Exactly. And that was addressed to me with Perce Pearce along.

The last thing that I saw of Walt, Perce was saying in front of me, "Now, Walt, I want every address you'll be at on the continent, so that when the trouble starts I can get in touch with you." A really reassuring kind of a statement to start the film!

The picture started just a day before Walt left. The set was the Bristol Courtyard, where the carriage brings the Squire, the Doctor, and little Jim, to begin the adventure.

Early, through the main gate of the studio, came an entourage of cars -- with Walt, Marshal Tedder, other swells, all pretty well loaded. It was about 9:30 in the morning. They got out of the cars to observe the scene. I turned at a disturbance in the courtyard, and who was in the middle of the set telling everybody what to do? Perce Pearce. With the brown hat on.

I took his arm and said, "Look, Charlie, up in your office there's a lot of pictures on your wall that don't look even to me, why don't you go up and straighten them?" (Laughs) That's the last time he was on the set.

I never saw Walt Disney during the production after that at all. It was his total contribution to my welfare as a director of the film.

Much later, when I was supervising the cutting for a while, and Watkin was still in London, I went up to Watkin's flat one afternoon, and we shared a bottle of beer. I gave him this same plaint, that I had been waiting for the Disney magic, etc.

He listened, and said, "Well, you want to know something? How much time do you think I had with Walt?"

I said, "You must have had a lot of conferences with Walt to get all those wonderful lines into the screenplay."

He said, "I had less than you did. About five minutes or so." Fantastic.

ADAMSON: This was the first totally live-action picture they did, wasn't it?

HASKIN: Yes. There were bits of bad luck, such as Bobby Driscoll getting deported because he was an American citizen without a work permit. He was too young to be working, and we contrived a defense that he was an American citizen, therefore he wasn't subject to British child labor laws (laughs) which, of course, the judge laughed off. At least he agreed to let Bobby stay in the country six weeks -- not to work, but to prepare the appeal.

We grabbed him and threw him on the stage. I had to shoot Little Jim Hawkins out of that picture in six weeks, from beginning to end. Doing close-ups with all the other actors present, for background or offstage voices. I finished Bobby Driscoll in six weeks. Then we went back to court with him all dressed up.

The judge said, "Get out of England." Deported him! (Laughs) Oh brother! Now, I suddenly had the task of beginning the film all over again, using a little English boy younger than Bobby was, as his double. To fill in all the longer shots, and other action with and without Bobby -- his close-ups being already shot. Nobody but a technician like myself could ever have kept it straight.

ADAMSON: Did this happen very early in the shooting, so that you didn't have any leisurely shooting time with him at all?

HASKIN: It was during the first week or two. A disgruntled prop man who got fired went to the Bucks County local court and lodged the complaint. Cunningly, he didn't complain about Bobby Driscoll violating the child minimum age law, but stated that an American citizen was working without a labor permit. Reason for no permit: Bobby was too young! If it hadn't been for my own technical ingenuity, I'm sure the picture would have been in a mess; God knows what would have happened to it. As it was, a certain smoothness of characterization and dimension was missing, I thought.

The apple barrel scene didn't come off well -- I had to shoot Little Jim at the time hiding in the barrel separately, without the rest of it.

A most difficult job to create a scene with any cohesion. . . .

Being long since off the payroll, I finally returned to America, leaving Perce and the cutter hacking at the film in Denham. Time passed. One day, I got word from the studio that the film had arrived in final cut. Walt was going to have a showing. I was invited to see it.

Honestly, I never saw a worse massacre in my life. I found out they'd already seen it, and had asked me to see it, so I could try to straighten it out. Perce and this English cutter, Alan Jaggs, had really messed it up.

Walt said, "How about taking over and re-cutting it?"

I took Larry Watkin and a copy of the script into a cutting room with the picture. The trims were still in England, so we unglued the whole damn thing, putting the rolls in the rack. Laboriously, we put it back together the way it was written and shot. Lacking the trims gave it kind of a staccato effect here and there, but at least it told its story straight.

That was my final association with Walt. Perce was my enemy. He's since died, is now relieved of all of his pain, I guess. God rest his soul!

ADAMSON: Didn't you have some trouble with Robert Newton?

HASKIN: No more than anticipated. I knew his reputation when I went over there. He was a British actor steeped in the full tradition of rep -- he came up the tough way in the provinces.

Right off, I figured, the best way to generate some personal enthusiasm in this guy was to suck him in as my helper with production problems. He knew all about English theatre.

He was hung over when I first met him. I said, "Well, there will be about eight weeks before we shoot. Why don't you go fishing? When you come back you'll have the job of casting the most delightful part in the show -- Ben Gunn." Ben Gunn was the crazy guy marooned on Treasure Island. When they found him, he begged, "You haven't got a piece of cheese on you, have you, matey?"

So Bob went fishing in Ireland for a week. He came back sunburned, his health restored. I kept drawing on him for advice about production problems, and got him hunting for a real good character actor to play Ben Gunn. We had almost landed Alec Guinness, but he was tied up for run-of-the-play at the Savoy Theater.

Bob generated lots of enthusiasm and interest in the picture, and he became a good member of the team. Throughout the shooting he came to work sober and full of good ideas. . . .

But he was unfortunate. The booze had really taken an advanced hold on him. He was unable to portray his concepts fully when the camera was rolling. Something going on in his subconscious, and when the camera turned, he stiffened up and became a bit mechanical -- losing the charm of the role, the fantasy of Long John Silver.

Long John Silver was a complex role. All of the early scenes with the little boy were like father and son -- they were tender, sensitive scenes. In rehearsals, I would just drool. I lived in the expectation of getting some outstanding scenes; but the minute the camera would start, he would stiffen, and the charm vanished. He gave a performance, but never one with that original genius shown in the rehearsals.

ADAMSON: He's just tremendous in the picture. I think he's great.

HASKIN: Yes, but only up to half potential. I tried to trick him during the scenes around the inn with Little Jim, where he gives the boy the little pistol -- they're charming, pure, enchanting Stevenson.

I would start the camera unbeknownst to him, and walk in and say, "All right, let's rehearse this thing."

I would drift aside to get out of the camera range. I'd say "Let's see how it looks." He knew subconsciously, and he'd tighten up. He couldn't break it.

Once I had the same problem with a test of Paul Draper, at Warner Bros. He was a great dancer, Broadway star, good-looking man. He looked like a Fred Astaire.

We'd stand and carry on a conversation, but the minute a camera'd start, he'd stutter. A terrible stutter -- couldn't get a word out. (Laughs) Well, I tried tricking him with a camera --

ADAMSON: Was this when you were shooting COLLEEN?

HASKIN: No, I was making tests at Warner Bros. with Zachary Scott, Paul Draper, and people from New York. This guy would have been a great bet to develop into a star. He was a top Broadway dancer, but damned if he could get a line of dialogue out with a camera rolling.

ADAMSON: The camera itself unnerved him, even though he had a stage presence?

HASKIN: Yes. Even though he didn't know it was going. He was not hip to movie procedure. I had the camera at times shoot through a hole in a black flat. I'd even get the cameraman to wander into the set with me with the camera still rolling -- every trick I knew. But you couldn't fool his subconscious. (Laughs)

ADAMSON: One more thing on TREASURE ISLAND. Did you find Larry Watkin a good writer? Were you able to shoot the stuff the way he wrote it?

HASKIN: Yes. Yes, he was terrific.

ADAMSON: Rather than shuffle the stuff around?

HASKIN: He had a flair for period stuff. One of his novels was about the time of the American Revolution. I was delighted with the screenplay. I think that it could have been improved as a film by a little better handling of this cast on my part. My only plea is the problem of Bobby being deported; I actually shot the picture twice. . . .

On seeing the film later, I thought it could have been improved by a better interplay between the principals. But never, in the double shooting, was I able to bring the actual relationships alive. Bobby Driscoll wasn't there when I was shooting the major version of the picture, and the little English boy was just an ordinary child actor.

Bobby Driscoll was a truly great actor. He'd been in eighteen films previous to TREASURE ISLAND. One day out on the quarry location, he said, "I can't understand why Long John and I are such friends at this point, and then later, I'm acting like I hate him."

I said, "Didn't anybody ever talk to you about how relationships change between actors by what happens in the story?"
"No," he said, "no."

I explained relationships an actor has with another to make scenes.

He said, "Oh! I see."

That night he rushed home and read the whole script over again. (Laughs) In a different light . . .

The tragedy of this fine child star was that he had been a natural, unaffected person up to the time he appeared in court for sentencing. Suddenly he saw himself as having international importance to the British government and the British law. It turned this kid's head. Suddenly, he became a sophisticated adult in his thinking.

It wasn't too long after that he was taking dope. He finally died of an O.D. He was just ruined by the notoriety. I often wondered how guilty I was, and yet I couldn't really put the finger on myself. We had a wonderful working relationship. The kid put on no airs at all -- he was just a naive young fellow, and took direction immediately. He had a great sense of the mechanics of screen movement. He was obviously headed for a career as a star, and hell, to think that by the time he was twenty-three or twenty-four, he was dead.

His parents never had any conception about what being an actor was doing to his childhood. He was all on his own.

ADAMSON: TREASURE ISLAND was a successful picture, wasn't it?

HASKIN: Yes, it was. It did well at the box office in the U.S. and abroad. It had several national runs on network TV, and then they split it in half. Then Walt got the idea of utilizing all the characters for the Pirates out at Disneyland.

ADAMSON: The Pirates of the Caribbean.

HASKIN: Yes, the Pirates of the Caribbean. Then they put the film on the shelf. It was reissued a couple of times on the Walt Disney weekly program, and then went on the shelf again. It would certainly bear theatrical reissue. It was well made.

ADAMSON: Disney did other films in England that were a lot less successful.

HASKIN: Yes.

ADAMSON: Why was it that you never did any of the other ones?

HASKIN: Oh, mostly my disagreement with Perce. Perce blamed me for all the problems, as well as the deportation.

ADAMSON: Perce had Disney's ear, I guess.

HASKIN: Yes. He was a confidant.

But, I had had hopes I would become the centerpiece of the British program. I liked England. Let's just say, it didn't work out that way.

ADAMSON: Could we talk a little bit about GREAT EXPECTATIONS and a scene from TREAURE ISLAND?

HASKIN: Oh, yes. I had always admired David Lean as a fine director. He was responsible for the biggest individual shock scene ever filmed. The scene of the little boy running through the moors to the cemetery to put flowers on his mother's grave, encountering an escaped convict.

I made an exhaustive study of why that scene generated such audience response. They'd always gasp and fall in the aisles. Under any conditions, it never failed when -- BOOM! -- Finlay Currie, the convict, is revealed. The reaction was always tremendous.

I determined to apply my analysis to a scene in TREASURE ISLAND to attempt to duplicate the psychological premises Lean had developed.

The scene was with Little Jim Hawkins after the masthead action where he shot Israel Hands, and Israel fell into the sea.

Jim was left alone aboard the Hispaniola. Then he went ashore, soon to be lost in the jungle.

Night fell, his terror growing. Eventually, he came to familiar territory. He spied the stockade where he left the Squire and party. He hurried forward, relieved that he's saved. He wrested the door open. It was dark inside. He rushed to the nearest figure, calling, "Squire, Squire!" The figure sat up. It was Long John Silver! He and his bloody-minded pirates have taken over the stockade. The Squire and party are gone.

I wanted to see if I could duplicate the shock value of GREAT EXPECTATIONS.

My analysis of GREAT EXPECTATIONS is as follows: the boy is alone, running in small figure through the moors at evening -- the only living thing onstage. The sky is very ominous. The moor is dotted with clusters of gibbets, all dangling loops of rope -- no bodies in any of the ropes, they're just suggested by the gibbets. This is the hanging-grounds, evidently, a nearby prison. The boy is aware of the gibbets in the close shots of him running along, and you see he is frightened almost to death. Fear is building in his mind which transcends anything that might actually be there.

It is a matter solely of imagination. The boy's images are terrifying him out of his socks. His pace is stiff -- inside he's ready to scream. Suddenly, he arrives at the gate. He looks back at the moors in terror, opens the gate, goes inside. He's in a safe haven at last.

As the camera pans him away from the gate, it reveals he's in a graveyard. Nothing's alive, nothing at all. He crosses, coming down out of his panic.

He comes to his mother's grave, relaxes and begins to think of her.

He plucks some wildflowers, places them on his parent's grave, kneels down, composing himself to say a prayer. The camera whips: right on top of him is the biggest sonuvabitch you ever saw in your life with a knife in his hand, sweaty, bald headed -- a convict's suit on -- Finlay Currie. Gasp!! (Laughs) He grabs the boy!

Well, everybody in the theatre fell in the aisles at this point. My analysis was that the audience had participated fully because it was not betrayed with any realistic touch -- no other figure on the moors, no bird in the sky, nothing alive but the little boy, and his imagination. The fear was purely imaginary and yet the conditions were such that the audience was so sympathetic and rooting so much for him in his panic, that they lost themselves and they became the boy, kneeling with him. Finlay Currie was assaulting <u>them</u> -- BOOM! That's the first piece of realism that entered this whole cleverly conceived succession of shots.

Well, I applied the formula to the scene of Little Jim Hawkins. He was coming off a dreadful thing, the encounter with Israel Hands, in the crow's nest. He had to shoot him with his little pistol and had caught a knife, sticking in his shoulder. He had to pull it out, climb down the rigging, stagger off the ship, start through the jungle. Get lost.

My concept was that nothing could be real. That the terror would be in his mind. It became darker and darker, his imagination would bring him to panic. He would finally break out of the jungle.

I selected a shot on the backlot at Denham with some gigantic trees. They're a normal kind of tree, not tropical, but they have trunks six, seven feet through, and they're 150 feet high. The boy, running through these tremendous trunks, would be dwarfed. There would be a sense of the whole forest and jungle threatening this innocent, helpless little child. When he comes out of the grove, there would be a swing shot traveling with him, on his back, through the jungle -- with a brief glimpse of the stockade ahead.

Then, cut to his face, with relief beginning to dawn. He runs to the gate, and goes in the compound.

Every step toward the door of the stockade, he is coming down off this panic -- which is actually only imaginary. He opens the door with a smile, calling "Squire!" and rushing into the arms of the nearby figure, alongside the stove. The man sits up saying, "Har har. It be Long John Silver, matey." (Laughs)

Well, that would have duplicated GREAT EXPECTATIONS!

Unfortunately, the shooting of the exterior stuff was given over to the second unit to meet budget requirements. Russell Lloyd, Second Unit Director, under careful guidance of Perce Pearce, whom I had banished from the set, decided to scare hell out of Little Jim with crocodiles bellowing in a swamp, birds flapping wings, and beasts calling -- completely destroyed the effect. It became a traveling circus.

ADAMSON: There was nothing you could do with the soundtrack? The picture itself was wrong?

HASKIN: Yes. The picture was wrong, producing the fear, not by the boy's imagination, but by real terror. How could you hope to match the real terror of Israel Hands, knife in teeth, appearing over the edge of the crow's nest? Then throwing it? Followed by Jim shooting him between the eyes? Then Hands falling seventy-five feet into the sea below to his death?

Well, that's all the real terror one small boy could take.

Certainly, he wouldn't care about a crocodile in the weeds or a bird flapping by, threatening to carry him off. It was all a lot of extraneous crap.

ADAMSON: Perce Pearce directed this stuff?

HASKIN: He was telling Russ Lloyd how to do it. In the final editing in Hollywood I chopped most of it out.

A little footnote might be added: Lean didn't quite achieve perfection. In spite of the fact that it blew the audience out of their seats in the theatre. Finlay Currie could have been delivered by camera movement with more impact, more on his face, I thought. But why quarrel with success? (Laughs) . . .

ADAMSON: I noticed that your coverage was much more complete in I WALK ALONE, much more elaborate, than in a lot of the others -- SILVER CITY, WARPATH, all of those.

HASKIN: Well, those were a special type of film -- meaning low budget. I had to compromise.

In that kind of picture you start with your camera on wheels, maintain the action without a cut as long as you can because it takes less time to shoot than standard breakup. Then you jump in at the finale for a quick close-up or a cross angle or something. I never did cover those films -- cheating all the way, because of low budget. There was no money to make them properly.

ADAMSON: I was going to ask if they were B pictures.

HASKIN: Yes, they were.

ADAMSON: Well, how did you get some of those incredible scenes in them? I kept thinking, I'm watching a B picture -- then you'd have these amazing sequences.

HASKIN: Well, they don't take any longer to stage if you know what you're doing, and you have good stuntmen. WARPATH, for instance, had battle scenes and Indian stuff that was as good as CUSTER'S LAST STAND and a lot of other Westerns.

ADAMSON: Yes.

HASKIN: WARPATH and all those B pictures were exploitation pictures, so-called by Nat Holt, and his ilk. He had a contract with Paramount to release them.

He and Harry Templeton, his production manager, would go around the country hunting for some big gimmick.

WARPATH was made entirely in Billings, Montana. They made a deal with the local farmers to utilize various spectacular sites in the foothills of the Tetons, the rivers, etc. Plus a windfall: use of the entire Crow Indian tribe from the reservation, in return for a set donation to the tribe. No individual payments, or anything, and these guys doing stunts! Falling into the river, and everything else.

ADAMSON: So this would be cheaper than having Hollywood stuntmen?

HASKIN: Oh, yes. Furthermore, the year before there had been a country fair in Billings, and some of the big buildings were standing. We used them as stages to build sets.

We took generators and equipment up there, and made the whole film in Montana, utilizing the Crow tribe, with their horses, for nominal fees only. The locations were just spectacular; like Remington paintings of the days of the Plains Indians.

ADAMSON: Yes, it seemed a lot like John Ford: use of the Cavalry, and the real beauty of the land.

HASKIN: Yes. I conceived several scenes of spectacular effect -- the departure of the wagon train, for one. I began by stationing the outriders. If I'd had two more days to shoot that sequence, I could have made it really outstanding . . . the wagon train heading into hostile Indian country with only a small Cavalry escort.

As it was, it took two-thirds of the day to get one big long shot and a couple of medium shots, and that was the end of my schedule. Next day I had to shoot the close-ups on the wagon and hurry on to something else.

ADAMSON: How much time did you have to do the whole picture?

HASKIN: WARPATH was shot in twenty-three days, complete.

ADAMSON: That's almost nothing.

HASKIN: I know. However, it was not only twenty-three days' shooting, but twenty-three nights' toiling with the writing. I had read the script and it didn't make sense, so changes were necessary.

Eddie O'Brien would sit with me in a corner of the hotel lobby after dinner, he was good at dialogue -- and I would block out a re-write.

I'd work most the rest of the night putting it on paper, then arrive on the set in the morning, bleary-eyed, 6:30 or 7:00.

Nat Holt, producer, would be there, and I'd hand him the pages, and he'd look at them and say, "Well, you know more about it than I do," and he'd hand them back to me. That's what I'd shoot for the day. (Laughs)

But I was in good health and I just reassured myself that with a twenty-three day schedule, I could stand on my head that length of time. I just kept plowing away.

ADAMSON: Monte Blue was in that picture, wasn't he? He was one of the guys crossing in the wagon train.

HASKIN: Yes. Monte prolonged his career by playing bits for many years. He was a star, originally, then fell on thin times, and he had to eat. He was a great rider, though. He had worked in Westerns for many years.

ADAMSON: Why Edmond O'Brien? I'm real curious as to the whys and wherefores of that casting.

HASKIN: Well, I did about three or four pictures with Eddie. He was a hell of a good actor, number one. I didn't particularly think he was the most exciting leading man, you know, he was a little pudgy, and kind of beat-up looking, but he would give it a real college try, in everything he did.

Christ, one day he had to mount a horse in a hurry. He went clear on over it, head first! (Laughs) But Eddie was a commodity with assets you had to consider carefully when casting a picture like that, because he was solid on dialogue, he was sharp, he played his points quickly. He didn't require much direction. Matter of fact, he didn't need much. You didn't have to tell him where he came from and what his aunt did to him as a child, and all the other horseshit a Kirk Douglas needs to get into the mood.

ADAMSON: (Laughs) Did you cast him in the picture?

HASKIN: No, Holt cast him. I agreed heartily. I loved him, we were good friends. It was up to Holt and Paramount. O'Brien had a name of sorts, sufficient to carry one of those exploitation pictures, as they called them -- the exploitation being the Crow Indian tribe fighting in a battle that makes Big Horn look like a tea-party. We always had good supporting players behind him, among the men; but we never did get particularly hot casting our leading women. Yvonne de Carlo was in one of them, and ZaSu Pitts played a comedy role in DENVER AND RIO GRANDE.

ADAMSON: You say you'd known ZaSu Pitts in the twenties?

HASKIN: Yes, yes. When she was just a girl. Took her to the first nightclub she ever went to in Los Angeles. (Laughs) She was from -- I don't know, Petaluma or some such town in California. Why this girl ever made it in films is a mystery to me. She wasn't even conventionally good-looking. I think originally Stroheim was attracted to her because of her innocence and vulnerability. He cast her in GREED. It must have been some sadistic impulse on his part, judging by the kind of part she played.

ADAMSON: He thought she was an extremely good actress.

HASKIN: Oh, yes, I don't doubt that. But a type that Hollywood never dreamed of as a leading woman. God, not in the era when she got her start.

ADAMSON: Well, she became a comedienne. She did good little funny bit parts.

HASKIN: Well, yes. Not in GREED, though. She was a very pathetic figure. But she turned out to be a hell of an actress, as well as a wonderful person. She married Tom Gallery, and they had a scad of kids. I had never thought of her as a female -- you know, for any lecherous dailliance -- but she obviously was quite fecund. She died of cancer later. It was a tragic thing.

We also picked up Dean Jagger -- he was loose for some reason -- on WARPATH. He was excellent. And Forrest Tucker. We had quite a cast in that film. Anytime you cast just below the star level, you can find a lot of excellent actors available, with pretty good names -- just hanging around ready for an assignment.

That's why Eddie liked playing in these films. His fee wasn't excessive. He was the exploitation man's darling. He not only worked for Holt, but for several others -- he did DOA, an excellent film on low budget. He wasn't a name that could carry a top drawer movie except as a supporting player, like SEVEN DAYS IN MAY or DAYS OF WINE AND ROSES, but he could star in the lower echelon.


ADAMSON: Is there anything else you recall about WARPATH?


HASKIN: Don't tempt me! Memories about the Indians are vivid. Donald Dearnose was the marshal of the Crow tribe. He became a friend of mine. His chief function was to go around to the jails in Billings on Monday morning and collect the braves in his truck and take them back to the reservation. (Laughs)


ADAMSON: Who was this guy, Robert Yellowtail?


HASKIN: I guess he was the old Indian. There's quite a tale there. He originally posed for the Buffalo nickel. His profile was pure Plains Indian of the most noble sort. At the time we made this film, he was a very old man, and he had left the reservation, according to tribal custom, with what he had on his back, to trek alone into the high Tetons, to await his end in communing with the Great Spirit. If the Great Spirit chose to spare him, he would come back; if not, he'd die up there. The coyotes would eat him, I guess.

We had them send a messenger from the tribe that he would be needed for our picture. A brave took a horse and went up to his camp at the snow level of the Tetons, and brought him back to be in the movie. Right in the beginning of the picture there's a close-up of him chanting. He had a big headdress. One of the authentic touches of the film.

ADAMSON: That was all, he just came back and did that?

HASKIN: Well, afterwards he also played extra in various scenes. I don't remember him riding a horse. I had had this idea that we should open on a big Indian head, and that's how it came about. We brought him down specifically for that. Naturally he stuck around on the payroll the rest of the picture.

ADAMSON: Did he ever go back into the Tetons?

HASKIN: I think I remember that he did, yes, and died soon after.

ADAMSON: Back to the Great Spirit?

HASKIN: I think so. That was his intention, anyhow, when we left.

While I was up in Montana, doing WARPATH, I got word by phone that Sol Lesser wanted me for a TARZAN film. I don't know why, but I faced myself and I said, Well, every director should have the experience of making one TARZAN for Sol Lesser. So I agreed to do it. . . .

After WARPATH, I returned home and into the mad, mad world of Sol Lesser. (Laughs) Honest, I went into the studio one night to see some rushes, and as I passed by the projection room, I looked in. The projectionist was fit to be tied. Startled, I said, "What the hell's happening?"

The projectionist shrugged and said, "I'm running your dailies backwards."

Lesser had ordered him to. His excuse: "Sometimes it looks better that way." The guy was a madman.

In the cast were Lex Barker and the young Dorothy Dandridge, the most beautiful creature I had ever seen in my life at that time. This was before she became famous, and before Phil Moore got hold of her and gave her style, and before the days of CARMEN JONES and all that. She was just a budding young black actress, and she played a princess in Africa in TARZAN'S PERIL.

As I say, I had figured it would be part of my bringing up as a director. To get mixed up with Sol Lesser once. (Laughs) I did and it was a real wacko experience. TARZAN'S PERIL was one of the better TARZAN's, I presume. It wasn't quite as crazy as some of them.

We, of course, used a chimp as Cheetah, the monkey. Al Antonucci, the trainer, carried a billiard cue, and would knock the chimp stiff every other minute to get some obedience out of it. (Laughs) It was not a fond memory, though, or experience. More a test of endurance.

ADAMSON: Did you shoot that completely on a stage?

HASKIN: Yes. Fred Ahern, who is big in TV now, and is quite famous, had taken a crew to Africa, and had staged a lot of stock shot type of things -- the tribal dances of the Watusis, some of the scenes in the original story of going down the rivers. Then we matched up the stuff on the stage.

ADAMSON: They shot this for the picture, or had they just shot a lot of stock shots?

HASKIN: No, it was shot for TARZAN'S PERIL. He went there before I ever heard of TARZAN, and they had eight or ten reels of this stuff, which was to be matched in. It was quite well done. I matched the action of the stage to the exterior long shots. With the help of Arthur Lonergan, art director, Karl Struss on the camera.

ADAMSON: So you did that between WARPATH and SILVER CITY. Then you didn't make these three Edmond O'Brien Westerns as a group?

HASKIN: No, I didn't. The only thing that I remember distinctly about the TARZAN thing was that I made more damn money on it than I ever made on any film in my life. Before, or since! (Laughs) I got fairly fat on it.

There was an award Lesser gave me of $10,000 for some mistake he'd made. I don't recall the details of it, but I made $50,000 or $60,000 off this thing. (Laughs)

After that, I made SILVER CITY and DENVER AND RIO GRANDE, also Nat Holt twenty-day-wonders.

ADAMSON: Done on the same kind of schedule as WARPATH? Twenty-two or twenty-three days?

HASKIN: Yes. DENVER AND RIO GRANDE was made near Durango, Colorado, up at the little town of Silvertown which was at 14,000 feet altitude, utilizing the gimmick of the little narrow gauge railroad that runs from Durango up through the mountains and gorges, alongside this rushing big river, on up to Silvertown. Silvertown itself is at about 12,000 feet altitude, and the pass leading over into Colorado is 14,000 feet.

Going to the location from Denver, we flew over this pass in a DC-3, with the windows open. That put us at 8,000 feet above Army regulation for oxygen-level -- (laughs) the Army goes on oxygen tanks at 9,000 feet.

Actually, the day we flew over this 14,000-foot pass, there was an apprentice stewardess in the plane, and <u>she</u> was the one who fainted! (Laughs)

We had a big camp catered from L.A., 2,000 feet higher than Durango, up the road in sort of a meadow, with tents and commissary and all the necessities. We housed the whole company there for the duration of the film.

ADAMSON: Were the interiors done there, too?

HASKIN: No, we did those back in the studio. Holt didn't like to do that, because the studio cost him extra, you know. The thing about WARPATH that was the windfall was finding those fairground buildings. Johnny Goodman, our art director, used local carpenters and built all the sets inside.

ADAMSON: The trains that ran on that narrow gauge railroad -- were they authentic old trains?

HASKIN: Oh, yes. Property of the Denver and Rio Grande Railroad Company. It was in actual operation -- what for, I don't know -- nor what they carried up to Silvertown or down from it -- the trains were mostly freight cars. How often it ran, I don't remember, because we had our own train, and seemed to pre-empt any activity the railroad was up to. Eventually we got two trains and ran them together.

ADAMSON: That's what I thought was so incredible, so great. You actually ran the two of them into each other?

HASKIN: Yes, I still have a steam gauge off one of the locomotives. I use it as a doorstop now. Nat Holt salvaged it, and had a brass plaque put on it. To commemorate the trainwreck!

ADAMSON: (Laughs) I'll have to look at it some time! That's just amazing. I really enjoyed the picture because there was so much authentic stuff. I mean, they're actually on the train, not just a lot of studio shots.

HASKIN: The interiors of the cars, etc., were shot up there. Frank Gruber, the writer, wrote Western books. They were published, why I'll never know, because a reader couldn't tell what was happening in them. He was on contract as screenplay writer by Nat Holt. Nat loved his work, because he worked cheap.

By God, his screenplays just would not play. Even his characters in his stories didn't know what the hell they were doing, and the dialogue was puerile.

So again, for me, it was a save-your-ass job of re-writing. I didn't <u>want</u> to re-write this stuff, I was forced to. You never hope to achieve any level of excellence in that kind of set-up. You can bring it up to mediocre, just make it play, that's about all. WARPATH, with a better script, could have been an outstanding Western film. It is just too heavy a burden to write all night and shoot all day, and expect a quality product.

ADAMSON: Well, of the three, the one that made the least sense to me was SILVER CITY. I could not figure out what the plot was, or when you were in a flashback.

HASKIN: I couldn't either. Barry Fitzgerald had something to do with the goldmines and assays and lumber -- a sawmill, and a lot of crap -- I don't know today what it was all about. I certainly know that I didn't then, particularly.

ADAMSON: The movie seemed to be structured around the three action scenes, which were good scenes -- you had one at the beginning, one at the end, and then you had one in the middle. I thought maybe the one in the middle you might have invented, just to put it in there, because everything else was all talk-talk-talk.

The guys were all drunk and they needed them to work in the mines, so O'Brien had them get into a fight, and as they all got knocked unconscious, he threw them into a truck and took them up to the mine to get the work done. There were some nice bits in it.

HASKIN: I don't remember it. I know there was some comedy here and there that was pretty good.

ADAMSON: You also did something I have never seen anybody else do, successfully: you did undercranked shots in a sound picture -- in a 24-frames-per-second picture, you had shots made at 12 or 16 frames per second. It worked well.

HASKIN: Yes.

ADAMSON: I have never seen it before. It's wonderful. You had a real sawmill in that final scene, didn't you?

HASKIN: Oh, yes.

ADAMSON: Edmond O'Brien and this guy were really running around in a sawmill?

HASKIN: The other guy was John Dierkes, a mediocre actor. They ran all around this lumberyard, and over logs floating in the pond where they were stored.

ADAMSON: It looked like O'Brien was doing his own stunts. I don't know how much he was actually doing, but I had the impression he was really running through there some of the time, leaping on the logs, and so on.

HASKIN: Eddie was pretty athletic, he did most of the stuff. He did all of his riding in WARPATH. He was a gutsy guy.

ADAMSON:   He seemed kind of a latter-day Tom Meighan. That was sort of the style that Meighan worked with.

HASKIN:   Yes. I suppose that Eddie had an idea that these pictures might do him some good if he could establish a character that the audience would pick up and like. He was the indomitable guy -- nothing phased him. He was ready to take a swing at anybody, Sterling Hayden, or anybody that walked by. Eddie was a very resourceful guy to have around on one of those ad-lib jobs. On DENVER AND RIO GRANDE, riding up in the morning on the train to the location, he and I would go over the dialogue and re-write it for the day's work -- which is not any way to make a picture, but there you are.

ADAMSON:   That was the one I really enjoyed -- DENVER AND RIO GRANDE. I thought it was just a lot of fun, all that train stuff, and the running around.

HASKIN:   Yes, and Sterling Hayden was quite good in it.

ADAMSON:   Yes. And Dean Jagger. I thought he was tremendous. A real interesting character: the guy who ran the railroad.

HASKIN:   Yes. It was a class performance. Of course, he is a hell of a fine actor. But, as I say, the three Nat Holt pictures could have been whipped into shape if, for instance, on WARPATH, instead of hiring me the week before we went up to Montana, where my efforts to prepare the show were limited to getting the right equipment together and so forth, I could have had the normal four to six weeks on the script with a good screenplay writer. We could have <u>made</u> something out of these things. But there was no adequate screenplay at all. Holt would buy one of Gruber's books or stories, and Gruber would take out the chapter headings and put it together in a screenplay in a very sloppy way. Then Holt would schedule it, and away we'd go.

ADAMSON: Didn't it cost a lot of money to take two trains and run them into each other?

HASKIN: No, you see, Holt was a conman. He'd get these deals together -- the picture'd be named DENVER AND RIO GRANDE -- it all became an exploitation deal between him and the Denver and Rio Grande Railroad. The hierarchy came over from Denver the day of the wreck and watched from behind barricades.

ADAMSON: Did you have a big crowd to watch this?

HASKIN: No, a couple of dozen or so people -- various functionaries from Denver, and a couple of local people, that's all. It wasn't a big crowd, because it was dangerous to be too close to it. Our cameras were 1,000 feet away.

ADAMSON: Were you shooting with long lenses?

HASKIN: Yes, and we had unmanned cameras in barricades up closer. The dynamite blew a big iron pump off the side of one locomotive, and it was like a projectile. It went through the air, right over our heads and whacked into a tree, knocking a branch off, far behind us -- would have decapitated anybody it hit.

ADAMSON: Did you have dynamite on the trains?

HASKIN: Yes.

ADAMSON: How many cameras did you have on it?

HASKIN: About four I think. It wasn't the greatest wreck that anyone ever staged. It didn't really give me much of a thrill when it happened, because a long shot didn't mean anything -- it was just those two tiny little trains and -- POW! -- a big puff of smoke.

ADAMSON: (Laughs) Well, you held the damn shot for about sixty seconds! All the smoke's pouring out and the whistle's moaning, and it was funny. The film felt a lot like Keaton's film, THE GENERAL. Was there any inspiration there from that? He ran a train over a burning bridge, and it just collapsed into the river.

HASKIN: No, I don't remember ever seeing THE GENERAL.

Early in my directing career, I found out the hard way that such a stunt is only as important and thrilling as the shots leading up to the actual crash.

The principle is illustrated by the circus guy who dives off the high tower into a tub of water. When he dives, you blink your eye and when you open it, he's on the floor taking a bow. You've seen nothing. So, to make an act of it, every step he makes going up the ladder, the drums roll and the announcer tells you -- "That daredevil" -- and he poses up on top and looks down and flexes his muscles and gets ready to go. He figuratively says, "Now here I go." BOOM! -- half a second later, the stunt is over.

The same way with two trains colliding. Only as effective as the buildup.

I never had the time on the shooting schedule -- it was all taken up getting the damn thing rigged. It cried for enough shots with those trains coming together to get a rhythm of shortening distance between them -- closer, closer, closer, and then it's -- WHAM! It's all over!

Like the Battle of San Jacinto in a film I did at Allied Artists, THE FIRST TEXAN. It was thrilling because of the time I spent on the Americans getting their field pieces into position early in the morning without the Mexicans discovering them. It was all quiet and sneaky, so that it built and built -- here comes another cannon! You show that, then cut to the

Mexicans having beans for breakfast, showing they don't know about it.

Finally, the Americans fire the cannons, and the thing is soon over. Melodrama depends for its effectiveness on the steps of setting it up.

ADAMSON: I thought you had a lot of effective stuff -- trains coming right into the camera, etc.

HASKIN: I ran the train into a mirror and flipped it out of the way at the last second.

ADAMSON: You had the camera mounted on the train a few times. It's a real nice piece of cinema. . . .

I think we're up to WAR OF THE WORLDS -- a very big subject. . . .

HASKIN: Yes, it is. WAR OF THE WORLDS in its day was as exciting as CLOSE ENCOUNTERS OF THE THIRD KIND or STAR WARS today.

You know how it all started? Don Hartman was vice president in charge of production of Paramount Pictures. Before the picture started, he tore up the script and threw it in his wastebasket and said, "I don't want my name on this -- I won't have anything to do with it. It's a bunch of crap!"

Luckily for us, we had Y. Frank Freeman, Jr. as collaborator on our group. He organized a secret meeting with D. A. Doran, executive; Y. Frank Freeman, Sr., studio head; George Pal, producer of the film; and myself, as director, in D.A. Doran's office, to discuss the matter.

Mr. Freeman asked, "Byron, do you believe in this? Can you go make a good picture out of it?"

I said, "Yes, I sure think so."
He said, "George?"
George Pal said, "Yes."
To his son, "Frank, you believe in this picture?"
The three of us said, "Yes."
He said, "All right, make it."

That was over the head of this vice president in charge of production.

ADAMSON: (Laughs) Who said this?

HASKIN: Y. Frank Freeman, who ran the studio. We had his son, Y. Frank Freeman Jr., "Pete" Freeman, as co-producer.

We made it, and it was a highly successful picture.

Hartman's memory was very short. About two-thirds of the way through, he saw the rushes with us of Los Angeles being destroyed, and exclaimed, "Jesus! I never knew this would be so exciting!"

I said, "What the hell did you think the evacuating of Los Angeles was going to be, a tea party?"

ADAMSON: Who was D.A. Doran?

HASKIN: He was a sort of head man of all operations without any authority on any of them at Paramount. He was in an anomalous kind of position. He had been with a big publishing house in New York at one time. He knew authors, he knew stories, he knew people, he was affable. He'd show up at all the cocktail parties and not drink very much. He was always the first man there, you'd sit for fifteen minutes and try to make conversation with him, and it was impossible. A nice guy. After he left there, he went to MGM. And, of course, there you can get lost, with these funny jobs that God knows what they represent. D.A. Doran never had any authority to fire anybody, but he was always in on all the secret councils. (Laughter)

Now you can't tell me that a picture which has in it, credibly, the destruction of Los Angeles, along with the rest of the world, by invasion from outer space, etc., could not have been hyped into something as big as CLOSE ENCOUNTERS OF THE THIRD KIND and STAR WARS. It was that important in its day. There was nothing in competition with it at the time it was made, and it did have terrific impact in the theatres where it was run.

It had great audience identification. That's the one thing that made it big, that this could be happening to people in the audience.

It took a year to make those special effects. I went out to the Fijis, to Australia, and made HIS MAJESTY O'KEEFE, and came back and Gordon Jennings, Special Effects head, was just cutting the last of the special effects.

A year later, and he hadn't completed them! Knowing this would be the case before I left for Australia to make HIS MAJESTY O'KEEFE, the last thing I had done was to cut in sketches. I made these sketches personally of the missing special effects shots. So, instead of just leaving blanks, we photographed these sketches of all the action of the Martian invasion. In the dubbing room, I made tracks describing what was happening in the sketches. With these all cut in, it was possible to run the picture as a finished product.

ADAMSON: In the studio.

HASKIN: Hartman had a projection room at his home, and he asked for it to be shown out there. Our group went out there and ran it in the projection room. At the finish Hartman was blown down.

He said, "Well, that's one hell of a job of picture making!" (Laughs) He was absolutely agog. I didn't remind him that he had thrown it in the wastebasket.

ADAMSON: Did they have trouble selling a film like that?

HASKIN: Paramount never did know what to do with it. They put it out as a routine production. Now, you know about the hype on CLOSE ENCOUNTERS OF THE THIRD KIND and STAR WARS. The biggest hype you ever heard of!

ADAMSON: They were advertising STAR WARS a year before it came out.

HASKIN: Of course they were, and it was not all that fantastic -- I mean, if you analyze the component parts. It's great, I love the picture, and it had the spirit of something we need in this day and age. As did SUPERMAN, and as BUCK ROGERS will, and STAR TREK, and all this stuff.

It's that you've got to be reassured that there's something to enjoy and laugh at.

With that kind of hype, WAR OF THE WORLDS would have been just as big. . . .

My participation in and contribution to the finished product was at least fifty percent of everything. Barre Lyndon and I wrote the story line, It was my decision to modernize the story. As you know, The War of the Worlds by H. G. Wells is set in the late 1890's.

ADAMSON: Doesn't it take place in London?

HASKIN: Not even in London. Out in the country, with vicars and old British gardener characters . . . The threat to humanity in the original War of the Worlds was an antiquated machine looking like a water tank tottering around the country on creaky legs, blowing whiffs of smoke, frightening a cast directly out of Agatha Christie -- the vicar and the butler and other rural characters.

Second guessing, in lieu of what happened afterwards -- the success of the nostalgic period in AROUND THE WORLD IN 80 DAYS -- WAR OF THE WORLDS might have had an impact, leaving it in the 1890's of the H. G. Wells version. At the time we were preparing it, we had to consider the atomic bomb and the impact of that technology in the world. I thought surely we should modernize it, which meant a new story, with new characters. We ignored the people and the complications of the original and created a new story line with new characters and complications.

ADAMSON: What about the Orson Welles version?

HASKIN: Orson Welles frightened America to death with a radio broadcast. He actually didn't frighten America to death -- Walter Winchell said that the broadcast of his small radio program was a dramatization, not real. Because Winchell had a big audience, millions screamed "What is the disaster Winchell is reporting?!"

So everybody ran for the hills.

Welles didn't have much of an audience for his little Mercury Theatre broadcast.

I saw the transcript of it. It was fairly well put together -- it was about a radio news reporter watching creatures and machines threatening New Jersey towns. The reporter told it as if it was actually happening -- "Oh, there they are, coming! There goes a farmhouse! . . ."

It too went into the wastebasket, along with the H.G. Wells personal story.

We decided that our protagonist, in order to reveal what the hell was going on with the modern technique of atomic age weaponry, should be a physicist. So we made our leading man a physicist.

My chief concern right from the start was to stress audience identification. To keep the whole thing at a level of a threat to everyday humanity. Our girl, we made into a smart young teacher, daughter of a local preacher. Locale to be a place where they have picnics and square dances -- a country atmosphere, with little people.

Our prologue was a series of drawings by Chesley Bonestell, showing machines heading toward earth -- an invasion! Voice-over to be Cedric Hardwicke, speaking in a haunting voice about creatures from outer space.

The opening scene was at the small town near Pasadena. A movie was letting out with local people standing around the lobby and discussing the show. Suddenly in the distant hills, there was a fireball falling. It started a fire. So the invasion, unknown to these spectators, was underway.

Unfortunately, I couldn't bring myself, and Barre Lyndon couldn't either, to break with Wells on the finale, because it violates all rules of dramatization to introduce, in the third act, the force that's going to solve the dilemma of the plot. You do not drag somebody into the third act who solves your story. This is the "safely out of the well" technique from the old serials -- you know, leave Pearl White hanging on a cliff, and next week's episode, she's in the bank cashing a check -- you're "safely out of the well."

Anyhow, De Mille read it and gave his critique. George Pal, as producer; Pete Freeman, associate producer; and Barre Lyndon and I, met him in a story conference.

He said, "Well, your leading man is a messenger boy, he has no authority over the events of the solution."

You see, God is the character Wells introduces in the third act, who sends germs to the Martians, cold germs, actually. Wells was ordinarily pretty supercilious about his climaxes, anyhow.

Nevertheless, I couldn't see how we could in honesty call it "H.G. WELLS' WAR OF THE WORLDS," and have Gene Barry kill off the Martians. (Laughs)

ADAMSON: With some kind of atomic thing.

HASKIN: Well, we threw the atomic bomb at them and it had no effect. All to prove that humanity was really in trouble.

(Laughs) If man's most powerful weapon has no effect on the invaders, it becomes high irony that tiny germs, to which mankind is immune, are fatal to them. That sounds pretty good when you read it, but in the weird way you have to tell a story on film, it doesn't play -- it's negative action.

It's an invisible element. There's no way you can show disease germs attacking the Martians so that you can juice it up into any kind of suspense. You have to show the conquering of the Martians simply by having them suddenly waver and drop.

This, you know, is not the way you stage drama. One has to have two parties in a conflict, with hopefully both equal in power, until suddenly one overpowers the other in an unexpected manner. That's the fundamental way.

But we stuck to Wells. I was as responsible as anybody for a lot of the major turns. The constant re-occurrence of the religious note came from having nobody solving our final dilemma but God. It became expedient to ring a few church bells to get some kind of ominous feel to the goddamn thing.

I really had pleasure with the picture -- it was fun to shoot. I had a hell of a good special effects man on the set. He maintained hoppers of burning stuff to drop in front of the camera. The actors would run down the street and we'd drop hoppers of bricks all around them -- always keeping it a real disaster. I tried to re-create at times the unreality that I remembered from the San Francisco earthquake. I don't know if it succeeded too well, but I wanted to stress the total helplessness of humanity. Nobody can do anything. Everybody's on the run. And there's no help. Until God gets to work!

Even the weird plane dropping the bomb on them fails. The effect was sheer terror. It was a good film.

ADAMSON: Yes, it's really kind of miraculous, the way everything fits together -- the special effects and the acting. I like Gene Barry's characterization too.

HASKIN: Well, he wasn't the easiest guy to handle. At the time, his professional credits consisted of playing in a group of sexy young men, in Mae West's act in Vegas. In the need for a feeling of terror, from everybody in the set, I over-accented it. Barry, excited, played the whole disaster in every shot. His attitude was reminiscent of THE CABINET OF DR. CALIGARI, like nothing human. It was probably my own fault. I was violating a basic principle. The higher the scale of melodrama, the cooler it has to be played. You play against the material. Barry was trying to play the destruction of Los Angeles, not playing against it. He was losing the feeling of bravery under stress. It's axiomatic in disaster that you must defy it, and keep your wits about you, putting up a good fight.

ADAMSON: Did you work with the editor on the cutting of the film, too?

HASKIN: Oh yes.

ADAMSON: Marvelous rhythm.

HASKIN: I worked months in the stop-and-go-room (where the scene may be run backward and forward, and stopped at will). I would run each little sequence then back it up, run it again, take frames out here, there, and everywhere. It really was a meticulous editing job. Everett (Douglas), the cutter, was in charge, but I went through the whole film three times after it was in rough cut.

ADAMSON: Remember that incredible moment after the girl's father actually gets killed, when you have all these cuts, and no single shot is repeated once, you just go "KABOOM, KABOOM" -- with each "KABOOM" you've got a different set-up, a different kind of shot, close-ups and long shots -- just incredible.

HASKIN: Yes. It's a shame that such technique had to be in a Paramount production. Paramount was run by an empty desk in New York. It was the only company whose every house-

telegram could be interpreted legally as meaning yes or no. (Laughs) You pick it! They had no idea how to market and hype an exploitation picture such as WAR OF THE WORLDS.

Even without the Martian shots, it was potentially a great war picture. God willing that it'd never happen, but if Russia and the United States had started hostilities, you could have substituted the Russian invasion and have had a hell of a war film.

Every time I ran it, I had a light perspiration on my brow, because I felt identification with the victims of the disasters.

It could have made a fortune -- with about six months of solid hype before it was released.

Originally, we had Bill Holden cast for it, but the budget wouldn't stand it. It was made for $1,450,000. Pete Freeman, son of Paramount's owner, and I went to the accounting department to check it out. As a matter of curiosity, we investigated what part of that $1,450,000 was overhead and what had actually been spent on the picture. What actually showed on the screen was $635,000. Less than half the money. The rest was overhead. I remember one little item -- $90,000 for settlement of a company dispute with the grips labor union, having nothing to do with WAR OF THE WORLDS.

It was studio policy. I used to do the same thing with the Special Effects Department at Warner Bros. Scripts would come in with no special effects in them at all, and I'd charge them $4,000. The production manager would come running down, and I'd say, "Well, what do you want me to do, pay for this department myself? I've got six cameramen, getting money. There's a hundred guys working." All films had to share the upkeep.

ADAMSON: You started to explain how you got to do this picture --

HASKIN: Oh, yes. Well, I had never met George Pal. I had seen his DESTINATION MOON. At that time, I thought that it originated with his preparation, which it didn't. I found out later that it was from a lineup that Aubrey Schenck and Chesley Bonestell and I had worked on years before. How it got into George's hands, I don't know. It doesn't matter, either.

Before DESTINATION MOON, I went to General Service Studio, and Aubrey Schenck had had these sketches of Chesley Bonestell's of a trip to the moon. Bonestell is the greatest space artist, with sketches in galleries, museums and the like. He's living in his old age in Carmel now. He was one of my eight matte artists at Warner Bros. Bonestell, the Llarinaga Brothers, Hans Bartholovsky, Paul Detlefsen . . . They're real weirdos. (Laughs)

ADAMSON: They all had bizarre names!

HASKIN: No more bizarre than *they* were. I used to stand outside the matte room door and listen to them. By the hour. Discussing life. Whew! And painting at the same time.

ADAMSON: In reference to the DESTINATION MOON "line-up," do you mean a series of drawings?

HASKIN: Yes, a sort of sketch continuity that had gaps in it, but from which came the lineup of DESTINATION MOON.

But that's neither here nor there. George had done it, and I had certainly heard of him. I had heard of his Puppetoons, also.

I was at the Pathé Studio in Culver City, doing TARZAN and I got a call one day from George Pal at Paramount. He said, "Hello, hello -- Byron Haskin? Well, this is George Pal . . . I have a picture I'm getting together -- WAR OF THE WORLDS. Are you interested in directing it?"

I said, "Sure. . . ."

ADAMSON: You weren't on one of the Edmond O'Brien pictures then?

HASKIN: No, it was TARZAN at that point. Afterward, I did a couple of O'Briens before they scheduled George's show. I went over to Paramount and met him. That's where I first met Pete Freeman, who became a close personal friend -- a wonderful guy. A very decent fellow and had a lot of talent, but too good-natured and always in the shadow of the great man, Y. Frank Freeman, Sr. A young man has a hell of a job transcending that kind of a set-up, and the old man a martinet and a bastard too. So Pete was just a lost soul from the beginning. He became a heavy drinker. But he was a great guy.

ADAMSON: How did you come to do HIS MAJESTY O'KEEFE?

HASKIN: Well, after I WALK ALONE, Burt Lancaster and Harold Hecht had kept in touch. I never took these guys seriously. (Laughs) I can't understand why. Wallis said that Burt was a Brooklyn bum who'd never get anywhere. I didn't believe that, but I didn't take Burt too seriously as an actor. Harold was a lightweight. The day I got back from the South Pacific, after shooting HIS MAJESTY O'KEEFE, Harold was on the TV singing like a bird at some Communist trial. . . .

ADAMSON: Getting back to the film, Burt Lancaster was in it?

HASKIN: Yes, with Joan Rice and André Morrell, and Benson Fong, and assembled characters. The pattern that I'm dreadfully afraid is going to come out of all this about my films, is a massive complaint of conditions and things that might have been. (Laughs) But Jesus! Incredible, what happened.

ADAMSON: Things went wrong on this one, too?

HASKIN: Oh! Did they go wrong! Just whose fault it was, I don't know, but they had the rights to one of the most interesting books that I have ever read, His Majesty O'Keefe -- a real story, a story of real people. O'Keefe was an adventurer in the 1870's in the South Pacific, around the islands of Yap and the Sonsorals. Historically, he was shipwrecked on the island of Yap.

I don't know how deeply we should go into this, but it's interesting to me. It was a story about the time of empire building among the big nations -- Germany, England -- all vying for colonial territories, "blackbirding" natives, wringing out profits. It was the time where England was under Victoria; the sun never set on British soil. Yap and the surrounding islands were rich in coconuts but the natives were lazy, wouldn't work. They could lean out the window and pick a banana -- why should they harvest coconuts to make copra for invaders? So, the big nations finally gave up on the area. There was one little outpost on the island maintained by Germany; a couple of guys sitting there drinking beer, but nothing of importance.

O'Keefe was shipwrecked on Yap. The natives adopted O'Keefe. He observed, among other things, the odd monetary system, inquired of its history. He learned that at certain seasons of the year, it was the custom for the young men to rig bamboo rafts, and cross the open seas, 228 miles, to a chain of miniscule islands called the Sonsorals, composed mainly of chalk sandstone. It could be easily quarried. These guys worked like demons for six weeks or so, chopping out blocks of this sandstone and shaping them into stone wheels.

ADAMSON: Large things?

HASKIN: Some would be two feet in diameter -- others six and eight feet, with a hole in the middle, like a doughnut. They would load the wheels onto the rafts and head back to Yap. The stone had a peculiar religious significance, as well as monetary. They were called fei, and the possessor of a wheel was adjudged wealthy. If you had a little wheel, you were middle class. If you had a big wheel, you were rich. The wheels were distributed according to the hierachy of the tribe, by the Medicine Man.

ADAMSON: Sort of the pecking order.

HASKIN: Yes. Often tragedy happened. The young men were never seen again. Due to some storm. This added to the religious connotation of the process. They would distribute this stuff. When a guy got the fei, he'd lay it outside in his garden -- the weeds might grow over it, and it'd disappear, but he was still a rich man. He had privileges because of it. Nobody worked in the whole damn place. They ate what was on the trees or what ran by the front door, and that was it! (Laughs)

O'Keefe observed all this, along with the great stands of coconuts -- absolutely bent over with nuts. . . . He hitchhiked his way to Hong Kong -- Chinese at the time -- and entered into partnership with a Chinese dentist who owned a junk. O'Keefe made a deal for the junk, manned it in Hong Kong. Also marrying the dentist's daughter. He sailed back to Yap, gathered up the young Yapese men, and took them to the Sonsorals. They quarried the sandstone, filled the ship with it, and returned to Yap.

O'Keefe tied up at the dock and said, "For each amount of fei, I get a work party."

He organized it so he could harvest the coconuts, becoming a big wheel in the copra business. He instructed the Yaps in how to resist the Germans, the English, and the French. He forestalled all efforts to take over his operation. He was the only one who could make the Yapese work, you see, because of the fei. (Laughs) He never revealed his secret. Maintaining a monopoly in the area. Upshot of it was that he was actually crowned "Emperor of Yap and the Sonsorals." His Yapese friends elected him Super Chief, and they crowned him, giving him a sceptre, and put him on a big throne.

With the passage of time, he fell prey to one Bully Hayes, a freebooter in the district, who eventually killed him.

Now that yarn was not a bad blueprint for an adventure movie. Especially on a big budget.

A decision was made to shoot it in the Fiji Islands -- at the time a British Colony.

I think everybody involved was caught up in expectancy of making a big commercial success. I don't understand to this day what kept the project from coming together.

In retrospect, I believe we could have let the story play as it was, perhaps eliminating the historic death of O'Keefe.

However, during the preparation, there was a new writer every week. Finally, they'd gone through all the writers in town. It'd always end in a terrible row. I'd see writers go flying down the hallway. Eventually, I hoped to be able to help a bit, but Hecht and I went to London for some casting. Then I had to go to the Fijis and organize the logistics. Ted Haworth was art director, a very good man. Norman Demming was a super production manager. Demming had already been out there six months, organizing hundreds of Fijian women to make costumes all over the various islands of the Fijis. A maritime tribe of natives in the Lau Islands were constructing a big double hull war canoe which would seat sixty a side -- a real big bastard.

Our headquarters were in a resort at Deumba (pronounced N-DUMB-BA) Beach, on the edge of the jungle. They had constructed cutting rooms, housing bures (huts), and a big stage in the jungle nearby. It wasn't big by Hollywood standards, but it would house all the interiors. The hardwood support beams were so heavy, I wonder how they ever got them upright. The problem was to make it soundproof; rains happened every five minutes there, and drops came down like golf balls. It looked like solid water outside the porch of our main building!

Upon arrival, I went into Suva -- we were preparing it for Hong Kong. I checked costumes being made. We even made a stab of getting the local Chinese to work. There was plenty to keep me busy.

Of course, I did not know that while I was doing all this in the Fijis, Warner and Hecht had had a big row back in Hollywood. The whole damn project had been cancelled!

While we're working away in the Fijis, and every airplane and boat in the Pacific bringing stuff, the project is dead!

Hecht did one of his famous miracles of recovery, got a terrific writer, Borden Chase -- who wrote RED RIVER and a lot of important films. Borden and Hecht ad-libbed a storyline to Jack Warner. I don't remember where the hell Burt was at that juncture. I think he had come to the Fijis himself. Setting up a trapeze in a rented villa, throwing himself around on the rings right out in the jungle.

Back in Hollywood, Hecht and Borden sold the story line to Jack Warner. It was put back on the schedule. Hecht, with Borden's arm firmly in his, boarded an airplane and flapped out of town. (Laughs)

ADAMSON: Before he could cancel it!

HASKIN: Yes. Now this was about twenty days before the shooting of the production was to start. Where the hell was the script? (Laugh) By the time Borden Chase was established in Fiji, he had forgotten the ad-libbed story line completely! (Laughs)

Borden and I met. He fell on my neck like I was manna from heaven. He said, "I'll write the script right under the camera. You and I will make this film. It'll be the greatest melodrama -- " All the bullshit that goes on between writers and directors! Harold and Burt and Jim Hill observed this relationship with sour looks. After about three such conferences, I realized what was happening. We were having a conference all right, but nothing was ever written down. The m.o. was that when the slightest little bit of action was suggested, Burt would jump up and act it all over the room, breaking chairs and jumping over things, explaining as he went: "I'd get them here and throw them down and jump on their necks -- see, Borden, like this!"

After which, he'd fall back to regain his breath. About three o'clock everybody would rush to the cabinet and drink -- Scotch was fourteen cents a glass in this freeport.

Well, this could go on just so long. About five or six days, with pressure building, building, building -- it's now ten days from shot #1 in Suva -- and not page one of the screenplay had been written. (Laughs)

Finally, Borden Chase, who had a short fuse anyway, blew. They were all in a villa about seven miles from our Deumba Beach headquarters. It was a big expensive, double-story villa. Well, when Borden started blowing, the others went out the windows, in all directions.

Borden tore up every paper in the place he could get his mitts on, leaped out the front door with a weapon, threatening to kill Burt, plus Harold, and Jim Hill, all three of them. He went out looking for them along the beach.

ADAMSON: What was this over?

HASKIN: Over all the interruptions and distractions in writing the screenplay of the story! Nothing ever written. Borden as the writer couldn't see any progress at all. He doesn't know what they want, he's getting no help from anybody. Every time he starts to write a line, they kill it, and Burt takes over with his acting. It just became Amateur Night in Dixie. Which the picture became, practically all the way through.

So, back at the beach -- they all run and hide in the swampgrass. Borden is after them with a big knife. As he's wandering up and down the beach, they're spying on him. (Laughs)

He can't find them, and finally gets tired of walking, sits down on a stump. Over on the dusty road nearby, a car drives past with a big Fijian at the wheel. He's driving it with one bare foot on all the controls -- brakes, gas pedal, clutch.

Borden yells and runs over, jumps in with the Fijian, and they disappear.

He ended up in Suva, forty-five to fifty miles from headquarters.

ADAMSON: Suva is another city on the island?

HASKIN: Yes, the main city. Deumba was no city -- only a little resort. So, he is in Suva and he quickly gets drunk. Now Borden had a heart condition -- never should drink at all.

Another day or two goes by. The now-chastened vipers back in the villa decide to send a Trojan horse into Suva -- Jim Hill -- with a plan.

Jim goes to the bar and pretends to get drunk, cursing Hecht and Lancaster. Borden, sitting close by, says, "I'll drink to that!" (Laughs)

Jim, the Mata Hari, joins Borden. Together they curse the whole venture, particularly Lancaster and Hecht. In three days, Borden can't drink any more. Jim gets him sobered up, and suggests: "Well, you can't get off the island -- Harold's got all the air tickets in the safe, and he's the only one who has the key. If you want to leave the island, you'd better write something." (Laughs)

About six had days later I got page one of the script. It had nothing to do with what I'm lining up to shoot, of course.

That's the way the picture began. The script was written in Suva by Jim Hill and Borden Chase, avowed enemies of Hecht and Lancaster. It became a kind of routine; a messenger would sneak by the window and Jim Hill would drop him the package of pages they'd written. The messenger'd hop in a car and tear up to Deumba Beach, arriving at about 11:30 or 12:00 at night.

Harold would take it into his office in this big cutting room unit, sit there with a bottle of Scotch, and rewrite it, have a stenographer pound it out, and I would get it in the morning to shoot. (Laughter) This is what's known as a real nerve test for a director.

What it became was just a narrative featuring Burt's new caps on his teeth. Tremendous grin he had with all these new caps, a few athletic feats, and the story was "From Here to Dere wid Boit." It had no construction at all. I did the best I could with it. It made a lot of money, and it still runs on TV quite often.

But some of the weirdest things have happened on TV to it. I'm going to try to organize a counter suit to those responsible, for $48,000,000 for defamation of my character and skill as a director, for what I saw of ROBINSON CRUSOE ON MARS the other night. And what I have seen in the past of HIS MAJESTY O'KEEFE. Anybody, embarking, as I am, on an authentic How-to-direct-pictures-book, has been maligned and defamed and scandalized and scratched up and down on the wrong side, by what they do, the half-assed, half-witted cutters for TV. Not just taking things out. I refer to TOO LATE FOR TEARS. They're driving along Mulholland Drive at night, a car passes them and throws something in the back. They arrive in their apartment house garage and find the object. It's a suitcase full of money.

I actually saw that film run on TV where the cut was made from driving along on Mulholland Drive to them in the apartment with a satchel of money!

ADAMSON: (Laughs) No explanation!

HASKIN: Just as crazy as the cuts they made in ROBINSON CRUSOE ON MARS; the cuts made in HIS MAJESTY O'KEEFE. For instance, Burt Lancaster, who's shipwrecked on the island of Yap, sails on a lugger for Hong Kong. The next cut is him sailing back to Yap with a junk, a new first mate, a new bride! Without explanation, back where he started from.

ADAMSON: (Laughs) So his activities in Hong Kong are a mystery?

HASKIN: You don't know where or why or what, which is the whole crux of the story.

These abuses have got to be corrected some way or another. I know that this is a long standing hassle which should be backed by the Directors Guild. Anyhow, I know a good lawyer who might take it on contingency and see what he can organize out of it.

ADAMSON: It would have to be an organized kind of a presentation.

HASKIN: Yes. It would. But he's not bashful. He'd probably begin by naming $50,000,000 damages, which would rattle their bones a bit. And he can get a basis for legal action together for it . . . he's a smart cookie.

In the making of HIS MAJESTY O'KEEFE: at times, I enjoyed making many of the scenes.

After a while, peace reigned between Harold and Burt and me. Particularly during the scenes of Burt returning from the Sonsorals with the junk, with all the fei aboard. Borden Chase, by then, was feeding us some real detailed script pages.

However, for the whole coronation he wrote one line: "Burt is crowned."

This involved 1,000 Fijians, 200 of who are in special costumes, dancing rituals.

I just staged it all out of my head, harking back to memories of old comic strips.

The pageantry made it a saleable picture.

Later, one of those supercilious MGM officials, Bernie Smith, when I was suggested for a picture at MGM, said, of all the Hecht/Lancaster films, the worst one was the one I made -- you know, HIS MAJESTY O'KEEFE. Thumbs down.

Actually, because of TV sale, O'KEEFE made more money than any of the others. It played again and again on TV in the weirdest kind of editorial mayhem you ever saw. You can't tell what the hell's going on half the time. Just a lot of natives, and beautiful scenery.

Our sound stage was built in the jungle. I had designed a method of killing raindrops on the tin roof: putting a screen above it -- to break up the rain. It would dull it down enough to record dialogue inside.

Due to some oversight, this device was cancelled. When the rain came (laughs) it sounded like cannon-fire inside. Even without the rain, sounds of the bulbul birds hopping around on it were deafening. (Laughs)

ADAMSON: You mean you designed this thing, but it was never put up?

HASKIN: Right. Even today, when I reminisce, the whole period from beginning to end was pure nightmare. Nobody could believe the atmosphere of a film like that. Everybody was so caught up in cabin fever, after three days they hated everybody else with a deadly hatred. In the damn dining room, everybody would pair off into different corners.

I'd always come in early so I wouldn't have to sit with <u>anybody</u>. I'd sit facing a corner, and eat the glop.

The ship never seemed to arrive from New Zealand with meat, so we ate what we called "glop" -- mostly curry over the top of whatever. Some kind of fish, or the local cat.

I don't want to go deeply into what liquor did to the whole enterprise, either, because many of the splendid staff had a problem with alcohol. When they indulged the problem, they were no longer splendid members -- they were bums. That's what happened to the screen on the roof of the stage. (Laughs)

Ted Haworth was art director, but in the middle of the show he got word that Hitchcock wanted him in Toronto, Canada. He blew.

ADAMSON: I CONFESS.

HASKIN: Yes. Haworth left W. Simpson Robinson, an old British scenic painter with a cowboy hat and a few cans of paint in his hand, to carry on the job. He became the art director. Immediately Harold cancelled all the expensive sets. After that we just shot ad-lib crap.

It had been understood firmly that Harold would come down, stay three weeks, then go home and let us make the film.

My wife, Terry, and several of the loose company members gave a farewell party for Harold, with a big banner in the resort barroom: "We love you, Harold."

The party lasted all night with the cheap whiskey. Next day Harold woke up with a terrible hangover, remembered the banner. "They love me so much, I can't leave." (Laughs) And he stayed during the whole damn picture. Oh brother!

ADAMSON: Do you recall anything about making THE NAKED JUNGLE?

HASKIN: NAKED JUNGLE, yes. Again I say, without any equivocation whatsoever, that unless you have a good story that you believe in, and it's well prepared when you start a picture, you're lost as far as really coming off with a first class movie. That's what happened with THE NAKED JUNGLE. Originally, we had Phil Yordan, writer, and again, the producing team of George Pal and Pete Freeman. Phil Yordan and I established a similar relationship to that with me and Barre Lyndon on WAR OF THE WORLDS.

The property we were to make was a classic short story: "Leiningen Vs. the Ants." It was a story about a plantation in the upper Amazon of Brazil, invaded by a swarming of soldier ants. The owner's lifetime of toil is destroyed by them. The ant invasion is very vivid and very ghastly.

We had to fabricate a personal story. A logical format became the story of the plantation owner to whom tragedy happened in the end; dramatically, as compensation for tragedy, we gave him love. That's how the story developed.

Pete Freeman it was who suggested characterizing the owner as a weird recluse, who advertises for a picture bride in the New Orleans papers. Indicating our sex relationship.

We worked the story line out, potentially for a young Leslie Caron, a waif, a gamin -- some poor servant girl with a heart of gold but very vulnerable. This choice to make credible the bizarre fact of a woman marrying a complete stranger on a plantation far up the Amazon. Phil Yordan agreed, and soon had a hell of an interesting screenplay going.

Meanwhile, Paramount had a loose commitment with Eleanor Parker. They had lent her $75,000 for her husband. In return she had given them a commitment for one picture. So, with that dangling around, and our picture getting ready, Don Hartman, exec, performed a magic bit of casting: "Eleanor will play the girl!"

Now, as to type, there is some difference between Eleanor Parker and Leslie Caron! Eleanor Parker is a grand romantic beauty -- she, at that time, was very lush, and age had not ravaged her. She was a haughty kind of actress, reflecting it in appearance even, not to mention that she visualized the part as coming up the Amazon with three trunks of candy-striped blouses and parasols, like a society belle.

Now that Eleanor Parker was assigned to our film, we had Edith Head making sketches of these wonderful costumes to be worn sailing along the Amazon.

Our screenplay, as developed, was an exercise in futility. It had to be changed drastically to fit the casting. Meaning, with an imminent starting date, we were practically starting with no story.

ADAMSON: It had to be changed?

HASKIN: Let me describe what happened. We had a big huddle in Hartman's office. Our production group with George Pal was there, and a new writer, Rannie MacDougall, who was going to take over the task. Don Hartman asked him what he thought of our story and he said, "Considering the problem you have, I think it needs a bit of re-focusing." (Laughs) A nice way of putting it!

Don Hartman then makes a stern statement to Freeman, "Now Frank, I want you to listen to what is said in this conference, and back me up. That's how this story will be."

"Yeah, yeah," said Y. Frank, the tyrant.

Hartman then sat back and began telling about a trip he had to New York where he saw Dial M for Murder on the stage. He describes the whole play from curtain to curtain. Finally, he turned to us, said, "Well, I guess that covers everything. Let's get this show on the road." Boom. The conference was over!

This is not exaggerating one iota: that's all that was said at that meeting. George and I and Pete just sat there grinding our teeth. We knew there was no credibility to our new story line. The minute you'd see this dame coming up the Amazon with trunkloads of finery, in the candy-striped blouse, straw sailor hat with veil, an umbrella over her arm, you had to be in the realms of fantasy -- not trying to tell anything real at all, just amusing the audience with a piece of phony casting.

However, Rannie MacDougall was a slick writer. He had begun as a radio writer, knew dialogue well. Some of his dialogue was fairly sophisticated.

During the shooting when we got into the action with the ants, it became good melodrama, but the personal story never got off the ground. In spite of all the added bolstering statements about her knowing the planter's brother in New Orleans; that she'd lost a husband, that after all the tragedy to her, she decided she'd come here, you never believed that this impressive woman, with all this impact of beauty and sex, would ever, on God's green earth, sail up a river to marry a stranger. (Laughs) Absolutely you couldn't believe it then, you can't today.

ADAMSON: Well, wasn't there dialogue to that effect, asking her why she did this? She said, "Well, I wanted to get away from New Orleans," or something.

HASKIN: Of course there was. You couldn't let it go undiscussed. But I didn't believe any of it. Do you realize what she was doing? She debarks from her steamer at a lousy little port, gets into a stinkpot riverboat with Romo Vincent -- CHUG, CHUG, CHUG -- sails up the Amazon for days.

ADAMSON: What bothered me was that that whole plot seemed to have very little to do with ants coming and eating up the plantation -- I wish the ants had entered sooner. Halfway through the picture, everybody starts talking about the "Marabunta" and I thought it was wonderful from that point to the end of the film.

HASKIN: "Marabunta." Yes. I coined the word myself.

ADAMSON: Tremendous. Then, this guy floating down the river in his boat, just a skeleton, when you've still got no idea what could have killed him -- I just thought that was one of the most incredible things I'd ever seen. It was wonderful, but it took so very long for that kind of thing to start happening.

HASKIN: I know. Well, that was the construction of the story. I followed the screenplay -- I didn't ad-lib any of that. There hadn't been enough time for Rannie to revamp the story thoroughly. He did well for what he was faced with. Some fairly smooth dialogue; some of the scenes were pretty good. But, there we were . . .

At this point in my career, I must say that my fortunes were in the ascendant, starting with WAR OF THE WORLDS, then HIS MAJESTY O'KEEFE, and THE NAKED JUNGLE. I had generated the most priceless ingredient for a successful director: excitement.

To illustrate. In a producer's conference, when they're talking over a project, talking about who to get as director, and several names are mentioned, invariably when one name is mentioned, everybody gets excited. This is a mystique that you help to create about yourself by a subconscious projection of self-importance. Letting yourself be considered a wizard of sorts. I had been cultivating this angle about myself -- I had let myself become part of the myth of Hollywood. I'd been in town a long time and was known as a wizard for a lot of things -- cinematography, special effects and the like.

Right at the peak of this, wouldn't you know, I left to go to Australia with Bob Newton, Joseph Kaufman, Marty Rackin, and Mark Evans. To make a synthetic version of LONG JOHN SILVER and a TV series. Throwing away all that precious excitement, as well as an assignment to make a picture with Wallis, with Martin and Lewis in a circus, which was a heavy assignment. Damned if I didn't sail out to Australia, and stay there a year and a half. When I came back, MCA, my agent, was so mad at me that they wouldn't speak to me.

We had our own company -- a Panamanian corporation called Isla de Oro. Jesus, the fantasies were flying like gnats on a summer eve. A guy named Joseph Kaufman, a producer of sorts, Robert Newton, Marty Rackin, and myself, along with Mark Evans, who is now TV Production Manager of 20th Century-Fox, went out to Australia. Kaufman had a promise of money from Louie Wolfson and some other sharpshooters. We were going to make twenty-six episodes of LONG JOHN SILVER and a feature.

ADAMSON: The feature was done and released. What happened to the TV episodes?

HASKIN: Kaufman stole them and ran them and got money out of them, and they disappeared. I don't know. They had quite a run, because we shot them in color. That was before there were many color series, and just on the basis of the fact that they were in color, they had runs. He kept the money and ate well and finally died. God catches up with all these characters eventually, I guess.

Going to Australia was not only disastrous from the standpoint of me sacrificing this priceless ingredient which I had spent so many years getting, but it was disastrous financially. None of the terms of what I was to get out there were fulfilled. The terms of our participation deal were a laugh. All my efforts to get the eighteen-month exemption from Internal Revenue, for being in foreign residence, were also a laugh, because there was nothing to exempt from. A real disaster.

ADAMSON: You never got money?

HASKIN: No. I got paid a bit, but I left there completely dead broke. All the extra payments I was to get for this, my living expenses, and this, that, and the other, were all welched out somehow, including a set fee for each week that they all got except me, and I don't know why.

ADAMSON: What about Newton, did you have any more luck with him now than before?

HASKIN: Well, for a short period, but -- and that's the reason the series couldn't be brought off -- he got to where I couldn't shoot a whole line in one take. I'd have to break a line two or three times, and get sometimes only a word before he'd fall off the stool, he was so stiff. He'd get drunk, roaring around town in a car all night, and how the hell he didn't kill himself or fifty people, I don't know. It was disastrous.

Not too long after we got back, his wife and his young son had left him, and moved to the Garden of Allah, and he was still up in Benedict Canyon in the house. He phoned them and said he'd stopped drinking, and he wanted them to come back. So they went back for a conference, and as he took a Miltown from his pocket and raised it to his lips, he fell dead in front of them. And that was it. The end of a great actor.

ADAMSON: That was right after this whole episode?

HASKIN: Not immediately, but not too long after....

ADAMSON: So you weren't too happy with Newton on LONG JOHN SILVER, or with the whole experience in Australia.

HASKIN: Oh, well, that was hardly a professional job out there. It was highly experimental and was one of the big mistakes of my life, ever to join up with these idiots. But in fanning it around out at Newton's house and Marty Rackin's house out in Benedict Canyon, it seemed so nostalgic of my boyhood and adventures in the Far East and so forth.

At this point, I had been to Australia on HIS MAJESTY O'KEEFE, and I had met certain Australians, and I had the entré. When we started this LONG JOHN SILVER venture as a TV series and one feature, there was no decisive thinking about where to do it -- maybe Europe, or wherever there was a source of material and workmen and actors.

So, as long as it was for the American market, I settled the deal and said, "For God sakes, you have to have English speaking actors, you can't do it in Yugoslavia. It'd cost you too much money to import people." We settled on Australia, because I had been there and had done a lot of sub-casting there for HIS MAJESTY O'KEEFE -- Guy Doleman and various guys who'd been brought up there to play parts. So that's what located us in Australia.

It was just so glamorous, the whole idea of being part of the corporation. We incorporated in Panama, the Isla de Oro Corporation, and we were all going to get rich -- it couldn't be resisted. At which point, I think I mentioned, I had just got a foot in the door through MCA, and I had two big assignments in the wind, and one that was definite -- the circus picture with Martin and Lewis, not that I would care much about making it, but it was an important film at that time. It was part of the charisma, the excitement element that you have to build on a person like a director in order to raise his rates and get him into the big league.

Particularly, there was the doublecross we underwent by the owner of a firm, a well-known wrecker of the financial world: Louis Wolfson had pledged $450,000 to the enterprise, which he reneged on as soon as we got there. There were a couple of knickknacks like that.

We were supposed to have something like $75,000 minimum per segment of this little TV series we were making, and it turned out we were lucky we had $11,000 or $12,000, for the last ten or twelve of them. We were just using nothing. They were nice people in Australia, but I came back broke.

ADAMSON: What was the first film you did when you returned to Hollywood?

HASKIN: THE FIRST TEXAN -- Allied Artists.

ADAMSON: You had story problems on that.

HASKIN: Well, I didn't have any story problems. My problems were nothing except that I had an absolute conviction that the thing wouldn't sell. And it didn't. It never has paid out. I agreed to a deferment on it, and I've never been paid out since. I think even today, and this is God knows how many generations later, I get letters from Allied Artists' holding corporation or something, giving me a statement, and the cost always overrides the income. (Laughs)

It followed dead on the heels of a tremendously successful picture called WICHITA, with the same idea of that period of time, and the same star, Joel McCrea, made by Jacques Tourneur. WICHITA had all the excitement and a natural gimmick working for it -- the Marshal posts an edict at all the trails leading into town -- "No guns allowed in town." Every time the Marshal takes a walk from his house over to the store, you wonder which cowboy is going to find out that he means it. (Laughs) That's a great gag.

Anyway, THE FIRST TEXAN was well written, and Walter Mirisch was the producer. We had a good cast -- Felicia Farr, Joel McCrea, and Jeff Morrow. It played very well. It was a great experience for me.

I finally ran across the man I consider the greatest pure cinema actor I ever worked with -- Joel McCrea. With a minimum of any kind of outward stylized movements, such as theatrical effects, he could sell ideas like gangbusters, mostly with thought -- inner thought and timing. I used to watch scenes on the set, and I'd print them, and I'd think, Jesus, there wasn't anything to him -- and I'd see him in the rushes the next day, and it'd knock you off your seat, because of the hemming in of the camera on the sidelines, focused on McCrea. He really was great, a very fine man. I enjoyed the association greatly. Another testimony that you can put as much effort into a film as you do into an Academy Award Winner, and it can turn out to be a bust.

ADAMSON: Your problem was not so much the script as the story -- wasn't that it?

HASKIN: It was the story, yes. You see, this is one of the lessons I learned along the line, and I kept learning up to the day I quit -- and I learn today about films -- the first thing I found out was the trap of slick scripts that wouldn't play. This script would play, but it would play to no avail, because rooting interest was lacking. If you don't have rooting interest, forget it. By the end, the <u>ushers</u> are outside smoking. The projectionist is reading a book.

ADAMSON: Just because the guy avoiding a fight doesn't make a good conflict.

HASKIN: Yes, it cannot make anything of a film. It was a very spectacularly shot film -- we used a ranch out at Thousand Oaks, and we had cavalry. As far as I'm concerned, I'm rather proud of the staging, and the acting was well handled, and scenes were together -- the picture plays like sixty, but to what avail?

Santa Ana is daring the guy, and the obnoxious Mexicans are taking things over, they're kicking hell out of the poor bastards at the Alamo -- offstage, naturally -- and it just doesn't work. It's a defeatist concept, and you couldn't, of course, <u>reveal</u> what McCrea had in mind, so he had to have a stiff upper lip to resist all these entreaties to please stand and fight, to even go down and be killed, but at least go into history as something other than a coward.

Mirisch didn't believe my complaints -- nobody did, and I don't think they cared much afterwards, either. They got their fee out of the making of it, and that was it.

ADAMSON: Then CONQUEST OF SPACE followed that?

HASKIN: Yes. CONQUEST OF SPACE was made after THE FIRST TEXAN, back with George Pal at Paramount.

The most pungent memory I have of CONQUEST OF SPACE is: on the first morning of the picture, I went downstairs in my place on Marmont Lane, 900 steps down to the street, and my pet rabbit had escaped out of its cage. He was hiding in a little hole under the ivy, and I reached in to get hold of him, and my back went out. I was seized with spasms in the sacroiliac area that were intolerable. I managed to struggle the rest of the way down, got in my car and went to the studio. They got the masseur, Jim Davis, who immediately started rubbing me, and we went off from there. I got so that during the shooting, I had a sign made for the back of my chair, "Condition Unchanged." (Laughs) That's the way I shot the picture.

Technologically, the concept was good. You see, if these stories that don't turn out hadn't shown great promise to begin with, you wouldn't be so upset about it. It was a story just far enough into the future to be realistic, of a space station 1800 miles out with a crew on board that were up for a duration and then supposed to be taken back, who had not been taken back.

Somehow, the functioning of the shuttle back and forth was being improved, and these guys had been up there for a year, instead of three months or six months or whatever they were up for. They were always in communication through visual electronics with their loved ones and the world, but overstaying their period and quite disgruntled about it. That to me, was always an interesting idea that could have been developed into something. They were up there and preparing a journey around the planets, with a free space vehicle, with no streamlining, never to be brought into contact with air. This great big bunch of tin cans and fuel reservoirs was what they were going to travel around in and orbit several of the planets including Mercury, then go back to the space station. From the ringleaders of the group aboard the space station, the crew was selected for this journey.

There was a personal story introduced into this thing, which was utterly incredible. Walter Brooke was commander of the expedition and Eric Fleming, the boy who lost his life down in South America, and was in RAWHIDE out at MGM, was his son. They're aboard this same expedition to circumnavigate space and go around these planets.

This, I think, was originated by Pete Freeman, who at that time had a maudlin relationship with his father, and this father/son thing was the biggest thing in the world to him. Somehow he got this thing into it. Though the writer we had, James O'Hanlon, thought it was oversentimental, Freeman went for it, and there it was!

It ended up with the father, I think, panicking at a crucial moment with an earthquake on Mars, and the son having to take over, and all this crap. Events in space are so gigantic, if they'd shot each other full of holes like a colander, it wouldn't have meant anything! Absolutely. A personal complication in that scope is just tawdry, it's sophomoric. I don't know how the picture did, and I wouldn't care to know much. It didn't have any TV run, I know that.

ADAMSON: It didn't?

HASKIN: I never heard of it being run. The effects are spectacular -- we used a lot of traveling mattes -- taxis up in space going here and there and everywhere . . .

There were two great scientific matters that I handled with a common touch. One was to explain to the audience how these magnetic shoes operated and to introduce their very existence. I cut to Phil Foster seated in his bunk, being melancholy about the whole thing, and he reaches down and unlaces his shoes. I had him on a wire, and immediately he rises up and bumps his head on the ceiling. (Laughs) So they pull him down, and say, "You dummy," and there's a little rough explanation. This showed, visually, the reason they were attached to the floor.

When we got to Mars, there was a question of explaining the condition of Mars, which later, in ROBINSON CRUSOE ON MARS, I continued. It was that it's a dead planet, which is all that we know scientifically about Mars. Now, with all these hooligans fooling around in CONQUEST OF SPACE on Mars, I picked on Phil Foster again to explain. They're digging in this red sawdust, and he drops his shovel and says with great disgust -- "Look at this stuff." He picks up a handful of it, and he says, "No bugs, no 'woims,'" then he looks around and he says, "and no people." (Laughs) And drops it. Now, Mars is a dead planet, without going into any deep scientific logic to prove it.

ADAMSON: You dramatized the explanation.

HASKIN: Yes. "No bugs, no 'woims,' no people." (Laughs)

ADAMSON: I was surprised at CONQUEST OF SPACE, because I thought it had a lot less authentic feeling than WAR OF THE WORLDS or any other science fiction thing that George Pal had done or that you had done.

HASKIN: Well, the personal story and the technical story -- oil and water. We had Werner Von Braun on the set all the time.

ADAMSON: Really!

HASKIN: As a technical advisor. He kept it straight, but I don't know -- it's a mish-mash thing.

ADAMSON: It was a mish-mash. Some things were technically very right, but then other things didn't make sense at all. When they got on Mars, they were wearing helmets but their hands were exposed. I couldn't understand that.

HASKIN: I had some things in CONQUEST OF SPACE that I was rather proud of. One was that they took this highly complicated vehicle around all the planets, and orbited Venus and what have you, and came back. And no single word was ever said, on how the hell it ran, nor did you ever see any of the multiplex contraptions being yanked around or wheels turned at all. It was tacitly assumed that this expert crew was running the vehicle. If you had started in trying to make it credible, and showed the space vehicle being run, you wouldn't have had room for anything else, because it would have been very complicated.

ADAMSON: You mean, just to explain how it ran and how the controls worked.

HASKIN: Yes, yes, and the dialogue -- the commands of the "frammis and scrammis" stuff, and all that. I avoided it. I said -- "We'll talk about none of it. Out!" So, because there were so many people, they had to walk upright in the ship, and the assumption was that they had on magnetic shoes on a magnetic track, which gave them an excuse to be walking around upright without floating. It would have been too much to expect to make them free-falling all the time. . . .

ADAMSON: Well, that takes us to THE BOSS, which I've seen, with John Payne.

HASKIN: Yes. It played fairly well, but it was about a subject that was very dear to Frank Selzer's heart -- Prendergast and that era. I think Selzer was a young man in that era, and undoubtedly felt the sting of all the stuff that was going on, but I think, when it was made, that the people couldn't have cared less. Prendergast didn't mean anything, and John Payne had lost his draw. It was very difficult to hold him down to any semblance of human behavior. In the dressing room he was the greatest artist since Beerbohm Tree, but he'd get out on the set and walk through it like a wooden log, or ham it up to the point that you couldn't believe. But that's not an excuse. It was just an uninteresting era of past skulduggery that I think by contrast with today's world, was just a pantywaist proposition of a few gangsters in Kansas City shooting each other down the stairs and that kind of stuff. It didn't have what THE GODFATHER had -- relative threads of connection with today's problems. Prendergast was dead. It was unearthing something. Besides, it was made on a very short budget. It didn't make any money either.

ADAMSON: One thing I thought was interesting about that was the guy's wife, the girl he marries because the girl he wants turns him down. Remember the girl that he finally marries out of a drunken rage? It's one of those situations where the script called for her to be completely unattractive, but no producer will put a completely unattractive woman in front of the camera.

HASKIN: But we did. (Laughs)

ADAMSON: Well, you end up with somebody who maybe looks less appealing than the starlet, let's say, but who is really all right as far as the average moviegoer is concerned. I really thought you got over that problem in an interesting way -- with makeup, I guess. Her face was shiny. She wasn't disturbing to look at.

HASKIN: Well, we didn't try for a good looking woman there. Gloria McGhee played Prendergast's wife, and we had Doe Avedon for something else. . . . It's kind of remote with me. The only stuff that I found much excitement in was the gangsters.

ADAMSON: You had a fight scene in the beginning, and there were other good moments. A good scene at the end, too -- the stalking scene in the cement factory.

HASKIN: Up in the grids of the stage.

ADAMSON: Is that where it was done?

HASKIN: Yes.

ADAMSON: That kind of thing was nice. FROM THE EARTH TO THE MOON, I have not seen . . .

HASKIN: JULES VERNE'S FROM THE EARTH TO THE MOON is the true, full title of this. It was made in the old nostalgic way that it was originally written. The first half of it was as good in certain ways as AROUND THE WORLD IN 80 DAYS. Great actors -- Joe Cotten, George Sanders, a whole flock of very competent people -- and the costumes were lovely, the settings were good -- we used Chapultepec Castle for Barbicane's house and palace. Up to the time that the damned missile was fired out of the cannon to go to the moon, it had a strange sort of nostalgic authenticity.

Joe Youngerman and I discussed that at full length later -- "What the hell happened to you on that film?" Jesus Christ! What did I have to do with it? But I don't know what could have made it into a good film. It just lost all sense of credibility with this obviously phony looking projectile with big rooms in it and step ladders and that twirling sort of gyroscope contraption and so forth, all manufactured by Mexicans out on their front lawn for a fee. (Laughs)

The guy that made the big twelve-foot gyroscope with blades flipping around which was supposed to hold us steady on course, bought it back after the picture. He put it on his front lawn, and he'd sit in the living room and turn it on. RRRRRRR -- the thing'd go like an eggbeater out there -- it'd kill anybody if they walked into it! (Laughs)

ADAMSON: Well, I guess what we should do is go to LITTLE SAVAGE and so forth.

HASKIN: A trained seal was brought down from P.O.P. (Pacific Ocean Park) in Hollywood for THE LITTLE SAVAGE, and the Mexicans had built a cage for it, of which the bottom half was water, and the top half was the screened-in area with shelves, so it could hop up and look around and then go back in the water. It had been hastily tarred, and the tar leaked off into the water. They dumped the seal into this thing without examining it too closely, and the tar got in his eyes and he went blind. He was the best seal P.O.P. had, a trained seal, which is worth a lot of loot. So we shipped him back to Tijuana and then they picked him up in a truck there, and sent down a seal that was really something -- he loved nothing but human flesh! (Laughs)

I guess the guys up at P.O.P. were mad -- "Gonna get even with those bastards!" Well, the seal was supposed to be pals with our young boy, the "Little Savage," but he loved the taste of flesh, and would savage him at every opportunity. The other impulse he had was to get out to sea and the hell with this whole thing. So about two times a week, he'd bust loose and start across the beach, which luckily was a wide beach, and we'd catch him before he'd hit the ocean. Impossible . . .

We went down, fully cast with Arline, whatever her name was, as the leading woman, who had been cast in Hollywood; Pedro Armendariz, who was playing an old pirate; an unknown young boy; and a seal from P.O.P. I should have had my head examined, and just declared myself into a looney bin, instead of doing this thing. EL PEQUEÑO SALVAJE. (Laughs)

We met Miguelito Alemán in Acapulco. He had a place there with the Mexican Army guarding the road so they'd see that he wasn't disturbed. (Laughs) And he had his father's yacht -- Alemán (Sr.) had been president . . .

I got most of this data from a very sharp Mexican named Ignacio Valdez, who had been a lieutenant in the detectives of the Mexico City police. He ran a rental service with Cadillacs, and was my driver with his Cadillac. Ignacio and I became quite good friends, and he would tell me all the inside stuff. We drove by the opposition party's headquarters, and he told me that the Party of the Revolution paid for the rental, their excursions in the countryside to electioneer, and all. The opposition was supported by the Party of the Revolution -- under the table, of course.

ADAMSON: I see, so there would be some opposition.

HASKIN: They were allowed a certain amount of money to paint farmers' fences with their signs, which means they had to give the farmer some money, paint the fence, and he'd vote for you, along with all his family. That's the standard electioneering procedure in Mexico -- to go through the countryside and pay farmers and paint the fences with the name of the candidate, amounting almost to a signed contract to vote your way.

They would even supply, according to Ignacio, hecklers for the opposition candidate, so that they could make the newspapers with protests and fights out in the boondocks and little villages. (Laughs) That's all bought and paid for by the Party of the Revolution, which has been in power ever since the Mexican Revolution.

The opposition never had a chance. They'd get one percent, two percent of the votes, that's all. But they could claim it's a democracy. Actually, it's a dictatorship of this party.

I remember particularly, one day we went by and there was a huge fifty-foot painting on the front of the building, of the opposition candidate. Ignacio said, "They paid a lot for this!" (Laughs) . . .

Anyhow, we were talking about Mickey Alemán -- Miguelito -- who was a butterfly of sorts around Mexico. He had a new mistress, Christiane Martel, a French woman who could barely speak English and had never acted in her life. Ever with the ear out for a piece of change, the producer is discussing the picture we're about to make, with Miguelito, who says, "Well, my girlfriend, Christiane, is very ambitious to be in a film, and I'd love to see her in a part like that with no other competition." So the deal is made -- Boom. For $35,000 she is cast in the part, the other dame is dumped, and $35,000 passes into the coffers.

The script was nothing. I undertook to re-write the script at night and shoot it in the morning of the next day. It was a bad script, believe me. I had depended too much on sort of an over-sentimentalized relationship between the boy and the seal, and the damn seal we finally got liked nothing better than human flesh -- particularly that boy's flesh. If they got within five feet of each other, the boy had to go to First Aid, because the seal would nip a piece out of him.

ADAMSON: Did he ever nip anything significant?

HASKIN: He never killed the kid, no. But he could have done so.

ADAMSON: A large hunk of flesh or anything?

HASKIN: Yes, he put some good nicks in him. The boy needed a couple stitches now and then. Pedro Armendariz was going to kill the goddamn thing, because every time he'd get near it, it'd take a nip at him, too.

All these scenes I had written where the boy has his arm around the seal and they're looking off into sunsets, now become separate shots of the boy walking through the jungle and then a cut to the seal going along to show that he's following the boy. (Laughs) Jesus Christ! Whatever I had in mind became impossible.

That was that, and the dialogue was forced. I tried to get a flavor of Melville into the old pirate lingo. I saw Pete Armendariz doing a dubbing job in Mexico City of it afterwards, for the Spanish version. He was fantastic at lip sync, a real sharp guy. But these bombastic terms, straight out of Melville, that I had used so heavily in the dialogue, translated into Spanish, had me rolling on the floor. (Laughs) I got a copy of the Spanish script -- I have it around somewhere -- a direct translation of the script I wrote for this dreadful picture.

ADAMSON: Do you know enough Spanish to find it funny to read the Spanish translation?

HASKIN: Oh, yes. Because a great many of these bombastic pirate type words, you just add "o" on the end of them and there they are. For instance, the word "catastrophe" is "catastrofico" or "cataclysmico."

ADAMSON: Did you want to talk about JET OVER THE ATLANTIC?

HASKIN: My friend Clarence Eurist was production manager. He had been a prop man when I was at Warner Bros. in the early days, and we'd been friends for years, so he and I were confidants. I was finished with the show, doing pick-up inserts and crap for the last day on the stage in the old Stahl "America" studio, a very good one there. Clarence came on the stage, and he was very pale. I thought he'd encountered a ghost or something. He kind of staggered a little bit, and motioned to me, and dived behind a flat. I went over and asked, "What the hell's the matter?" He said, "I -- I just left him." I said, "Left who? What are you talking about? Calm yourself, settle down, Clarence." "Bogeaus," he said. "In his office. Sonuvabitch . . . !"

What happened was this. The picture to that date, with all bills paid and everything complete, had cost $185,000. It was with George Raft, Margaret Lindsay, George Macready, Guy Madison, Virginia Mayo, Ilona Massey, Anna Lee, Venetia Stevenson, Mary Anderson -- the marquee wouldn't look bad with this cast on it, and with the airplanes and this, that and the other. It had some scope. $185,000 we had done it for. It was all paid now, and Clarence was proudly looking over (Benedict) Bogeaus' shoulder -- Bogeaus was sitting with the budget in front of him and the cost sheets. Bogeaus said, "I've had a lot of expenses on that script."

Now, he had promised me that he was throwing his script in, if I would take this deferment, see? And he'd just toss in the script. So he marked down $25,000 for the script in the budget -- he writes it in by hand. Then he said, "It cost me more out of pocket" -- and wrote, "$25,000 cash disbursements."

Clarence says, "Hey, what the hell is this? You can't do this!" And Bogeaus says, "Fuck you. It's my budget, I'll do anything I want with it!" And another $25,000 goes on it, for some other undetermined item. $75,000 at one stroke! This gave Clarence a heart attack, after all this work he had done to shave corners and get special permission to use the whole Mexicana Airlines free, and all their facilities in the headquarters down there. The clerks and janitors, even, played themselves for nothing, and you couldn't even tip them, because Clarence was smart enough to hire this guy named Carlos Musquiz to play a steward aboard the plane. It was a little tiny part, but Musquiz is a brother to the wife of the president of Mexicana Airlines, and for this big part he gets -- all the way up to the top the guy put the order -- "Give them anything they want, and not a penny's cost. Not even a tip." Believe me, you couldn't tip one of those little Mexican guys, even behind a flat. You'd try to slip them a few pesos -- "No, señor, no, no" -- he'd be fired if he took it. They even sent the whole interior, all the seats and the windows and everything, of the entire Brittania, which was one of the biggest airplanes ever in existence. They had spare parts enough to re-equip the whole interior. The Brittania itself had, several months previously, failed to make much altitude on a take-off and landed on its belly and busted in half. The repairs were just completed. They turned that over to us as a prop -- the big Brittania, four prop-jet whirligig engines -- all this stuff. So Bogeaus slaps on $75,000 while Clarence is watching.

Now we finished, and flew back to Hollywood. We're sitting around the outer office of Bogeaus' partner, a renowned exhibitor thief, gassing with him a little bit about the picture and what to expect from it. He says, "Not a bad movie for $350,000." Now, Bogeaus on the way up had slapped more on it. (Laughs) God Almighty!

It was released, and every time the income got close to the cost, they'd slap another $75,000 on it. So I had no possible chance ever, of getting any participation money. George Raft, who was supposed to be pari passu with everybody from the first dollar of the gross, did this whole trip for an agreed $5,000 and a hotel suite on top of the Fenix Hotel. His girlfriend came to stay with him and meals and everything were supposed to be paid. Well, he was looking for Bogeaus to kill him, because he never got a nickel -- except the bills for the hotel stay. (Laughs)

ADAMSON: (Laughs) You mean he never even got his $5,000?

HASKIN: Nothing. Bogeaus swore to Raft -- "Even if the picture never makes a dime, you'll get your money. First money comes in, you get it." That's the way he got George Raft to go down there, but it was never put on paper just quite that way. (Laughs) Well, Bogeaus is dead, God rest his soul for his sins. He was a phony from way back.

Chapter Eight

## THE EARLY SIXTIES

HASKIN: SEPTEMBER STORM was also THE GIRL IN THE RED BIKINI.

ADAMSON: Why was the title changed from THE GIRL IN THE RED BIKINI?

HASKIN: On a certain day during the shooting, I sent the Spanish assistant director up the hill to get Joanne Dru in the red bikini for her first shots on the beach, where she's to go up onto the point and stand there as the hero goes by in an airplane and sees her.

After a considerable wait, she came down in a brindle brown full-length bathing suit. I said, "Hey, hey! You got on the wrong costume?" She comes over to me and says meaningfully, "You know I can't wear a bikini. I've got stretch marks all over my belly from the kids I've had."

ADAMSON: You were supposed to magically know this?

HASKIN: I had no idea. How the woman had the nerve to sign up for the film, knowing that wearing a bikini was the mainstay of the script -- the title was THE GIRL IN THE RED BIKINI! She needed the money, I guess.

But that wasn't even the bottom of the barrel -- the whole script and the whole operation was ridiculous.

We had Bob Strauss and Mark Stevens in leading parts. Both were good actors. After production, Mark stayed there and took up residence in Mallorca. Mallorca was so beautiful, I longed to live there myself. It's a real peaceful place: rolling, sloping little hills, full of <u>almendres</u> (almond trees).

The biggest industry is smuggling. All night, from your hotel room, you could hear: CHUG, CHUG, CHUG -- boats coming into the docks, full of cigarettes and other goodies. Juan March was the smuggling baron. He'd been instrumental in helping Franco to take over. We used the Juan March smuggler's warehouse, before it was completed. It took up a whole block about eight stories high, with a concrete basement -- it looked like a Bekins Van and Storage warehouse.

You could get anything you wanted -- Lucky Strikes, Marlboros, made in the Canary Islands. (Laughs) Actually, we had to have a 100-horse Evinrude motor to blast the water alongside the yacht, to make it look like it was moving. In four days we had our motor. Where they got it, God knows, but it came through Africa. We used it in the picture, and then (Edward L.) Alperson sold it back to the smugglers. There was constant haggling in the corridors of the hotel. He got what he paid for it! The warehouse wasn't yet commissioned, so we built the sets downstairs, using a generator from Italy for lighting, along with a gang of garlic-smelling juicers. (Laughs)


ADAMSON: Do you have anything to say about ARMORED COMMAND?


HASKIN: Oh ho! This could legitimately have been called a Haskin film, except that I didn't like the thing in the first place. I took it as a breadwinner -- when you get low in dough, you've got to take a picture. Ron Alcorn, an eccentric, to put it mildly, had produced a TV series called CITIZEN SOLDIER in Germany utilizing the training facilities of the U.S. Army station there. He had some kind of hold over some high muckamuck general -- who later got into a lot of trouble back in the States. This general had sent through his permission to give Alcorn anything he wanted, and Alcorn had used all the tanks and ammunition and soldiers for nothing.

ADAMSON: To do CITIZEN SOLDIER?

HASKIN: Yes, his TV series. It never did come off, but it had the core of a decent idea. CITIZEN SOLDIER is self-explanatory -- all our kids in training, and the things they get into, in Germany -- it could have, with proper writing and directing, become a hit series. There's no doubt about it. But Alcorn maintained importance by his access to all this equipment and personnel in Germany.

He, I found out later, had gone to the Library of Congress, and got the records of what happened during the Battle of the Bulge, and other subsidiary action. He cribbed incidents, got together a story of sorts and wrote a script from it. With this communiqué from the general in Germany that the deal still stood, he sold it to Allied Artists.

He called me. I went over and we discussed the whole thing. I was impressed, too, with all the equipment and men he had going over there, at the U.S. Army training grounds.

It was an odd kind of a story. Opening with a wintry sky, snow-covered roads, ruined landscapes of war's passing, broken trees, etc. A limousine hurtling along the road pulls off into the snow. From it emerges a German soldier. Next out, a beautiful dame, Tina Louise, in a fur coat. She pauses for a moment, then she walks briskly away into the bleak snowscape. The German soldier shoots her. She falls. He jumps back in the limousine and goes.

Well, that's a pretty mysterious opening -- you kind of got excited about that. The next action you see is a squad of G.I.'s in a halftrack cruising in the snow. They encounter this unconscious wounded woman shot through the shoulder. They pick her up, put her in the halftrack, and take her back to the little headquarters village of the American forces. Secretly, this woman is a spy. The thing has been all planned. When she was shot, it was done carefully by a sharpshooter, through the shoulder. It was the means to place her, and get the secrets of the U.S. Army plans. The story goes on from there in like vein. Not bad.

We went over to Munich, and with full cooperation of the U.S. tank forces, up to Schmidtmulen. Unfortunately, when we arrived in Bavaria, the snow had not begun yet. It was impossible to do the exteriors, so we went into the interiors. I had Burt Reynolds as a young G.I., and Earl Holliman as corporal, along with others. A good cast.

The screenplay was somewhat amateurish, but I figured I could make corrections. The first day I'm on the stage, I thought, to establish rapport, I should defer to this producer. He's sitting in his office down the hall. At some minor dilemma onstage, I thought, Well, this is it. I'll consult him. So I took the script to his office, and he said, "Hi. Sit down." I explained the dilemma. He said, "Well, I don't want any dissension on this picture. You decide." The next day he left for Kitzbühel. To learn to ski! (Laughs) I never saw him again for weeks. Not until the middle of the tank battle.

He showed up in charge of it, along with the general and all the other brass. You know, to keep his act alive with the brass. He proceeded to screw the battle up so badly you didn't know who was fighting who.

Long ago I had learned that in fast action, the director must have a definite chart of the action geography -- the enemy goes right-to-left, the heroes, left-to-right. No matter what the hell happens, that's the way they have to go. Your northern hemisphere audience is used to maps with north up top, east to the right, west to the left. So the enemy comes from the east and the good guys come from the west. Eventually they have to meet. Unless you keep the directions straight, they end up shooting themselves. Well, the quickest thing an amateur does is "cross the road" -- "Got a hell of an angle over here!" Now, the Germans are going the same way as the Americans. Who the hell are they firing at? They're all in tanks, with or without a swastika, you know. (Laughs) A mish-mash.

They began shooting the battle while I was still in Munich. There was a whole village on the firing range, all ruined -- houses blown to pieces. We had mined the village for a tank attack -- Jesus, a hell of a thing! It would have made a great sequence. I had sent my cutter, Jimmy Lester, to supervise the geography of shooting, to keep it straight, right-to-left and left-to-right. Naturally, to get rid of him, Alcorn put him up in the top of a tower, and went off with all the brass to shoot it however he wanted. Bejesus, surrounded by the general and the whole tank brass, nobody quarreled with the way Alcorn said to stage it! The whole tank corps was to come over the ridge, full speed, firing. Well, of course, they're not going to hit anything rolling at that speed. A tank has to come to a stop, aim the gun, shoot, and then go ahead. Just like soldiers in the woods -- they don't run around shooting their guns wildly while they're running -- they get behind a tree and fire, and run to another tree and fire. This is simple Indian fighting. The same with tanks.

When I finally got there, all long shots had been shot. But I was able to re-establish the regular ABC's of tank fighting for the intermediate action. It was a very spectacular thing.

Oddly enough, the picture didn't make any money; I often wonder why. Marty Ingels was the comic, now married to the mother of Shaun Cassidy. We had some priceless G.I. humor, I will say, very authentic stuff that Alcorn had collected.

Finally, we returned to the U.S., and I'm immediately off the picture. Allied Artists took over, and Walter Hannemann, of Allied, cut the picture. I was invited to the first running. Every bit of humor had been carefully snipped out and dropped into the barrel. Not one comic line was left! Of course, it had all been G.I. low beat stuff, which, in a projection room, doesn't look like much, but will throw an audience into the aisles! This I had learned early. Somehow, just the little three-frame beginnings of this comedy stuff, or endings of some of it, had remained in. When it was previewed, you could hear the audience start to roar, and then it would be cut off. So it became straight melodrama, with no relief.

ADAMSON: The jokes never did go back in?

HASKIN: No, no, no. No, I had no say at all. I can remember how I never have felt so alone in my life as I did up there on the tank firing range. I was carrying this film alone. I had got acute bronchitis, with a fever of 103-1/2, but I couldn't leave the job. The picture would disappear. Who the hell else was around? The production manager was in Munich, loaded, at his desk, didn't know what the hell the score was. I had Germans on the staff: Frank Gothke, a good assistant, but with no executive potential. And Alcorn was in Kitzbühel, Austria, learning to ski. There was just absolutely nobody even to consult about what to do or how to interpret the script. I was light-headed a great deal of the time, but I couldn't quit. I just kept going.

ADAMSON: When you say carrying the film, you mean supporting the production?

HASKIN: Yes. It was all dependent upon me. Period. Ernie Haller happened to be over there, and was cinematographer, but he was worse than I'd ever been on the camera: he didn't pay any attention to what was happening with the action, as long as he could make it look pretty. (Laughs) But the film played, finally. The last big finale was supposed to be the division general standing on the corner in this little village of Schmidtmulen, reviewing the whole tank corps passing by. Taking their salutes. It's a sort of a glory ending to the whole thing -- while the American forces kick the shit out of the Germans, and stop them at the Bulge, and a few other knickknacks. I had a hell of a job getting these fifty tanks placed in the narrow streets of the village. No chance to rehearse. About 11:00 a.m., I'm ready. I turn to Gothke, and I say, "All right, bring the general."

"What general?" he says.

"Oh," I said, "So-and-so . . . " Whatever his name was -- some actor we picked up in Europe.

He said, "Oh, he's back in Vienna. In a stage play."

It had been a month since we'd last used him. (Laughs) The guy wasn't ever there!

In the instant, I had to re-write the whole ending of the picture to something else completely -- play it off the G.I.'s, Earl Holliman, Burt Reynolds, and the boys, on foot, instead of giving it the glory finish with the tanks. Well, such an ad-lib is completely maniacal, to have to do this with a scene, but I suppose that, in review, these things that happened to me were to educate the fool. (Laughs)

ADAMSON: (Laughs) What happened in 1962? Were you making CAPTAIN SINDBAD then, which was then released in '63?

HASKIN: Yes. In the winter of '62, we made CAPTAIN SINDBAD.

ADAMSON: So after ARMORED COMMAND you stayed in Germany?

HASKIN: No, I came back to Hollywood. I was looking for a job, I think.

ADAMSON: How did you end up back in Germany again to direct CAPTAIN SINDBAD?

HASKIN: Well, the King Brothers and I ran afoul of each other. Leon Chooluck was with them as production manager, and I knew Leon. He suggested me and we had conferences, made a tentative deal, and then, at the last minute, Frank King started to give me a per-diem which wouldn't even keep me in a tent over there. After long argument, I said, "Well, forget it, I have been there before. I'll just go home, and read books, do something else." And I did. After about eight days Frank King said to Leon, "The guy must mean it." Leon said, "Of course he means it. He's in dead earnest." King says, "Well, O.K., give him what he wants." On ARMORED COMMAND, I had found out what things cost in Germany, and they were trying to chop me in half. (Laughs)

Anyhow, we went over to do CAPTAIN SINDBAD. I was assured that there were all kinds of facilities in the Bavaria studios, everything you wanted. I got there and it was absolutely Mack Sennett, 1917. Nothing there. One rear-projection machine, without even flame carbons, so the background was all-over blue. Their optical machine was not much. No modern facilities for special effects at all. I thought, "What the hell am I going to do?" So, having been pretty good at tricks in my youth as a cameraman, I decided to make all the effects in the camera. Now this was quite a decision to make. And I did. I had Lee Zavitts, from HIS MAJESTY O'KEEFE, and he is tops. He made the miniature dragon with nine heads that barked like a dog.

ADAMSON: Was that some kind of puppet or was it machine-powered?

HASKIN: No, it was on wires. It was a horrendous job to hide the wires, but we succeeded. There were a lot of sequences which eventually were cut out. I couldn't convince Frank King that you cannot fight with something invisible and get anything out of it on the screen. We had a whole big sequence that took weeks to shoot, of an arena, with Pete Armendariz fighting and killing an invisible monster.

ADAMSON: Like FORBIDDEN PLANET -- the footsteps in the sand.

HASKIN: Yes. It doesn't mean anything -- unless you've got an equal, at least, preferably a stronger, villain than your hero, but Frank King just wouldn't realize it.

ADAMSON: You shot a whole sequence of the arena, and it was cut out because it didn't work?

HASKIN: Yes, weeks of work, up on towers and big grand-stands full of people --

ADAMSON: It's still there in the film, but it's a very short fight.

HASKIN: Well in a thumbnail sort of a way. All the opening of the picture was re-cut and transformed into something else.

The thing that really stumped me was shooting the miniatures of Sindbad's ship -- in June, the tank was still eleven inches deep in ice. (Laughs) You can't sail a miniature ship on ice, so we had to wait until it finally thawed out. For the twister that is supposed to be the major part of that sequence, I had concocted an idea of a tank with front and back glass, filled with water with an impeller down at the bottom, and a valve to let the water out as the impeller set it whirling. Like a bottle turned upside down and spun, the water formed a perfect spiral cyclone effect. I intended to double it over the sea shots, even conceivably let Tommy Howard in London put them together later.

But it took so long for this tank to thaw out, that one day in June we were sitting on the border, with Frank King there, and my contract ran out. We still had all this crap to shoot. I said, "Well, what about it?" There was still ice on the damn tank.

ADAMSON: An exterior tank?

HASKIN: Yes.

ADAMSON: There was no way to heat it?

HASKIN: No. Too big. God. Half a block in size. He said, "Well, I tell you -- we'll settle it later." I said, "Do you want to give me a ticket, and I'll go home?" (Laughs) So he was a little panicked about that. We quickly ad-libbed a tentative deal. Finally, the ice broke up and we launched the ship, and started the wind machine. It was icy goddamn weather -- there was snow two feet high on the curbstones of Munich, in the middle of June! That's how cold a winter this was.

ADAMSON: Is this freak weather?

HASKIN: Well, not freak, particularly. It's cold up there so close to the Alps. We finally finished the ship shots. Then I started in to make the hurricane -- this water spout. So we filled the glass-sided tank with water. Lee Zavitts snapped on the impeller, and the water began to spiral. I got about eight frames of the most beautiful water spout you ever saw in your life. Then the pressure blew the glasses out of the box! (Laughs)

Well, this would take at least two weeks' work to put in new plastic or something, so we abandoned the whole thing. In the picture, there is no water spout. I went up to London and sketched out all the shots for Tommy Howard to fix up, which he didn't do. Whatever the reasons, the company finally arrived out at MGM with the picture.

ADAMSON: Tom Howard has a credit on the picture. Did he do the stuff you wanted him to do or did he do something else?

HASKIN: Well, the King Brothers are the weirdest outfit that ever tried to make movies. Anybody that's been with them has a scar that lasts him the rest of his life. They took over the show and made sweeping changes, such as swapping the last four reels with the first four reels -- all such little things! They re-cut the whole beginning -- into what? I don't know what the hell it means. They ordered Tommy Howard to matte out the ocean background of the ship shots. They wanted to have the rocks passing by, you know.

MGM Special Effects Department worked out the technique on paper and sent it to Howard. The work couldn't be done in America because of the tax situation. Anyhow, the King Brothers hacked here and there and changed continuity and what have you. It went on and it was a fairly substantial hit. It was known as tops of the MGM summer season. A Persian fairy tale! And I'm telling you, it was ad-lib all the way.

ADAMSON: You mean stuff was shot for one purpose and then used for something else?

HASKIN: Yes. The basic fairy tale was more or less preserved -- Guy Williams as Sindbad is in trouble with the

Rajah, and the Rajah cannot be killed because his heart has been removed to a tower up past all these terrible valleys of smokes and wolves and all these fantastic trials and tribulations. To kill the Rajah, you've got to go up in the tower, which is guarded by forces unknown, find the heart on its silk pillow, and stab it to death.

Sindbad sets out to do this. Guy Endore wrote the story and the screenplay, and it was later re-written in about a week by Frank King just before shooting.

ADAMSON: To effect an improvement?

HASKIN: To cut money out of the thing. But it was interesting to do -- a high challenge, I guarantee you. There were scenes of a dame who becomes small like a bird, and flies out through the window --

ADAMSON: Without her clothes on.

HASKIN: Yes. I remember a shot worth describing. Galgo, the court magician, is studying a big book of magic. He's got a tiny broom in his hand and he sweeps his arm with it to make it grow long, then sweeps it back to become normal again. During the preparation, an itinerant peddler went by with a small ocelot on a leash, and we hired it to put on Galgo's table, as set dressing, sitting on a stack of books.

ADAMSON: Yes, it's great. But that shot with the ocelot is not in the script?

HASKIN: No, no. No, it was an ad-lib. Frank King watches as Galgo sweeps his arm and it becomes long, and then sweeps it back into his sleeve. Now, Galgo is working out the technique by which he is going to reach his arm down the side of the castle into the king's quarters and steal the magic ring from his finger. (Laughs)

Frank says, "Hey -- why don't you have Galgo make the cat little?" I thought, I don't know. Why not? I said, "I think" -- this was early in the morning -- "about four o'clock this afternoon we can shoot."

I was using a big transmission mirror for most of these tricks. In other words, you shot through fifty percent and fifty percent reflected is from a right angle offstage -- so you can have action out here, see? Combined with action on the set. To explain the use of this simply, if I want the girl to become little -- I have a 100-foot dolly track offstage, at right angles. The girl is standing reflected in the mirror, seemingly talking to Galgo, who is being shot <u>through</u> the mirror in the set.

ADAMSON: Actually what the camera is recording is a <u>reflection</u> of her off to the side?

HASKIN: A reflection of her. It's equal in quality to Galgo through the mirror, and fitted to the proper size.

ADAMSON: Special effects done with mirrors!

HASKIN: Yes, of course. So to reduce the girl's size, we have her on a dolly of the 100-foot track. On cue, we start the automobile outside the stage, and -- ZOOM! -- the line attached to the dolly jerks her back, diminishing her rapidly. You cut to Galgo, and now you've got a little girl. You dissolve the tiny girl into a bird, and she flies out the window. Naturally, I've only described it simplistically; there's a lot of fitting to be done.

ADAMSON: Where does she have all the room to be dragged back without disturbing the background she's standing in front of?

HASKIN: Well, it's dark in the first place, but back there, on the wall of the stage, at the end of the dolly track, is a big painted backdrop of a portion of the set in exaggerated size blended to match into the composite set.

ADAMSON: So she's still in front of this background.

HASKIN: Yes. She's still in the set. That's what gives the illusion. You gauge the shot so that her feet remain on the same level in the frame -- only her body grows small.

Anyhow, this cat deal -- I have the cat on a dolly, exactly at the height of the top of the books he's supposed to be lying on. As the dolly recedes, in the reflection, he becomes a little tiny cat. The cat was beautiful. By luck only, the dolly move didn't alarm him. He even washed his face a little as he diminished. The tough part was lighting the cat's trajectory all smoothly. As he came back to normal size he gave a yawn. It was a tremendous bit of action. It took all day for one shot, because it started from nothing. Remember, there was not even a cat, originally. And it was all on the original negative in color. That's what is so fantastic about it. Having been Director of Special Effects for Warner Bros. for nine years, I had all these tricks at my fingertips -- it was just a matter of working out the mechanics. There were over 170 trick shots in the picture, all done in the camera.

ADAMSON: For CAPTAIN SINDBAD?

HASKIN: Yes. Our composite shots included straight shooting, reflected images from models and multiple exposures.

ADAMSON: So the ocelot shrinking was done in the camera.

HASKIN: Yes. Single take.

ADAMSON: That's great.

HASKIN: I dressed the table close to him with props, identifiable in size, so that he wouldn't look like he was dollying back -- he just got little.

ADAMSON: It's amazing that he didn't move.

HASKIN: Oh, yes. It was the greatest luck in the world. I just took the gamble the cat wouldn't jump down and savage somebody. It was a wild ocelot.

ADAMSON: Not trained?

HASKIN: Hell no -- liable to take a piece out of you!
(Laughs)

ADAMSON: (Laughs) How did the magician do all those scenes with him? Or was he mirrored in all those shots?

HASKIN: No, we had luck, that's all. Abe Sofaer, of course, is such a consummate actor -- he was Galgo, and he had magic, and why should he be afraid of wild animals! (Laughs) Abe was a great character. And Pete Armendariz -- he was a most enjoyable actor to work with.

Guy Williams got in a fight with the King Brothers over money. A big influence in casting Guy was that he is an excellent fencer. He expected an adjustment -- a fee to do the fencing himself. He did it on all the ZORRO series. "No, no," Frank King said, "that goes with the fee for the part." Guy said, "It's stunts. Hell, I might lose my eye. I'm going to get paid, or I won't do it." So it was an impasse. Guy said, "All right, I won't do it. Get a stuntman." They said, "All right. You don't do it." They sent over to London for Mark Evans' brother -- he was a fencing expert -- and he did the fencing. Well, this delayed it a lot.

ADAMSON: What did that cost the production, as opposed to what it would have cost to give Guy Williams what he wanted?

HASKIN: Yes, that's what I wondered. It doesn't make much sense. But it inhibited the continuity I wanted to do with the fencing, from close-up to action and all, without cuts. With a double, you've got to make cuts to close-ups of the principal.

Some of the effects were fantastic, really. They came off. A few of them didn't sell. But it was an interesting film to work on, like going back to the old silent days, like Leon Shamroy helping with the montage for WOLF'S CLOTHING, rewinding the film to the mark, watching the counter, putting it through again, time after time.

ADAMSON: Interesting. So is a lot of that stuff done in the camera -- like where the cyclone goes into the sea, and just at the point where it hits the water, there's this kind of splash?

HASKIN: Yes.

ADAMSON: That cyclone is not as good as what you described would have been, but --

HASKIN: Oh, no! I've fogotten what the hell that was -- I think it was a whirling bunch of cellophane strips that Lee Zavitts got together. It had no sinuous movement at all.

ADAMSON: No, it was a cartoon of a cyclone.

HASKIN: That film later came within a half inch of selling as a TV series -- SINDBAD or THE ADVENTURES OF SINDBAD. It was to be done in Munich. I would have been executive producer, and I had a hell of a deal with the King Brothers to do this TV series. I made a pilot at MGM for them, and used portions of the actual SINDBAD film to fill out the footage. The networks hassled for eight or nine months about whether they would or wouldn't buy it, and it went from CBS to NBC and ABC, till finally they cancelled out. I was all set to go. The Kings were, too. I could have got rich on that one, because I would have directed any amount of them I wanted to, for a set fee. They knew what I could do. (Laughs)

Frank used to stand around with his eyes bugging, along with our old cameraman, Eugen Schüfftan, in his eighties. Frank had found him in New York. He was supposed to be the daddy of all special effects -- yet he was agog the whole time on our picture. I had to light it and do all the special effects myself, (laughs) because Eugen just stood around in awe. Half the time the camera panned, his neck was in the shot! I put a guy with him to keep him out. (Laughs) He'd cackle, "Oh! I see what you're doing!! Heh, heh! Amazing, amazing!" He'd shuffle around in his Congress Gator shoes, climbing up and down the ship. I had to feel sorry for him.

ADAMSON: Was this the guy that created the Schufftan process?

HASKIN: Yes. The original.

ADAMSON: Which was with mirrors too, wasn't it? They scraped part of the mirror off --

HASKIN: Yes. It's funny, in 1929 I was in England. We sent over to UFA to put the top on a scene of Scotland Yard for a picture I was making with Herbert Wilcox. Schüfftan was the special effects wizard in UFA. And here in the late fifties Frank found him in New York, and hired him as a cameraman. Jesus. I almost dropped dead. Frank said, "Ah, he'll be fine, don't worry," chewing a cigar, and throwing it in the pocket of my chair. It was an experience even surpassing the one with Lesser on the TARZAN films.

ADAMSON: So Schüfftan was on SINDBAD --

HASKIN: Yes. He had done THE HUSTLER in New York with Jackie Gleason.

ADAMSON: As a cameraman?

HASKIN: Yes. And got an award for it. But I'm sure that all the New York cameramen that were also on it did the lighting and the panning and everything else. Because Schufftan was completely inept. Nothing against him -- he never was a production cameraman in the first place. So how could he have shot a black-and-white film called THE HUSTLER and gotten an award for it? It must have been shot by some of those good New York men, and they didn't get any credit for it.

ADAMSON: They were credited as camera operators.

HASKIN: Yes. Probably a good gaffer did the lighting, and away they went.

Guy Endore, our writer on SINDBAD, was very imaginative. He was a novelist -- he wrote scores of fairly successful novels, and he had a good flair for fairy stories.

I first went to Vienna to work with Herr and Frau Schlichting, the art directors on the film. They're a famous pair in Vienna. I worked with them at their atelier for a couple of weeks, running through the whole story and telling them what I was going to do with action and how much set I'd need, and so forth, because they were not as hip about settings for movies as much as they were good designers. They did create the palace and various other things, in fact, which they did beautifully.

ADAMSON: They did one sculpture which you actually centered on, to pan over and introduce the princess or something.

HASKIN: Yes. They had a good flair for that kind of thing. We were lucky, because it was all slapdash -- put together quick, cheap budget, ad-lib, done in the camera -- Jesus! The King Brothers should have such luck that I happened to be on the show.

ADAMSON: Is there any such place as Baristan, which is where it takes place?

HASKIN: No.

ADAMSON: Is that sort of Istanbul turned around or something?

HASKIN: Oh, something like that. Galgo -- they were all creations of Guy Endore's mind.

ADAMSON: Well, why don't we abandon all this crazy stuff and go on to ROBINSON CRUSOE ON MARS?

HASKIN: (Laughs) Yes. It's getting to be a saga of a loser! . . .

ADAMSON: You said before, it takes a certain personality to be able to direct.

HASKIN: Yes, yes. I often wonder if I ever had it, really. I could achieve fulfillment and great success on a film like ROBINSON CRUSOE ON MARS -- that was one of the most pleasant films. I laughed all the way through it, I had fun, everybody was congenial, because I was happy; there were no pressures. I went over, I think, $62,000 on a $1,000,000 budget, so the budget wasn't even a problem. And there wasn't a big bunch of egos to worry about -- there was Paul Mantee and a monkey, and Vic Lundin, a Tennesee mountain singer.

ADAMSON: Why was it that that worked out so well?

HASKIN: I guess, at that point, the Fates had decided to let up on me a little.

ADAMSON: (Laughs)!

HASKIN: It's about the only thing I can think of. I had been at Paramount and had directed films there. I had a reputation as the special effects director from THE WAR OF THE WORLDS, etc., and I had nothing to prove to anybody before or after. ROBINSON CRUSOE ON MARS was so obviously a director's tour de force, that there was nobody to interfere and tell me how to shoot it.

Mantee was practically an amateur and I didn't have Eleanor Parker or a lot of others who were pretty snotty, to worry about. I had thorough faith, as did my friend -- who did the special effects -- Larry Butler from Columbia, a terrific man. He swore "You've got a hit here, that's going to really go out and do a lot of things that you've been trying to do for yourself over the years." It might have, except that Paramount had it, and they didn't know what the hell to do with a picture of that kind, as they didn't with WAR OF THE WORLDS or those others. They could not sell an exploitation science fiction picture.

But to get back to ROBINSON CRUSOE ON MARS -- you asked why it was a happy film as far as I went. Not that I believe it's necessary to have a happy set. Jack Warner's credo was "Show me a happy set, and I'll show you a flop!" (Laughs) You know -- where everybody's laughing at each other's jokes. But it was a pleasant film, and it was fulfilling because the challenges were those you could figure out and meet, reverting almost to the feel you had on a camera -- that as a cameraman, you were challenged by this set, to light it and get the things out of it, and nobody did it but you.

There are many jobs in movies from which a director could derive his training which would be better than camera work. Cinematography is too all-absorbing. Later I thought I should have gone through editing. This is the real school to learn your number one responsibility as a director, where to put the camera when you shoot. That's you, nobody else. The actor can interfere with a performance -- he can take over his performance -- a hundred and one things can happen. But the one pure area of directing art is in formulating the shooting continuity. Hitchcock made his success in films that way. He'd go in his dressing room after rehearsal, make little sketches, and come out and give it to his assistant and say, "This is it. Shoot it any way you want." He'd practically be a spectator. He had started as art director. He made these little sketches, etc. His personal visualization is what made his films have class and penetration, because he knew where to put the camera. He knew how to mount suspense by the cuts he shot.

ADAMSON: That brings up two things. Do you know anything about Hitchcock and his use of drawings? He evolved into a method where the whole film was drawn out before they'd go on the set.

HASKIN: Well, sketch continuity of the scope, for instance, of a William Cameron Menzies production design, is a nice flossy luxury, but is not fundamentally sound. The sketch continuity that amounts to anything is what the director visualizes doing with his camera. I used to watch Lewis Milestone -- he would get his scene together and know what his shooting continuity was going to be, and then he would turn to this Russian kid, who was a pretty good artist, and he'd say, "All right, here's the shot. Now give me something exciting about this shot." Then the sketch continuity artist would embellish the viewpoint that Milestone had already picked. Not that Milestone was such a good man at shooting continuity. He'd always throw in these damn naked reverses, with no excuses for them. Suddenly everybody's jumping to the opposite side of the screen, because you don't notice background enough to be able to tell what is happening.

ADAMSON: Is that what you call it, a naked reverse? 180 degrees?

HASKIN: Yes, well, if you've got a railroad train coming at the camera, you can make a nice 180 and see it going away, and you've got some excitement. But for people standing, jawing with each other, if suddenly they leap -- WHIZZ! -- you've got to have an action that spurs the reverse. When three guys are standing here, if one guy whirls and walks back, you can go right to a reverse with him coming into camera -- watching his movement takes your eye away from all the leaping geography.

Remember that, philosophically, the director is a storyteller. He's got to tell a story without making the audience conscious that he's in there with more damn mechanics than it takes to put up the Empire State Building. . . .

During the production, the director is the only audience the actor will ever see. His approval is the thunderous applause of the audience; and if he sneers, the audience has given a boo. It's an oversimplification, but he is the surrogate audience for the cast.

ADAMSON: That's true. The director takes the audience's place during production.

HASKIN: And more than that. Because the actor, if he ever does go to see his film at a theatre -- it was made so far in the past, a year and a half ago or more -- that he can't even recall what he put together to make his scenes work. But when he's on the set, the director is the one who pulls certain strings and pushes a button and gets him to a dramatic level -- influencing him to get out of himself enough to give a good performance. He can look to the director and the director will nod, and the two of them will form that priceless rapport that in theatre becomes the single unit: audience/actor, caught up in the emotion of the scene. This is entertainment -- the evocation of emotions and mutual participation. The actor and the director have become one entity.

It was a hell of a job on TREASURE ISLAND. I had to become one with Bob Newton as Long John Silver. I could actually out-ham the ham, which helped a lot because he'd look at me and say, "Holy Christ, I'd better cool it off a bit!"

But back to ROBINSON CRUSOE ON MARS. I won't spend much time on the weird way Paramount acquired the story, because it's too obviously proof that the Mad Hatter runs the movie business. It was bought in England, as a treatment by Ib Melchior. Dancing girls on Mars, practically -- that type of thing. It had the theme of Robinson Crusoe, a man marooned in a hostile environment. The Crusoe figure on Mars encountered more monsters than there ever existed in science fiction, including man-eating fish. Behind every rock, there was Spiderman, or Wolfman -- just a conglomeration of crap from all the monster films ever made.

Somebody must have read it in London, or bought the idea from Ib in some pub, and then shipped it over to New York. Here I am telling it, when I said I wouldn't! The manner of its arriving must have hinted that it was important, that London approved it and wanted it made. Nobody even opened the cover in New York, but the order was given: "Send it to the Coast. Mark it 'shoot.' But low budget."

So it arrived out on the Coast, and they took it as the word of God that London and New York wanted this thing made. They hired Aubrey Schenck, the producer, to get a screenplay together and make it. Aubrey and I knew each other from previous meetings on various projects. He knew that I'd made WAR OF THE WORLDS at Paramount, and he called me and asked me to come in. I read the treatment and almost fainted.

I said, "Aubrey, this is a real piece of drech. Anything like this, in this day and age, would not make the Saturday kids' matinees. Let's try to put some dignity in it, and do what I believe is the key to successful science fiction today, which is get as close to scientific fact as you possibly can, and get real believable, credible incidents. First, let's make Mars a dead planet, no life at all." By that time Death Valley was being considered as the setting. "We'll pick every weed and avoid every semblance of earthlike erosion."

Well, we got John C. Higgins, a writer, and he and I sat down and wrote this bloody thing. We preserved a certain amount of scientific integrity, with a NASA gravity probe around Mars, from which an astronaut bails out.

We made exploratory trips into Death Valley, and I conceived a key to credible verisimilitude that it was another planet. I would abandon shots from the valleys, make them from up on the ridges. Death Valley had been seen in hundreds of Westerns, but they were all shot from the bottoms of the canyons, because that's where horses could gallop through. On the top of these weird-looking ridges of marshmallow sands, the vista was something else. It looked like another planet --

certainly not Death Valley. Additionally, I conceived making the blue skies red -- which later scientific knowledge proved to be right. The sky is red on Mars. These changes made it believable, that we were in an alien environment.

ADAMSON: Could you explain optically how this worked?

HASKIN: Well, it was wintertime, and the skies were deep blue. They formed a perfect traveling matte, in a great many instances. Barring that, some scenes were put through optically, frame by frame, matting out the sky.

So we established ourselves in a hotel up there and went to work. It became spontaneous, the shooting of this film, because there's only one person in the whole show for reels and reels. You have no cutaways, except to his viewpoint, and then you come back to him.

Now his progress from shot to shot must be continuous -- no jump cuts or what have you, or you lose your reality. I found that in order to believe the action, without having a lot of dialogue to describe it, I had to get into very close inserts. If our astronaut was going to turn a valve on, I would move in to where the camera showed only the fingernails of his thumb and forefinger, and the valve handle -- then he turns it from on to off, or vice versa, so the audience knows what is going on. It was quite a challenge.

In Death Valley, we proposed removing all the weeds. The Ranger disagreed. They were worthless little weeds, but he said, "You are to leave the environment just as it is." So we would wait till he was out of the way, and then the prop man would quickly yank them out. We also used that defunct volcanic crater.

Zabriskie Point was the central location. Moving Paul Mantee around was very difficult, because of the crinkly, slidey nature of the ground, nothing solid underfoot. Sometimes he'd sink clear up to his hip, when he'd step off of something. For his pressure suit, we'd picked a black shiny material. Unfortunately it kept breaking open at the ass. I'd get one take and -- Boom!

-- put him in a new suit. But Paul was wonderful with his patience -- he's magnificent in the film.

It took nearly an hour to change costume to make even a walk-through shot. In the beginning he wore his helmet, had as back-pack this omni-com communicator, wore gloves, and all the other instruments and junk. Then he's got to walk over the ridge and down the slope and exit off left. And he gets halfway up the ridge and his ass breaks out. You see what we were up against. We had to change costume -- another hour to take all that stuff off and put it back on. It was a real nerve test. But it was a good natured crew. Winnie Hoch was the cameraman. Being a scientist, he maintained scientific detachment. And Aubrey -- it wasn't his money making the picture, so he was happy.

ADAMSON: Was he in Death Valley with you?

HASKIN: Yes. We worked like buggery, I tell you.

ADAMSON: And you didn't have any problem with him?

HASKIN: Oh, no. No. We were good friends, and he was not an interferer. He delegated the job of directing to the director -- in the proper sense. It was a good relationship. Very rare, I have news for you.

ADAMSON: Now some of this stuff was designed by Albert Nozaki who had worked on WAR OF THE WORLDS. Is that right?

HASKIN: Yes. Al, a Japanese American, at this time, tragically, was going blind, but he did work on the vehicle, which was a very highly sophisticated modern type of space vehicle. He since has gone completely blind. He is a genius -- he was the designer of the original invading flying saucers for WAR OF THE WORLDS, and at that time was greatly involved with the settings. But it was Arthur Lonergan on ROBINSON CRUSOE

ON MARS -- Arthur Lonergan had done the big MGM film, FORBIDDEN PLANET, and was tops at that type of thing. We got a little bit tricky in the cave -- the cave shelter that Paul lived in.

ADAMSON: Wasn't that a set?

HASKIN: Yes, it was a set, but it was difficult to move around in, and the removable parts were so heavy and difficult to take out that generally I compromised the shot and left them in. (Laughs)

I can't think of any other film I've made, unless it was WAR OF THE WORLDS -- where I had such complete autonomy, and was alone on the set, all the time -- that I had as much genuine pleasure and fulfillment from as ROBINSON CRUSOE ON MARS. It was as fulfilling as cinematography had ever been. Everything I set out to do, I accomplished as well as one possibly could. And again, my friend Larry Butler, who did all the special effects on it, and I, were sure we had a hit of minor proportions. But once it was finished, it was in the Paramount inventory and as usual it escaped, it wasn't released. They just handed it to Charlie Boasberg, the sales manager, who never saw it at all. He put out some key 24-sheets with monsters being held off by weapons that were never in the picture. Geez, you can't believe some people.

ADAMSON: What was the title you wanted?

HASKIN: I wanted GRAVITY PROBE ONE: MARS (in red). It was an interesting idea, and it would have made it, changed the whole aura of the film, but Boasberg said, "Oh, they'll think it's a dock-a-mentary! We don't want a dock-a-mentary. This is a regular movie." He never saw it, he didn't know what was in it. I'm sure it would have been better off if people thought it was a documentary, than having it released with this comic strip title, ROBINSON CRUSOE ON MARS. It was the only thing of Ib Melchior's that remained in the picture. The only single thing.

ADAMSON: (Laughs) Was the main character's name Robin in Melchior's script?

HASKIN: Yes, yes. It was that corny.

Anyhow, Higgins and I got along beautifully. Higgins' only weakness was that he was a rock freak. He had a power saw at home and he'd cut and polish these rocks and make tables out of them. He knew every variety of rock that God ever created on earth. He'd get going with his typewriter, describing some of these formations on Mars, and he'd write two pages of rock data (laughs) -- beautiful essays on rock! So I let him go, what the hell's the difference? Whatever rocks your boat, I say!

ADAMSON: None of which ended up in the film.

HASKIN: No, no, no.

ADAMSON: Now, Winton Hoch knew something about Death Valley?

HASKIN: Yes. Winton was basically a scientist. I first met him years previously, when he was doing aerial camerawork as a specialty, on CAPTAINS OF THE CLOUDS, in Canada. Down through the years we had become good friends. He was suggested as cameraman, he was free, and he was good with color. Actually, he was better than most with color. So he was assigned to the film, and I had great pleasure in working with him. He had a quiet detachment of manner -- he had a lot of answers to everything, and a catholic interest in everything that's material, or immaterial, I guess, on or off the earth. He was also helpful in divining which of those funny-looking stripes in Death Valley were made by water erosion, telltale signs of Earth we were trying to avoid. We could accept wind erosion, but not water erosion. He could quickly tell you what the strata of the rock were caused by and so forth.

ADAMSON: That's interesting. While you were tearing up the weeds, how did you avoid all those footprints in the sand?

HASKIN: The soil is hard, mostly, where the weeds grow.

ADAMSON: But didn't you have footprints-in-the-sand problems? What if you had to take a scene twice?

HASKIN: We'd have to sweep it. Or pick a new spot. The one scene that I really tried to duplicate from the <u>Robinson Crusoe</u> story for a thrill is the one where he has conquered everything, and he's living off the fat of the land and has a sunshade, and a goat and a dog, and what have you, and he's strolling his domain down the beach. Suddenly, he looks down, and there's a big footprint. (Laughs) And he damn near poops in his pants. You remember that from the original <u>Robinson Crusoe</u>? Well, I tried to re-create this as follows: I picked a spot with some weird looking humps of ashes, about as high as, or a little bit bigger than, a chair. The astronaut is strolling through with the monkey on his shoulder. He notices a strange, ornament-like rock on top of one of these knolls, and he ponders. "That's odd, doesn't seem natural." It was just kind of an elongated, egg-shaped rock stuck on top of the hump.

ADAMSON: It was up there already?

HASKIN: Yes. He tries to move the rock a little, and wonders how it could have got there, how it could have remained there with the winds blowing constantly. Then he starts digging in the sand close to the monument. Suddenly he uncovers a bone -- a forearm, and hand of a human skeleton!

Later, he goes to find his astronaut companion, who bailed out of the ship after he did. He crosses a mountain range, spots the capsule by its reflection, rushes down, calls -- "Hey, Mac! Mac!" -- runs across the valley, gets up to where he sees it. We cut to Mac's hand, dead! He buries his friend and afterwards, there's the suspense scene of him seeing something moving, thinking it's an alien creature, firing a shot at it -- at which point his little monkey jumps up chattering. This scene is part of his conditioning to the raw atmosphere of Mars -- he starts back and he almost does not make it. His own oxygen tank is empty. Finally, he sees the monkey's still got his little oxygen tank, he takes it, and shares it with the monkey. The two make it back to the cave, where again he almost passes out. At that point he discovers oxygen coming out of the rocks. You see, the story of Robinson Crusoe is that of a man able to conquer a hostile environment, but with success, finally coming face to face with his own loneliness. That, he cannot handle. A good theme.

Anyway, ROBINSON CRUSOE ON MARS had pretty solid success, with frequent TV runs. I often wonder why it isn't worthy of re-issue, because it is a gorgeous film. The color is absolutely startling.

ADAMSON: Yes. There's a Technicolor consultant credited on the thing -- was he a latter-day version of Natalie Kalmus?

HASKIN: I don't know. Certainly nobody helped Winnie Hoch with the color.

ADAMSON: Richard Mueller is the name in the credits.

HASKIN: Well, he might have been technically assigned to it, but he wasn't on the picture that I know of. Winnie Hoch was the original Technicolor technician. He knew more about color than Kalmus did. Really.

ADAMSON: What about Farciot Eduoart?

HASKIN: Well, in lieu of spending a couple more days way in the canyon where Paul Mantee is crossing the mountain ridge, I shot some still slides of locales, and we made projection shots out of them later. Farciot got his little slide projector and tested them for days and days, and we eventually shot them.

(Laughs) They're not too good, but they filled the gap in the story.

ADAMSON: I was reminded of 2001, which would mean that 2001 would have somehow been influenced by your picture. I noticed that when you had the ships flying around, you cut to their red sensors -- you had these flash cuts, cutting in tighter and tighter -- which was what was picking up Friday's bracelet. That was used in 2001, I think.

Another thing that he (Kubrick) used was a shot that you had used in CONQUEST OF SPACE and also in ROBINSON CRUSOE ON MARS, which was a guy on a ship standing at a 90-degree angle to another guy just because the gravity was funny.

HASKIN: I delivered Mantee upside down into the cockpit of the space vehicle, with Adam West seated at the controls. Mantee enters through a chute from the other portion of the ship. We laced Mantee onto a shuffleboard, so that only the top of his body was free, and put him at this odd angle, floating, like he was weightless. They discuss what they're going to have for dinner. (Laughs)

ADAMSON: I thought it was an effective kind of angle in terms of making the extraordinary seem ordinary -- they've obviously done this a million times, and we've never seen anything like that before. They just go about like it's an everyday thing.

Could you talk about AFFAIR IN SUMATRA?

HASKIN: That was for the SCREEN DIRECTORS PLAYHOUSE, a prestige series at the time, which opened on the back of the man in the director's chair. He turns to the camera and tells you how wonderful he is, and then the picture follows. The one I made was with Rita Gam and Ralph Bellamy, as I remember -- nicely acted, written by a friend of mine, Mike Fessier.

AFFAIR IN SUMATRA was semi-Noel Coward in the jungle. (Laughs)

ADAMSON: So you were filmed in the beginning of AFFAIR IN SUMATRA? Talking about your career?

HASKIN: Yes. About this film, particularly.

ADAMSON: Now, I don't know if these various other things on my list are the titles of TV series or the titles of episodes.

HASKIN: I don't know either. There are a lot of missing links here. The first TV series I worked on of any duration was MEET McGRAW, with Frank Lovejoy, which was highly stylized. It was of some importance at the time. Lovejoy was a kind of white knight solving acute problems and then walking off into the sunset. He was a hell of an actor.

This series had a distinctive style, and it was the one on which I learned the necessary transition from feature directing to TV, which is a very tough way to go. You learn if you're going to direct TV, or else. It consists of tearing down your restraint as a feature film director, becoming an exhibitionist, using many things you wouldn't, in good taste, use in a feature, but which are routine in TV.

You stylize things. People do not face each other when they talk dramatically to each other, they both look over the left shoulder in the camera off into space, so that you've got two faces, one behind the other. There are all these tricks that have to be done -- you make violent zooms to look through a hole and discover something dramatic -- all of which is pure exhibitionism.

I made the transition and became a good TV director. I climaxed my career on TV with the series OUTER LIMITS. I was aide to Joe Stefano, the producer, and also directed half a dozen of them. Unfortunately, the damn series was cancelled because of considerations quite apart from the quality of the work, or even the cost of the films, although they kept running over budget. I was the only one who consistently made any of them for anywhere near the budget, or on time, either.

ADAMSON: What was the time and the budget?

HASKIN: Well, the time was six or seven days, and I've forgotten the budget figure -- it's irrelevant now in this day of the dollar being worth a nickel and who knows what cost means -- but they were moderately priced, saddled with a figure that was really too low. Even half again of the budget, which is what Stefano wanted, wouldn't have sufficed, because most of the directors would come in and just fool around, and run ten, twelve days' schedule. Two or three times the budget.

But I enjoyed that series very much. I was in charge of designing the monsters. A great deal of the inner planning of the show was in my hands. I supervised the special effects, which were very important.

It got to the point where the teenagers had begun to talk back to the monsters on the tube -- they'd whoop and holler when a new weirdo would show up -- which meant complete success. That show could have gone on and become a very important milestone, much more so than the Rod Serling things -- NIGHT GALLERY, TWILIGHT ZONE, and so forth. OUTER LIMITS had a different approach. It was much more visual, less theatrical, and therefore, for what it was supposed to be, it was much more honest, I thought. And they were damn well done. God. They used the very best players in town.

ADAMSON: Why did it die?

HASKIN: Well, if you want to know the nitty gritty of pure paranoia again! (Laughs) Joe Stefano was a classy guy. He was a hell of a fine writer, a well-educated Ivy Leaguer. He redecorated his offices in fine style and worked like a sonuvabitch. He would rewrite every script. He had style, and it showed. The quality was his entirely. But he had an annoying habit of receiving communiqués from the network censor, reading them with interest, and dropping them in the wastebasket. (Laughs) He knew, as a smart professional, that what they were complaining about was not in any way ever going to show on the film to offend anybody, because it just wouldn't play that way. But this of course offended the ogre -- the censor -- so the hatchet work started.

It came renewal time, and the network informed the executive producer, Leslie Stevens, that they would renew, but without Stefano. Well, Stefano was the series. Leslie Stevens had directed a couple, but he hadn't anything to do much with planning the basic thrust, the whole artistic integrity of the thing. So Stevens had to surrender to this edict, and they brought in Ben Brady -- who had killed many a good show in the history of TV. He was known as Guillotine Charlie around town. Among his notches: PERRY MASON, and RAWHIDE for MGM, with Clint Eastwood and Eric Fleming. That was a pretty heavy show to axe, but they managed it. (Laughs) And he did it to OUTER LIMITS -- in eighteen episodes. He killed it.

ADAMSON: Did it die at the end of its second season?

HASKIN: Yes, yes. It was not produced for the third season.

ADAMSON: So there can't be too many of them --

HASKIN: I think twenty-six the first year, and about eighteen or nineteen the second year, that's all. They became classics. They run and re-run, they're running right now. Amazing. I got residuals out of that damn show like you would never believe, and to the penny, and right promptly. I got all five residuals for domestic run, and I got residuals even for foreign sales.

I felt very badly about the loss of Stefano from the scene, because I knew what it would mean. Brady, to give him his due, was just not an inspired producer. The network had him on their hands with a contract of some kind, and with nothing to do, so along comes this series with no producer -- what do they do? Move him in. What the hell does he know about OUTER LIMITS? Doesn't matter. He's a "producer." This is the executive thinking of TV. I did encounter some interesting people during the time the series was in production.

I had Bob Culp, one of the greatest actors in TV. He hasn't ever become a big picture star, but he certainly had a flair. He was in ARCHITECTS OF FEAR and DEMON WITH A GLASS HAND, which I directed. FEASIBILITY STUDY I did with Sam Wanamaker. Geraldine Brooks was in ARCHITECTS OF FEAR. She's since deceased. TWO DAYS OF THE DRAGON was with Sidney Blackmer -- it was a hell of a good show, really.

ADAMSON: That was a little bit like INVASION OF THE BODY SNATCHERS, with duplicates taking over people ...

HASKIN: Yes. We made it cheaply and quickly. I thought it was quite good. I loved working with Blackmer. BEHOLD ECK was a silly thing.

ADAMSON: That was the 2-dimensional creature that had come into the 3-dimensional world. Peter Lind Hayes goes through a lot of the picture with his glasses on his forehead, leaving a different pair of glasses on his eyes -- it's kind of funny. Tell me a little bit about DEMON WITH A GLASS HAND.

HASKIN: DEMON WITH A GLASS HAND was made in seven working nights, at the Bradbury Building on lower Broadway, Los Angeles. We couldn't begin until it was dark, because the roof of the place is glass. Otherwise we could have made some good time. We had to wait until about eight o'clock at night when it was real black up there in order to shoot.

ADAMSON: Did you work all night then?

HASKIN: Yes.

ADAMSON: Was that time and a half?

HASKIN: No, we switched our calls to night and dismissed in the morning. Of course, we got indigestion, eating in those beaneries around there. But that is a landmark, that old building, and it's very weird with all the iron scroll work and the outdoor lift in the center of the plaza and that sort of thing. It became part of the environment of our weird story of a guy from some outer galaxy or somewhere.

What the hell he was going to do, I guess, was destroy the earth. I don't remember what his mission was. This was played by Culp, and he was actually a robot. We gave him a very intricate hand, manufactured of glass, with glass gears -- a highly complex piece of machinery. Then there was a place in his belly he rips open later, showing that his heart was just a big bunch of springs and gears. (Laughs)

ADAMSON: Like clockwork.

HASKIN: Yes. And damned if I can remember what the girl's name was originally who turned up in my karma as up for the part in DEMON WITH A GLASS HAND. She's the one in LITTLE SAVAGE who got bounced. Immediately, in the spirit of retribution or what have you, I cast her. Besides, she's a hell of an actress. She meanwhile had taken the last name of the dame who had done her out of the role in LITTLE SAVAGE -- Martel. She became Arline Martel.

ADAMSON: Why?

HASKIN: Oh, self-punishment or something like that. She's a weird kind of person. As you can see in the show. (Laughs)

Then I had my old friend Abe Sofaer whom I used in every film I possibly could. I used him in CAPTAIN SINDBAD in Munich as Galgo, the magician, I used him as the witch doctor in HIS MAJESTY O'KEEFE, and I used him as some weirdo in

DEMON WITH A GLASS HAND. I used him in several other films also. He's a great actor. He came over from England, from rep over there, Shakespeare, and the BBC. He was cast in THE ROBE as one of the senators.

That was a combination in Munich at the Ambassador Hotel -- the two people most unlikely to become friends: Abe Sofaer, old line English repertory player who bleeds only theatre; and Pedro Armendariz, wildcat Mexican star. (Laughs) Pedro was utterly fascinated with Abe's boring stories -- Abe could absolutely bore you to sobs. But to Pedro it was the most fascinating thing he'd ever heard. He even invited Abe to his home in Mexico City to stay as long as he wished. I thought -- Geez, this must never happen; Pedro'll shoot him after a week. I loved Abe, but Jesus, he was a bore. But not to Pedro! (Laughs)

ADAMSON: (Laughs) You liked Abe as an actor?

HASKIN: Yes. Oh, he was a tremendous actor, a terrific actor. But he'd tell these damn long-winded stories about repertory, some play he'd done, and what some actor said to him, and everybody'd be hurrying through dinner, while Pedro would sit there absolutely fascinated. (Laughs) I'd much rather listen to Pedro's stories about shooting up people at his parties in Mexico. (Laughs) He was a real wildman.

ADAMSON: In DEMON WITH A GLASS HAND, did you pretty much shoot the script as it was written? With no interference from producers?

HASKIN: No, there was no producer interference on the OUTER LIMITS series.

ADAMSON: Presumably this was under Stefano's reign.

HASKIN: Yes. Stefano was an astounding character for a movie producer, really. He would accord you respect as if you were the greatest director in the world. He gave any director he hired complete respect and complete autonomy over making the film. Naturally, ordinary changes and defects of environment, you have to accept and revise during the shooting. Culp was quite resourceful about business for the things he had to do. He would like to get up in a corner and dive out of it into the camera, and various things like that for shock effect. Culp was the consummate TV actor. As I mentioned, in accommodating yourself to direct TV you have to discard half of your rules of good taste you use as a film director. Culp was thoroughly aware of that. All his effects were theatrical -- he'd deliver himself with a bang whenever he came on, and do all those goddamn things to which you would ordinarily say, "Hey, wait a minute!"

ADAMSON: I was struck in the OUTER LIMITS episodes of yours that I've seen, by all the male/female relationships. They seem to be incredibly interesting, sometimes beyond what was there on the page.

HASKIN: Part of my concept of science fiction. This warmth between them was added verisimilitude. I injected those things into them. Particularly in ARCHITECTS OF FEAR.

ADAMSON: Yes!

HASKIN: I concocted the almost maudlin relationship of Gerry Brooks and Culp out of whole cloth. The little love scene they had, minor in importance, I developed into an honest, warm thing, moving the camera around the set to afford different vistas. Making it about nothing except love and affection. I developed a sort of haunting dimension of tragedy, almost, when later she sees him as the critter we called Willy Lumplump. You have to take such scenes completely seriously to get that kind of a dimension, and I just whipped everybody up and got some good results out of it, I thought.

ADAMSON: Yes.

HASKIN: I did not believe the story a bit when I first read it. I thought -- Oh Jesus, this is a real comic strip. The only way they could save the world was by posing an outer space threat to it, and people would come back together, instead of firing at each other with one of these damn atom bombs. It was very far-fetched, but that was the kind of series it was. It's like H. G. Wells says -- "First you give them the weenie and they swallow that, then you play the rest like the word of God." Absolutely. First you say, "A lot of flying saucers are invading from Mars." If they believe that, they're stuck. "Stick around, buddy, and we're going to be just as realistic as the Battle of the Marne." This is the key to good science fiction.

ADAMSON: It also worked that way in terms of the male/female relationship in BEHOLD ECK -- the Peter Lind Hayes episode. The girl was just a secretary, but she kind of figures she's his compatriot.

HASKIN: Yes. I thought that most of the OUTER LIMITS were rather cold and professional in concept. They did not have much humanity. I thought any little effort I could make to bring some recognizable human emotion into them, the better they would be. I had complete freedom to develop all such dimensions, as did all the directors.

I had a lot of fun with that series. I literally drew the original drawings of all these monsters in charcoal on a big pad. One of the most interesting monsters was Willy Lumplump in ARCHITECTS OF FEAR, I thought. He was Chicken Little and a lot of things. (Laughs) I hired a guy named Janos Prohoska who came into my office one day. He was a Hungarian acrobat who had an 8 x 10 glossy still picture of himself in which there was a table, a beer bottle, and him with one finger in the neck of the beer bottle, upside down, supporting himself with his finger, with his feet in the air. Well, this takes quite a bit of balance. I thought, Jesus, a guy who can do that has got some coordination. With these monsters, you've got to have somebody in them to move them, so I hired this guy Prohoska to work the monster on ARCHITECTS OF FEAR.

The way it turned out, with the chicken feet and all -- it took an acrobat to get inside it and make it walk! (Laughs) Even

Janos couldn't give it any speed, but he managed to move around. We hired him to work all the monsters after that. Later, he became Andy Williams' bear. Finally, he was killed in a plane accident -- damn shame. He was a nice little guy.

ADAMSON: I was curious what the gibbering little thing was in ARCHITECTS OF FEAR that was supposed to be the example of what Robert Culp was going to be. Was that a monkey in a suit? It was some bizarre little thing that kept hopping around. Was it something you just made up?

HASKIN: Yes. I added several such effects. You have to be real ingenious on a hot scare-show like that, to guide the audience to what they're expected to do, so you in effect become the surrogate audience yourself when you're planning the effects, and say, "Well, what the hell would scare *me* most? The first sight of Willy? Yeah, well, that would, sure -- " But I had long ago learned that the preliminaries to an audience shock are as important, if not more even, than the actual shock itself.

It's the old principle of the great act that couldn't make it in the circus -- the guy in an eighty-foot tower who would jump off into a spittoon. It never got over, because the minute he took off, everybody'd blink and he'd be in the spittoon and out. (Laughs) You've got to give them a chance to quiver first, and finally deliver the hammer over the head.

So I got a thought -- not only would humans be scared, but animals would also, so I figured out the hunting party that first discovered Willy Lumplump -- the guys have been duck hunting, and they're walking back through the woods. They've got a beautiful setter, a nice dog, and the dog hears something and runs into the bushes to investigate. Suddenly he barks, and in a panic, runs out of there. Which is enough to give you a bit of a creep. What the hell would scare a dog like that? Well, Willy's in there. So it all added up to pretty good scare stuff.

ADAMSON: Do you remember anything about Jim Danforth? Didn't he work on some of those OUTER LIMITS in special effects?

HASKIN: Oh, yes. We operated with the Projects Unlimited outfit. I forget all their names, but Jim was over there, and he was more or less the coordinator with the monsters, I think -- in the manufacture. The beneficent hand of George Pal was underneath somewhere; he invested the money to get Projects Unlimited going, I think.

ADAMSON: Is that how you got to be associate producer on the show?

HASKIN: Not necessarily. I had a track record of special effects, and knew all the special effects companies around town -- Larry Butler and all these characters -- and knew what they specialized in and what they were best at, so that I could put this one on that show, and that one on this show, and so forth.

I, however, did not take screen credit for it, because long since I had come to believe what Hal Wallis had told me: "I never trust a one man band. If you're going to be a director, don't try to be a director-writer, a director-producer, or this-that-and-the-other." It made sense.

ADAMSON: Why?

HASKIN: Directing is an all-consuming profession, believe me. If you get to the point where you really know what you're doing, and you're giving it a class job, you haven't got time for all this other crap. I'm not mentioning my opinion of what the art of producing is, in movies -- I've never found out yet, what the hell it is -- but writing is another art, entirely. Writing is a different means of telling a story, completely foreign to the whole mentality and decision-making process that a director has to exercise in telling the story for a visual/audible combination medium. One director out of twenty understands what the hell the full extent of this medium is. He may be great on dialogue, which is enough to carry him; he may be great on camera movement, and that's enough to carry him. To become a consummate, fully rounded director as a storyteller, in a medium that almost re-defines the story because of the way you have to tell it -- this is something, you know. Then, if you start futzing around trying to put this all on paper, it's too much for one man, for one mind.

The writer writes a story, and explains with full subtlety all the nuances and all the insights, and all the environmental auras and effects and so forth -- it can be written as prose as far as I'm concerned. I don't want a screenplay writer trying to tell me how to break up a scene, but if it's a luxury he enjoys -- as long as he puts in the information I want to know about the scene, it's all right. Of course, breakup came in with budgets and schedules. They're tools of the production department.

Half or more of the directors are temperamentally unqualified to be directors -- it's good money, that's one reason they have for being directors. The other is they've got a batch of little tricks that work, and so they're successful, because of a lot of reasons that have nothing to do with being qualified to be a director. It also gives the man awesome power.

The producer represents a lot of authority, but the director has the most powerful position, particularly over the artistic decisions. Therefore, he's subject to the envy of all the whole phony money hierarchy that is laid on top of a picture effort. Any guy up there who sees everybody rushing to the director as the important guy, has got to be envious.

"Directors, aw, you can hire them in bunches like bananas!" Warner used to say. "I directed the whole of Africa on Stage 10." He did -- a serial. (Laughs) Producers have to tear the director down, and they have to assume command of functions which will generate artistic acclaim for themselves. Although they may have not one talent in their goddamn skin, they've got to get some of that admiration -- so that all the sycophants who gather in the lobby at a preview rush up to them, not that bum the director.

ADAMSON: Isn't that a good argument for a director doing his own producing, though?

HASKIN: . It is, but how can he do it? You can't just walk out and say, "I'm going to produce this." I tried for years, never could get four dollars together to produce a picture.

ADAMSON: Because you hadn't produced one already.

HASKIN: Actually, I've produced a lot of them, but not officially. I produced one entirely in Munich: ARMORED COMMAND. The so-called producer wasn't even on the set, he was up learning how to ski at Kitzbühel. I produced WARPATH -- Nat Holt would hand the scenes from the script back to me and say, "Well, you know more about this than I do. Go ahead and do it your way." But that wasn't what it said on the screen. I produced TREASURE ISLAND, if you want to know the truth. Perce Pearce was around, but not on the set after I ran him off. (Laughs)

ADAMSON: Is it true that you did the pilot to STAR TREK?

HASKIN: No, I didn't do the pilot for STAR TREK. (Gene) Roddenberry, who had the idea, who eventually formulated the whole series, called me. He knew my reputation as a special effects expert and a director of science fiction, and asked me if I would like to be advisor in the preparation. He didn't have any staff or anything together at the time. I said, "Yes, sure. Why not? What you need on one of these shows, to ramrod them through, is an understanding person who knows when to say -- 'Take all the time you want' -- or if you're noodling, say -- 'Cut it out and let's get going.'"

Bobby Justman and Lee Katzin, who had alternated as assistant directors on OUTER LIMITS were both sharp guys. So I told Roddenberry he needed Justman, and he put him on. Justman was on for the pilot, and then he went to producing himself. I was there also. I supervised the planning of special effects, worked with NBC color people, and was sort of the standby expert -- I did not have any further function than that.

I don't think I had screen credit, because I didn't want screen credits that didn't say "Directed by -- ." (Laughs) So I was on it two or three months, got some good money out of it, and had a lot of fun.

ADAMSON: The pilot?

HASKIN: Yes. We made it in the De Mille Studios. It was with Jeff Hunter and Susan Oliver. We had a lot of good actors. Bob Butler directed it, and did a hell of a good job. It was beautifully made. What happened between that and the purchase of the series, I don't know. In the warfare of selling it to a network, a great deal of the original excellence was lopped off, I thought. It was pretty well made later, but nothing near the class of the original pilot film, because the standards were lower. They compromised in every direction. Jeff Hunter, who was playing the guy -- I didn't think he was a ball of fire anyhow.

Like OUTER LIMITS, it fought through a certain hit and miss audience interest, and then took off. It didn't really go to town the first half season, but by fidelity to the concept and continued exposure of the Mr. Spock character with the phony ears -- Leonard Nimoy -- and so forth, it caught on. The audience began to show an interest in the weirdos -- that's what the kids liked. Teenage kids become aficionados. Geez, it's a classic now.

Roddenberry supervised all the stories for a while, like Stefano did, and Roddenberry was a class concept man. He was never the writer Stefano was, but he had good concepts -- he avoided the comic strip kind of thinking that goes with a great deal of this stuff.

ADAMSON: I always had the feeling with OUTER LIMITS and STAR TREK, that they were fighting an uphill battle, because science fiction at that time, compared to now, just had no prestige -- it was just not considered to be a hot item.

HASKIN: No. Audience acceptance was indifferent, during all the science fiction films I made.

ADAMSON: But you told an interviewer once that you didn't care that much about science fiction.

HASKIN: I never did. It was a very difficult matter to pump yourself up to completely dedicated belief in the material, and unless you did, you were out of luck if you really wanted to make it believable. You take CLOSE ENCOUNTERS OF THE THIRD KIND -- by God, they had belief! They <u>believed</u> that thing. Everybody in that landing of the big ship, <u>standing</u> there in the weird lights, was as dedicated as Henry Walthall in THE BIRTH OF A NATION. For chrissake, they believed it was the word of God!

That is the secret, as I have firmly believed, to science fiction -- once you grab the weenie, that makes the story possible -- all men are born with no feet, or some such ridiculous thing -- once you believe that, then you can do anything, and it's got to have thorough verisimilitude of human behavior.

Audience identification, too, is vital. You see, the director, as surrogate audience, and the audience, must be sold the original gimmick. From there on, he leads the audience as much as possible in the action. If the action scares <u>him</u>, and enthralls <u>him</u>, it will scare the audience too. It's a hell <u>of</u> a job, and after you've done it once or twice, it becomes hard to rouse yourself again.

Actually I would have liked to have done adventure-type films, but aside from HIS MAJESTY O'KEEFE, I never really got into that field. I never got an opportunity, of any importance at least.

ADAMSON: Why was it, do you think, that you kept getting typecast as a science fiction director?

HASKIN: I was typecast as a science fiction director, but I didn't get any assignments. (Laughs) You know, every company in the business was making them, but they didn't jangle my phone to come do them. Then if I got a call for some interesting different style of film, it's -- "Oh hell, he's science fiction" -- and I was dead. Science fiction was not coming along too often. There are times I am amazed that I did the number of films I did. . . .

Chapter Nine

## THE POWER AND AFTER

ADAMSON: Do you want to talk about THE POWER now?

HASKIN: I hadn't done a picture for a long time. In fact, I was thinking of getting out of the business, which I did very shortly after that. Directing had become something about which I knew nothing in the new world. The fun had gone.

It was the days of EASY RIDER -- an industry metamorphosis, where "experience" became a bad word and anybody over twenty-five was through. The big transition began with BLOW-UP, considered the greatest thing since INTOLERANCE. One man's opinion of the scene is all that's needed -- forget plots and all that crap -- start from the beginning and go to the end, and that's all you do to make a picture!

The movie business in which I had made my living for almost sixty years was dead as the dodo, defunct -- the Golden Era of Entertainment, which is the kind of business I grew up in and earned my living at all those years. The advent of television actually didn't kill it overnight; the rot had set in years and years before. I knew when the Consent Decree was first mentioned in the newspaper, that that was the deathknell of the business I was working in. When a company could not manufacture, distribute and exhibit their product, they lost the hold on any kind of sustained security.

ADAMSON: So it became the kind of grab bag, hit or miss thing that it is today.

HASKIN: It broke Hollywood's monopoly on the business of making movies. For what? I don't know. Movies are not building a bridge across a river -- they're something that you either go to see or you don't, depending on if you've got enough money and if you feel the need to amuse yourself.

These so-called miraculous changes that came with the new freedom, where heroes were de trop, and plots were anathema, and two idiots smoking pot ride a motorcycle through an hour and a half, until some stranger wastes them with a shotgun -- I don't know what the hell kind of picture-making that is. That's what it turned into.

ADAMSON: That was the year after THE POWER.

HASKIN: Yes, I know, but the change had already started. The distrust of the experienced person -- "experience" was the worst word you could mention. At the time I was at the MGM studio making THE POWER, the hunt was on. It was like they were going to clear the rats out, if they had to shoot every one of them through the head. That meant all the old-timers, all the experienced personnel, the expert staff that MGM had spent fortunes and years in assembling, had to go. And they went -- while I was there.

All they'd have to do was find some guy with a little grey in his hair walking up the company street, and say -- "What are you?" "Oh, I'm in Wardrobe." "You were in Wardrobe. Out!" Boom. Or the drapery, or the properties, or anything.

A story about one man, amusing because he was quite wealthy and it didn't hurt him much: One of the last survivors of the purge at Paramount was Farciot Eduoart, who had been with them since De Mille was king. The new wave execution squad knew a big experienced department head was evading them, but he was very slippery, and he didn't show up; he'd stay away for days, and hide, and if he was there, he went through so fast, nobody could pin him. Eventually, they found him -- hah! -- in an office somewhere, and they quickly fired him. The end of Farciot Eduoart. (Laughs)

He had built a little Napoleonic empire of his own with a single subdivision of special effects called rear projection. He really didn't know special effects at all. I have patents and an Academy citation for developing the machine which he featured. He came over, and by the terms of the patent agreement, put up development money, and was allowed to -- I don't know what the hell the deal was, but he copied my triple background projector, which I had invented at Warners, and he made a career out of it. He had slide rules and the stages were marked with little numbers here and there, and you thought you were going to some future galaxy called Mathematica. (Laughs) Weird.

Gordon Jennings, a great guy, had his own stage and was doing all the rest of the trick work. Farciot would come in with all this pomp and shoot out the back window of a taxi and show you a New York street, which he did for forty years -- nothing novel.

Anyhow, this was all happening at the time that I was on THE POWER, and I knew the end was near. Fouad Said had equipped a big truck for running around the country with a lot of little lightweight lamps, and a generator in it and what have you. It was supposed to free the producer to go anywhere and make his film. What the hell, we'd had all these units when I made WARPATH. We made it in Billings, Montana! In a 4-wheel drive Dodge pickup, with a rising platform on the front of it. Ray Rennahan used it with a 3-strip Technicolor camera, big blimp on it, and we carried our lamps with us. What was new about Fouad Said? He had a lot of little lamps -- if you didn't watch out, they'd fall over, put a lump on your head. They didn't have enough stability to stand up without a man holding them. (Laughs) But it became something to talk about.

It was talk and image and bullshit -- that was the big metamorphosis. Nothing actually came out of it in the way of improvement of pictures, although they said -- "Oh, it's a new world!"

ADAMSON: It was more a cleansing out of the old system than a bringing in of anything new. I knew a lot of talented filmmakers in film schools, and the industry was not interested in them, or in using them or getting them --

HASKIN: I don't know where these monumental fakers came from -- from under what bush -- that were the vanguard of this "revolution." Of course, when James Aubrey took charge of MGM after I'd left, his first policy statement was that he was going to make all pictures like EASY RIDER. That's it -- now there's a policy for picture-making!

ADAMSON: He didn't make a single picture that was at all like EASY RIDER.

HASKIN: No. He didn't make any pictures that we could call pictures. Anyhow, I knew it was time for me to get out. At one time I was one of the most highly respected members of the picture-making fraternity, well known in every studio. I was elected President of the A.S.C. I could have, if I'd applied myself, become President of the Directors Guild, because I knew how to make people like me and vote for me, but it was just like it had all segued into Alice in Wonderland.

In the first place, I never knew how the hell you got a picture together, even in the days when I fit. And how the hell they get pictures together today, I have no idea. A guy like Francis Ford Coppola, who, through a couple of very fortunate things, does a gangster film that makes billions, gets $30 million to go throw away in the Philippine jungle. I don't think the picture will pay the cost of the negative. The mechanics of getting that kind of money together, I don't know where it comes from, or how it goes. And I don't care. I'm happy to be out of pictures, really.

THE POWER was a great strain, physically, on me due to advancing years -- I was over sixty -- and, while I was in good physical health, the night schedule, the kind of thing that I used to laugh off in the old days, was destructive. Very. The whole buttonhole-factory atmosphere of filmmaking had just ceased to be fun any more. It was a grim business. Like the garment industry.

ADAMSON: I wanted to ask you a couple of things about THE POWER. That was really one of the best casts you ever had to work with.

HASKIN: Best acting cast. Yes, they were excellent. All the cameo roles were name actors. The "new wave" pall over movies was to the point where experienced actors were suffering too, and strangers from nowhere were getting all the parts. Here sitting around were Yvonne de Carlo and Richard Carlson, and Mike Rennie, top quality professionals. And we had them all together.

I knew there was something wrong with the show, but I only got in on the "owl." I never had a whack at trying to re-dramatize the thing, to fulfill the premise, although ever since it was published, I thought the book (by Frank M. Robinson) would make a hell of a show. When first I learned what they wanted me for, I was very enthused about doing it, and I rushed down there and got put in an office along with John Gay, the writer. I'd been told, "Byron, you work with the writer now, get everything straight." All John Gay did was put in some niggling changes that he and George Pal had agreed to. Then -- "We go!" (Laughs)

ADAMSON: So, did the script follow the novel? Very closely? Not at all?

HASKIN: Not much.

ADAMSON: It became a kind of NORTH BY NORTHWEST.

HASKIN: It did? I'm glad to hear it became something. (Laughs)

ADAMSON: Well, it's this character suddenly lost, with nowhere to turn, and every time he turns up, he's --

HASKIN: Yes. That was a thing that I phased in powerfully, put an accent to, because I thought that could be a _film_. A guy who is caught in a weird circumstance of supernatural nature, who has been a graduate of a certain university, in a fraternity, and this, that and the other, suddenly on investigation can't verify any of his background, and becomes an invisible character -- who the hell is he? This was not relevant to the story at all, but it was interesting. Gay had it in there, but I stressed it and made a point out of it -- made the scenes about it bigger. Then the whole relationship with Suzanne Pleshette was so impossible to solve -- I didn't know what the hell she was in there for, aside from an obvious lay she had with George Hamilton. What the hell was the finish -- what was she going to do?

There they are at the finish, and they look up at this logo in front of the university, and mumble a line about "corruption corrupts and power is power" -- some doubletalk, and he walks away. I'm supposed to dolly off with him into the far distance, leaving her standing there. I actually got to the point of beginning to lay the dolly track for this thing.

She was sitting over in her chair, looking sorrowful, and I thought -- "What she's played is at least a human being up to here. Now what earthly credibility and excuse can I have that she would stand there, voiceless, and let this bum walk away from her?" I couldn't swallow it, and I couldn't tell her that that's what she had to play, because I knew she was waiting for me with a double-barrelled shotgun.

ADAMSON: (Laughs) She's kind of a tough character, isn't she?

HASKIN: Oh, murder! (Whistles) So, I quickly switched the whole idea and she goes away with him. This now meant that I had to put an accent in, previous to this. As they're walking down the hall, away from Rennie who has been killed, I had him (Hamilton) walking ahead, and she's walking four steps behind. She stops and he continues a couple of steps, senses that she has stopped, and turns and looks back at her. She gives him a weird look, and he goes back and takes her hand. So you've brought them together without dialogue. You can play things like this, and it sells as much as a dialogue scene.

The two walk out in a sort of a glory, and now we come outside, they stop, he looks up at the logo and makes the deathless remark, and walks off into the sunset. At least it played, and people believed this happened, rather than leaving her standing there with her mouth shut. She was the kind of a dame who would have commented on anything that you could bring up.

ADAMSON: Yes. Did you increase her importance? At the end she has a lot of the explanation of what has happened.

HASKIN: Yes. It was another failure of the script, that exposition had to be indulged in at the end -- it's like a Perry Mason story, where the whole last chapter is explaining why it all happened this way.

ADAMSON: But putting it in her mouth gives her some importance.

HASKIN: Oh, yes. I don't know who guided it that way.

ADAMSON: How about that incredible fight in the kitchen? I really thought it was amazing. I noticed that John Baxter commented on it too, in Science Fiction in the Cinema. It's made up of very simple elements -- the dishwasher, and refrigerator, and the burner going on the stove -- but it's great, it's a tremendous scene.

HASKIN: Well, that's pure movie, you know. You get big effects. You can write your brains out and you never get the effect, and they can talk for hours, and you never get that kind of shock. It's surprise and instant symbolism and things.

ADAMSON: How long did you spend working that scene out and doing it?

HASKIN: Oh, we had the concept of the refrigerator beforehand -- it had to be rigged so it would tip over, etc. The scene didn't take long in the shooting. I think it took a day.

When the car went into the water at the drawbridge -- to save money, they'd taken the motor out of it, and of course it went off the bridge and bounced up like an eggshell and floated! It wasn't the thrill you'd expect from a car going off of a bridge into a river. So I worked in the police car routine -- that was all extra stuff. We cut underwater, and Hamilton gets out of the car and swims to the shore, and now a weird light comes on him and we show two headlights come through the tall grass. Well, this looks like a big feral monster, you don't know what the hell it is, and it turns out to be a police car. The vibrating front wheel effect previously was another one that I added. I was trying in every way to put weird supernatural notes into this chase, to duplicate the way that I subconsciously remembered the book affecting me when I first read it. The screenplay didn't have anything of that sort.

ADAMSON: Did the book spend any more time dwelling on what the Power was, how it was achieved, and the evolutionary concepts? I liked all that stuff in the film, but it really was gotten over with very quickly. And then it proceeded into effect, rather than cause.

HASKIN: Well, it was based on the power of mind over matter: in certain repetitions every 10,000 years, etc., a human was born who could, through his concentrated effort, move matter -- that's what happened at the table to begin with, he moved things back and forth. That to me was a very intriguing idea, that a group of legitimate scientists conducting certain experiments -- in the book it's not quite as wild as what it is in the script -- develop and successfully display this kind of an experiment. Who did it? It should have been a complete mystery, a mystery treatment from that point on, to find out which one around the table -- the Twelve Little Indians format from Agatha Christie -- which one is the the one? But it stuttered and it rolled this way and that way, and avoided the issues, and it was a real punko development.

ADAMSON: (Laughs) Was the novel stronger?

HASKIN: Yes, I think so, although when you're throwing words around, you can create any kind of an effect, and it's a different way to tell a story.

ADAMSON: It is. What about those George Pal Puppetoonian kind of scare things, like the little soldiers that march and fire their guns?

HASKIN: Well, he had those accents in there, and he had that Projects Unlimited outfit with Wah Chang and the others. They were doing those for months before the picture ever started. That was all in and developed before I ever got on it.

ADAMSON: Did you find it a great joy, or more of a headache, to be working with such big names in the cast?

HASKIN: Oh, I don't know. It didn't mean anything much to me. I had worked with Yvonne de Carlo before, and directed her in two pictures, or three, I don't know. "In again, out again Finnegan" -- I knew all the people. Mike Rennie was a very down-to-earth guy, and there was no strain on that.

Suzanne, I think, possibly was puzzled about who the hell she was playing, as was I, and we didn't get along very well. I was packing a tremendous load, trying to organize the geography in my mind of where people are going and she wants to start creating moves of her own choice.

We got in a row and I told her, "Look, it doesn't matter to me if you go home. You don't want to go where I tell you, go home." She said, "Is that what you want?!" So we got into that kind of thing. (Laughs) I said, "It doesn't matter what I want. If it's impossible, don't stick around. But I do have a routine that I'm shooting that requires you to do this. It involves guys up at the top of this elevator trying to stop the wheels and various other knickknacks. Probably you haven't read the sequence in the script, because it's all in there." That didn't endear me to her either.

There were some effective things in it, individual parts, but the general disapproval of the management about the whole idea, about Pal, influenced the reviews. Daily Variety and the Reporter massacred it. It wasn't all that bad. I read the London reviews and they were quite good. Somebody over there wrote me and said it was a smash. Well, of course the nine dollars you get out of England -- it didn't matter.

ADAMSON: There is also a scene where George Hamilton kind of goes into space and decomposes into a skeleton, and it's all in his head. That was a nice scene.

HASKIN: These attempts to frighten by being weird are George Pal's stock-in-trade. He thinks if you whirl the body off into space and galaxies explode -- "Oh, eets terrific. Ooh!" He can't stand it. You can tell more with contact between two humans than you can with all these tricks.

ADAMSON: So you left the business formally?

HASKIN: With no regrets. I knew that there was no further use going the route of trying to get employment, and I made up my mind that that was the end of it.

ADAMSON: What about television?

HASKIN: During my tour, a couple of times I almost broke into the inner ring of the favored directors -- there are six or eight of them who shoot all the television series, and unless you're in that ring, you might as well forget it. You get just enough to subsist on, crumbs. From OUTER LIMITS, but for the bad offices of Mr. Brady and his friend Sam White, I would have jumped to MGM, to KILDARE and a couple of other shows going out there. Lou Moreheim, story editor, had left OUTER LIMITS and gone out there, and he had recommended me. They looked at ARCHITECTS OF FEAR, and a couple of things, and they said, "Well that's what we need, more stress on the romantic interludes in these pictures instead of all this talking ... about mathematics." But just as I was about to close with them, they went into a hiatus. (Laughs) The opportunity sailed by. I couldn't move, because they wanted me at OUTER LIMITS for ECK with Peter Lind Hayes, and by the time I finished that, that show was in a layoff. I just decided to retire, that's all. I processed my pension and away I went.

ADAMSON: How long was it before you left Hollywood and came up here?

HASKIN: To Santa Barbara? In '74 I was working on my book, and my wife, Terry, had written her first book, which was published. I helped her with that, and when we came up here, she was into her second book.

I spent about a year on my own book, for research, for material, and I got the whole spine of the book and chapter headings and a lot of research material during that year. Since coming up here, I have not been idle -- I haven't been retired at all! This writing is a damn sight more demanding of your time and attention than making movies.

ADAMSON: Do you have any thoughts on seeing your films on TV -- besides the fact that they're cut to ribbons?

HASKIN: Only occasionally can I override the indignation of what butchery is being performed. I was always so heavily involved with the editing that I know every cut that's in the film -- and to see all the structure that was agonizingly contrived to bring the thing up to where it could generate some suspense, ripped out by some punk in a TV station, makes it very difficult to resist seeing red, running and breaking the tube.

But I saw one that I enjoyed, that I didn't think too much of in the making -- DENVER AND RIO GRANDE. It had some interesting offbeat kind of sequences in it, and some good playing, and some good comedy.

ADAMSON: Yes, that's one of your early pictures that I like a lot.

HASKIN: I like WARPATH, aside from the over-complicated personal story. It had some good spectacle and some well-staged scenes here and there.

ADAMSON: Do you find you can be more objective looking at your films now than when they were new?

HASKIN: Yes. I never got a perspective on any of the work when it was new. It was impossible, I was too steeped in it, because I became very deeply involved, particularly in the editing and shaping it up, timing and so forth. I can now see flaws in THE NAKED JUNGLE, which I had always considered one of the slickest continuities I ever got together in shooting a film. In WAR OF THE WORLDS, I see the technical defects quite clearly -- the traveling mattes didn't fit in a lot of places. But it still has a lot of power, because it's basically got the impact it was supposed to have, a great deal of which was ad-libbed on the set.

Chapter Ten

## EPILOGUE

The nightstand clock was at 3:00 a.m. I was sitting on the edge of the bed in a robe, barefooted, muscles cramped from disuse. The book was heavy in my hands. I finished reading the last page, closed the covers. On the back, in gilt letters on shiny black, <u>Byron Haskin, Oral History</u>.

My mind refused to produce anything . . . only feelings, not thoughts. For hours I had been re-living my entire professional life as a filmmaker. The effect was profound.

A feeling of déjà vu stole over me. An experience like this had happened before. Bits of it began to reassemble.

It was 1923. I was twenty-three years old.

Memory of the climb came back. Up the mountainside, in wellnigh impenetrable thickets of scrub oak, blackberries, grapevines. My feet stumbled for footing on the slippery debris carpeting the long-disused wood-sled trail.

Sweat was running down my face, my legs were trembling from the strain, my breath coming in short gasps. My heart thumped like a runaway diesel . . .

Why would anyone in his right mind subject himself to such torture? What urgency could be driving me on, seemingly heedless of exhaustion, even if it killed me?

Bits of blue sky began to show through the lattice overhead. I grabbed briars with my hands, heedless, wrenching myself upward, breaking out into the clear. Before me lay a wide meadowland. The grass was high, electric green. Yellow buttercups, a few dainty violets, an occasional lily bent to the gentle breeze underneath the tapestry of shadows. A tiny brook meandered by, its banks lush with bracken and maidenhair fern. In the trees, blue-coated tree squirrels soared through the intermittent sunlight with the grace of birds. A fairyland . . .

My knees gave way, depositing me on a granite outcropping. I couldn't think. There was an air of expectancy . . .

It was one week since I'd driven up to the country, on leave from the Hollywood studio. My first big assignment as cinematographer on the Barrymore feature had come to an end. The stress and tension had just about done me in. With rest and recuperation imperative, I thought only of Grandpa Conrad's old ranch in mid-state. Nobody lived there anymore, the family long scattered, but it was where, as a child, my first memories began.

The afternoon I arrived I set out to hike across the fields to the small lake on the border. As kids, my Uncle Landrith and I had lazed on the warm grassy banks, learned to swim, frog-fashion.

Halfway across, my legs buckled, I sat down in the middle of the rows of bean plants, unable to go on.

Day by day I regained strength. My horizons began to widen with memories of childhood. There was a particular tantalizing impression about the mountains rimming the south border. I often paused in my hike, eyes fixed on the purple silhouette, wondering why. Was it something to do with the daily phenomenon, when the sun crossed the ridge, casting the whole valley side into shadow, except for one sliver of light lingering on a protruding benchland halfway to the top? Something seemed to be telling me I had been up there before, long ago . . .

Sitting on the outcropping, I began to sense that this was a new world. Everywhere else in the county was burned by the summer sun, here it was deliciously cool. Then I noticed that the premature shadow of the noontime sun was already inching through the trees toward the rim of the bench. My eye was drawn to a big circle of brightness on the otherwise dappled shadows.

A sense of excitement pulled me to my feet, drew me toward it. As I paused on the perimeter, the feeling grew. In this wide patch of sunlight stood a weathered stump four feet thick. Extending from it lay a blueprint in dust of what once must have been a mighty oak tree. Here and there segments of the trunk still remained, grey with the rot of passing years. Up above, the sky blazed, fiercely blue.

The whole remembrance came to life, I began to hear the voices . . . young voices. Uncle Lan and me. It was back in 1909, which made me nine years old, him seven. He was the youngest of Grandpa's brood of eleven. We were running around yelling with excitement over our first exploration into the world of finance, bound to make our fortune chopping firewood. For the first job, we'd picked the biggest tree on the ranch right up here on the benchland.

We began working the two-man saw borrowed from Grandpa's toolshed. By evening of that first day we were no more than six inches into the iron-textured trunk of the tree. We dropped our tools, wolfed sandwiches, milk and apples from a knapsack. Afterwards, lying on our bellies on the bank of the stream, drinking cold mountain water; then curling into khaki blankets on the grass. Not to sleep, but to put words to our wild dreams of fame and fortune . . .

After three days' labor with the saw we had made an adequate cut halfway through. Next, to chop a wedge on the opposite side of the trunk to "fall" our prize. All afternoon we chopped with double-bitted axes. Finally, late-afternoon, a muffled cracking came from the heart of the oak. We stopped work to watch. The huge canopy of branches began to quiver. Then the tree began to turn. We jumped away to the bushes. The monarch of the benchland seemed to totter forever . . . then gave forth a mournful groaning, falling majestically to earth with a crescendo of splintering screeches, and the impact of a major earthquake.

We stared out of the bushes, speechless. My own first reaction was to the glare of sunlight where but a moment ago had been nothing but shade. Slowly, a feeling of guild possessed me . . . guilt for the desecration of nature we'd wrought. Fouling the wonderland. The thrill of conquest left. We both got to our feet.

I turned to Landrith for reassurance, perhaps even for sympathy for the pain I was experiencing. I clearly remembered he seemed aloof from such turmoil, just packing his corncob pipe with tobacco filched from Uncle Don's humidor. I had an impulse to smack him.

My guilt grew and grew; I was aware of the nearness of an avenging God. I said, "We'll have to quit smoking, you know."

He paused from lighting the pipe. "Whatever for?"

I struggled to put it into words. His eyes remained opaque. I exploded, "How're we gonna stay in shape to chop all this wood if we don't?"

That scored where morality failed. He hefted the pipe, then threw it away among the bushes.

Righteousness overcame me for saving this callous sinner. I patted his shoulder. We grinned at each other, hurrying back to pick up the axes and begin the job of piling up our fortune . . .

Gradually, my mind returned from boyhood to 1923. A residue of our exultation remained with me.

Of course, the entire enterprise had finally collapsed. The huge trunk was too tough to saw off in segments; we opted instead to work on the small branches around the perimeter. Compromising our goals without the quiver of an eyelash. By week's end, we'd only stacked a fraction of a cord of firewood. It finally became evident that at such a snail's-pace we'd never chop a whole cord before the winter rains began. Tired of the job anyway, we picked up our gear, sliding down the old wood-sled trail without a backward glance . . . rushing off to new worlds to conquer, new dreams . . .

Standing by the edge of the opening, I was almost overcome by the vivid memories. All at once I turned to a nearby clump of bushes, knelt down, raking familiarly beneath. I quickly encountered a slim little wooden pipestem much the worse for the wear of years; all that time had left of Lan's pipe. Kneeling with it in my hand, a lump rose in my throat. I could not have spoken to save myself. An awful sense of the relentless passage of years struck me . . . Gradually, the exultation of nostalgia left me. I felt empty. The glimpse I'd been given of the past was altogether too real to handle emotionally . . . being privy to the childhood dreams . . .

Of what significance were they? If any? Was this to be my future, just then beginning? Futile dreams?

I couldn't accept it. It had been only the usual anarchy of being a child . . . God only knows how they ever grow up . . . !

I moved quickly to the stump, poked a finger at it to test the once formidable strength; it sank into the rotten wood without resistance. I whirled away, unable to cope with any more, hurrying down the wood-sled trail, slipping and sliding. The little pipestem fell from my hand unnoticed. . . .

I rose from the bed, placing the heavy book on the dresser. At age eighty-four, the future I'd dreamed about was over . . . professionally, that is. I had a sense of so-that's-all-there-is! Nothing more.

But slowly, my mind began building defenses. The time for dreaming dreams had gone; whatever they had been, here, between the covers of this book, was the record. So be it. . . .

The only tenable purpose for recording this Oral History could lie in how much value it is to newcomers today, wondering uncertainly just how it's going to be for them.

What we have compiled, then, is a record of the way it was . . . through my eyes. Without apology. It may not read like it at times, but I had a ball!

## Film, Television, Radio, and Stage Play Title Index

ACROSS THE PACIFIC, 59
ACTION IN THE NORTH ATLANTIC, 130-34
AFFAIR IN SUMATRA (teleplay), 268-69

ARMORED COMMAND, 241-45,246,280
AROUND THE WORLD IN 80 DAYS, 202,233
AS THE EARTH TURNS, 106,120

BABES IN ARMS, 101
THE BIRTH OF A NATION, 282
THE BISHOP OF COTTONTOWN (never released), 46-51,124
BLACK FURY, 106,120-24, 128
BLACK WATERS, 78
BLOW-UP, 283
BOBBED HAIR, 53-55
THE BOSS, 231-33
BROKEN CHAINS, 38-39, 41-43,45
BROTHER CAN YOU SPARE A DIME?, 117
BUCK ROGERS, 202
CABIN IN THE COTTON, 125-27
THE CABINET OF DR. CALIGARI, 206
CAPTAIN BLOOD, 127
CAPTAIN SINDBAD, 246-55, 256-57,273
CAPTAINS OF THE CLOUDS, 96,265
CARMEN JONES, 191
Christie Comedies, 57, 103

CINDERELLA, 171
CITIZEN SOLDIER, 241-42
CLEOPATRA, 33
CLOSE ENCOUNTERS OF THE THIRD KIND, 199, 201,202,282
COLLEEN, 128
CONQUEST OF SPACE, 228-31,268
COOK'S TOURS, 15
CUSTER'S LAST STAND, 185

DOA, 189
DAYS OF WINE AND ROSES, 189
DENVER AND RIO GRANDE, 188,192-194, 196,197-98,199,293
DESTINATION MOON, 208
Dial M for Murder (play), 221
DODGE CITY, 98
DR. KILDARE (TV series), 292
DON JUAN, 63-64,65,68,87, 107,164

EASY RIDER, 148,283,286
FANTASIA, 171
THE FIRST TEXAN, 198, 226-28
FORBIDDEN PLANET, 247, 264
42ND STREET, 101
THE FOUR HORSEMEN OF THE APOCALYPSE, 35, 36,79,86,92,94,142
FROM THE EARTH TO THE MOON. See JULES VERNE'S FROM THE EARTH TO THE MOON
THE GENERAL, 198

THE GIRL IN THE RED BIKINI. See SEPTEMBER STORM
GINSBERG THE GREAT, 76, 77
THE GODFATHER, 232
GOLD DIGGERS (film series) 101
THE GOLDEN COCOON, 59
GRAND HOTEL, 66
GRANDMA'S BOY, 152
GREAT EXPECTATIONS, 181-83
THE GREAT TRAIN ROBBERY, 15
THE GREATEST STORY EVER TOLD, 160
GREED, 188-89
THE GREEN LIGHT, 52,120

HEE-HAW (TV series), 41
HIS MAJESTY O'KEEFE, 201, 209-16,217-19,222,225, 247,273
Hold Your Horses (play), 76
HURRICANE'S GAL 37-38
THE HUSTLER, 255-56

I CONFESS, 218
I MARRIED A DOCTOR, 128
I WALK ALONE, 141-45,148, 153,154,155,159,184,209
INTOLERANCE, 36,79,283
INVASION OF THE BODY SNATCHERS, 272
THE IPCRESS FILE, 149-50
IRISH HEARTS, 75-76

THE JAZZ SINGER, 68,77
JET OVER THE ATLANTIC, 237-39
JULES VERNE'S FROM THE EARTH TO THE MOON, 233

KEY LARGO, 146
Keystone Comedies, 15, 88-89
KINDRED OF THE DUST, 30

LAWRENCE OF ARABIA, 80
LIFEBOAT, 80
LITTLE SAVAGE, 233-37,273
THE LIVES AND LOVES OF ROBERT BURNS, 82-84
LONG JOHN SILVER, 223-26
"Look for the miner" (Albers promotion film), 17-18,21

THE MAN FROM PAINTED POST, 24
MAN-WOMAN-MARRIAGE, 35-36,92
MANEATER OF KUMAON, 156-59
MATINEE LADIES, 74-75
MEET McGRAW (TV series), 269
THE MERRY WIDOW, 129
Mickey Mouse Cartoons, 168-69
MIDSUMMER NIGHT'S DREAM 117-19
MISSION TO MOSCOW, 117
MONSIEUR VERDOUX, 87

THE NAKED JUNGLE, 153, 219-222,294
NIGHT GALLERY, 270
NORTH BY NORTHWEST, 287

ON THIN ICE, 59
ON TRIAL, 70, 72-73
OUTER LIMITS (TV series), 269-78,280,281,292,293
  Architects of Fear, 272, 275-77,292

Demon With a Glass Hand, 272-73, 274
Feasibility Study, 272
Two Days of the Dragon, 272
Behold Eck, 272, 276, 293
PERRY MASON, 271
Peter Pan (play), 12
POTEMKIN, 61-62
THE POWER, 68, 136, 149, 283-92
Puppetoons, 291

RAWHIDE, 229, 271
RAZOR'S EDGE, 156
RED RIVER, 212
RIN-TIN-TIN (film series), 59
THE ROARING TWENTIES, 116-17
THE ROBE, 274
ROBINSON CRUSOE ON MARS, 216, 230, 257-58, 260-68
Romeo and Juliet (play), 146-47
ROOKERY NOOK, 80
Rookery Nook (play), 80

SCARAMOUCHE, 92, 94
SCREEN DIRECTORS PLAYHOUSE (TV series). See AFFAIR IN SUMATRA
THE SEA BEAST, 59-62, 87
THE SEA WOLF, 140-41
SEAL ISLAND, 167, 170
SEPTEMBER STORM, 240-41
SEVEN DAYS IN MAY, 189
SILVER CITY, 184, 192, 194-95
SINDBAD / THE ADVENTURES OF SINDBAD (TV series; never made), 254

THE SINGING FOOL, 68-70, 84
THE SIREN, 77
SKIPPY, 104
SLANDER THE WOMAN, 46
SNOW WHITE, 166
STAR TREK (TV series pilot), 280-81
STAR WARS, 94, 199, 201, 202
SUPERMAN, 202

TARZAN'S PERIL, 190-92, 209
TOL'ABLE DAVID, 39
Tons of Money, 80
TOO LATE FOR TEARS, 145, 159-60, 169, 216
TREASURE ISLAND, 115, 155, 280, 166, 169-84, 260,
TREASURE OF THE SIERRA MADRE, 139
TWILIGHT ZONE (TV series), 270

THE WAR OF THE WORLDS, 10, 134, 199-208, 219, 222, 230, 258, 261, 263, 264, 294
The War of the Worlds (Mercury Theatre radio play), 203
WARPATH, 184-88, 189-90, 192, 193, 194, 195, 196, 280, 285, 294
WHEN A MAN LOVES, 64
WHEN KNIGHTHOOD WAS IN FLOWER, 68
WHERE THE WORST BEGINS, 55, 58
WICHITA, 226
WOLF'S CLOTHING, 73, 254
WOLVES, 80-82
THE WORLD'S A STAGE, 45-46

ZORRO (TV series), 253

**Subject Index**

ABC, 254
Abel, Dave, 160
Action, staging of. See
    Directing, theory of
Adams, Maude, 12
Adler, Luther, 141
Ahern, Fred, 191
Albers Brothers Mills, 3
    advertising promotion and
        film for, 16-18,21,22
Alcorn, Ron, 241-242,243,244
    245
Alemán, Miguel
    234,235
Alexandria Hotel, Los
    Angeles, 26,27,46
Aller, Joe, 42
Allied Artists, 198,226,242
    244
Alperson, Edward L., 241
American Film Studio, 23
Amy, George, 131-32
Anderson, Mary, 237
Antonucci, Al, 191
Arliss, George, 143
Armendariz, Pedro, 236,247,
    253,274
Art background, B. Haskin
    See Education, B. Haskin,
        artistic training
Astaire, Fred, 177
Aubrey, James, 286
Autry, Gene, 18
Avedon, Doe, 232
Ayres, Hale, 18

Bacon, Lloyd, 69,130-31,132,
    134
Bank of America, 45
Bara, Theda, 86
Barbary Coast, San
    Francisco, 12-14

Barclay, Sir Reginald, 80
Barker, Lex, 191
Barnes, George, 134
Barry, Gene 204, 205-6
Barrymore, John, 32,59,60-63
    64-66,67,296
Barthelmess, Richard, 39,
    125,127
Bartholovsky, Hans, 110,208
Bartlett Alley, San
    Francisco, 12-14
Battles
    of the Bulge, 242
    of Franklin, Tennessee,
        46-50,124
    of Harper's Ferry, 127
Battleships
    Iowa, 40
    Mississippi, 40
    Oregon, 40
    USS California, 40-41
Black Hell (novel by M.A.
    Mussmano), 120,123
Baxter, John, 289
Beatty, William, 107
Beldt, Glen, 118
Bellamy, Ralph, 268
Berkeley, Busby, 95,98-101
    152
Bischoff, Sam, 156-57
Bitzer, Billy, 93
Blackmer, Sidney, 272
Blanke, Henry, 117,118-19,
    139
Blue, Monte, 59,67,73,187
Boasberg, Charles, 264
Bogart, Humphrey, 59,131,
    143
Bogeaus, Benedict, 237-39
Bonestell, Chesley, 110,204
    208
The Book of Knowledge, 4

Boone, Daniel, 2, 17
Boreham Wood, 114
Bradbury Building, Los Angeles, 272
Brady, Ben, 271-72, 292
Briskin, Sam, 77
British and Dominions Studios 79, 89, 85
Broening, Lyman, 28, 31, 48, 51, 160
Brooke, Walter, 229
Brooks, Geraldine, 272, 275
Brunton Studios, 28, 30-31
Bryan, William Jennings, 2
Bucquet, Harold S., 38, 47
Burns, Robert, 82, 83-84
Butler, Bob, 281
Butler, Larry, 110, 258, 264, 278

Cagney, James, 96, 140, 161, 162-63
Cagney, William, 140
Cagney Productions, Inc., 140, 141
Campbell, Colin, 45, 46
Canutt, Yakima, 98
Carey, Harry, 55, 101
Carlson, Richard, 287
Carnation Mush, 3, 4, 16
Caron, Leslie, 220
Caruso, Enrico, 12
Cassidy, Shaun, 244
Ceballos, Larry, 100
Cheetah, 191
Childers, Naomi, 30
Chooluck, Leon, 246
Christie, Agatha, 202, 290
Christie Brothers, Al and Charlie, 55
Christie Comedies, 103
Chang, Wah, 291
Chaplin, Charles, 32, 86, 154
Chase, Borden, 212-15
Cinematography, B. Haskin.
See also Directing; Warner Bros. Special Effects Department
assistant cameraman at Brunton, 28-29
assistant cameraman to Walsh, 34-35
cameraman for Holubar, 35-40
consistency, 164
first experience with, 16
lighting, 122, 128-29
multiple camera shooting, 70, 72, 78
photographing Colleen Moore in BROKEN CHAINS, 41-43
photographing Preparedness Day Parade, 19-20
using father's Universal camera, 21-22
Clawson, Dal, 46
Club Royale, 26, 27
Co-Artist Productions. See Truart Film Corporation
Cody, Lew, 27
Cohn, Harry, 77
Cohn, Joe, 43
Columbia, 77, 106, 258
Compson, Betty, 30
Consent Decree, 283
Coontz, Mel, 158
Cooper, Gary, 71
Cooper, Miriam, 30, 34
Coppola, Francis Ford, 286
Corbett, Bennie, 98
Corey, Wendell, 141, 157-58
Corrigan's Ranch, 158
Cosgrove, Jack, 110, 132-33
Costello, Dolores, 60, 63, 64
Costello, Helene, 63
Cotten, Joseph, 233
Cotton Club, 27

Coward, Noel, 269
Crosland, Alan, 68
Crow Indian tribe, 185-86, 188, 189. See also Dearnose, Donald; Yellowtail, Robert
Crump, Owen, 96
Cruze, James, 154-55
Culp, Robert, 272, 273, 275, 277
Curtiz, Michael, 95-98, 120-21, 127, 150, 151-52

Dandridge, Dorothy, 191
Danforth, Jim, 277-78
Davidge, Roy, 42-43
Davidson, Roy, 110
Davies, Marion, 62, 68
Davis, H.O., 44
Davis, Jim, 228
de Carlo, Yvonne, 188, 287, 291
De Courville, Anthony, 80
De Mille, Cecil B., 204
De Mille Studios, 281
Dearnose, Donald, 189
Del Ruth, Roy, 73, 75
Demming, Norman, 212
Denham studio, 115, 170, 175, 183
Denver and Rio Grande Railroad, 193, 197
Detlefsen, Paul, 110, 132, 208
Dierkes, John, 195
Dieterle, William, 117, 118
Directors Guild of America, 216
Directing
  vs. cinematography, 32-33, 134-37
  and producing, 278-80
  science fiction, 281-280
  for TV, 52-53, 269, 275
Directing, theory of
  action staging, 133, 243-44. See also Battles, Battleships
  cutaway technique, 152-54
  director as storyteller, 149, 151
  director as surrogate audience, 260
  dramatization, 143, 145-48, 227-28
  How I Learned to Direct Movies (by B. Haskin, working title), 148, 293
  naked reverses, 259
  preparation for, 128, 258
  qualities necessary for success, 161-63, 165, 222-23
  shooting continuity, 149, 152, 155, 163-64, 258-59
Disney, Roy, 169
Disney, Walt, 166-71, 173-74, 175-76, 180
Disney, Walt Productions (see also Denham studio; Mickey Mouse, Limited), 115, 166, 167, 168, 169-70
Doleman, Guy, 225
Donner party, 2
Doran, D.A., 199-200
Douglas, Everett, 206
Douglas, Kirk, 141, 143, 144, 145, 154, 188
Draper, Paul, 177-78
Driscoll, Bobby, 174-75, 178-80
Drop speed photography. See Film speed
Dru, Joanne, 240
Dubbing. See Sound on film, early days of
DuPar, Edwin, 88, 91-92, 116

Duryea, Dan, 145,159,160
Dwan, Allan, 31

Earle, Ralph Radnor, 17-18, 19,22
Earthquake of 1906, San Francisco, 4-10,205
Eason, B. Reeves, 162
Eastwood, Clint, 271
Edeson, Arthur, 95
Editing, 258
  early days of, 20
  of films for TV, 216-17, 293
  on THE WAR OF THE WORLDS, 206
Education, B. Haskin
  artistic training, 22,23, 103-4
  high school, 4,22
  primary school, 10-11
  school plays, 11
  University of California at Berkeley, 4,17,22
Eduoart, Farciot, 267-68, 284-85
Einstein, Albert, 109-10
Einstein, Mr. & Mrs. Albert. See Einstein, Albert
Electrical Research Products Incorporated. See Erpi
Ellis, Robert, 31,37
Endore, Guy, 250,256,257
Engel, Joe, 38
Erpi (Electrical Research Products Incorporated) 66,72
Eurist, Clarence, 237-38
Evans, Mark, 223
  brother of, 253

FBO, 44
Fabian, Max, 39
Fairbanks, Douglas, Sr., 24, 128

Family, B. Haskin. See also Haskin, Mrs. Byron (first wife); Haskin, Mrs. Byron (Terry)
  ancestors, 1,2,4,7,196,297
  parents
    father, 2,3,4,5,7,8,9, 12,16-18,21,22,40
    mother, 2,4,5,6,8,9,40
  sister (Rowena Catherine) 3,4,5,9,13-14,40
  uncles (Don; Landrith), 296,297-98,299
Farr, Felicia, 226
Fenix Hotel, 238
Fessier, Mike, 268
Film labs. See also Aller, Joe; Fox, William Studios
  Roy Davidge, 42-43
  at Goldwyn under Louis Physioc, 41-43
  B. Haskin's first job in, 18-19,21
Film processing. See Film labs; Editing.
Film speed. See also Hasman plan
  of Keystone comedies, 88-90
  of silent films, 88-90
  in SILVER CITY, 195
Fire king photographers, 94-95
First National Studio, 35,45, 46,111
Fitzgerald, Barry, 194
Fleming, Eric, 229,271
Flint, Motley, 45
Flynn, Errol, 120,127-28
Fong, Benson, 209
Ford, John, 158,186
The Forty Strong, 14
Foster, Phil, 229-30

Fox, William Studios, 86
Francis, Lee, 26
Frank's. See Musso & Frank
Frankenheimer, John, 162
Franklin, Sidney, 30
Frederick, Pauline, 70
Freeman, Y. Frank, Sr., 199-200,209,221
Freeman, Y. Frank (Pete), Jr. 199-200,204,207,209, 219,221,229
Furie, Sidney, 149-50

Gage, Fred, 73,92-93,113,129
Gallery, Tom, 189
Gam, Rita, 268
Garden of Allah, 224
Garfield, John, 141
Gaudio, Tony, 95,164
Gay, John, 287,288
General Service Studio, 31,156,208
Giesler, Jerry, 99,100
Gish, Dorothy, 80,82
Gist, Bob, 128
Gleason, Jackie, 255
Goldwyn Studio, 38,39,41,47
Goodman, Johnny, 193
Gordon, Huntley, 55
Gothke, Frank, 245
Goulding, Edmund, 163
Green, Duke, 53,98
Gribbon, Eddie, 90
Griffith, D.W., 15,26,44,154
Gruber, Frank, 194,196
Guinness, Alec, 177
Guthrie, Bill, 125,126

HMV. See His Master's Voice
Hagenah, Harry, 22-25
Haller, Ernest, 163,245
Hamilton, George, 288,290, 292
Harbaugh, Bill, 90
Hardwicke, Cedric, 204

Harlan, Kenneth, 53
Hartman, Don, 104,199,200-1 220-21
Haskin, Mrs. Byron (first wife), 135
Haskin, Mrs. Byron (Terry), 128,158,219,293
Hasman Plan, 90,113-16
Haworth, Ted, 212,218
Hayden, Sterling, 196
Hayes, Peter Lind, 272, 276,293
Head, Edith, 220
Hearst, William Randolph, 20,68
Hecht, Harold, 209,212-15, 217,218-19
Heisler, Stuart, 104
Hernandez, Carl, 47,49
Higgins, John C., 261,265
Hill, Jim, 213-15
His Majesty O'Keefe (novel), 210
His Master's Voice, 79,85
Hitchcock, Alfred, 151,218, 258-59
Hoch, Winton, 263,265,267
Hoffman, Otto, 77
Holden, William, 207
Holliman, Earl, 243,245
Hollywood, first impressions of in 1919, 22-27
Hollywood Hotel, 24,57
Holmes, Burton, 15
Holt, Nat, 185,187,188,189, 192,193,194,196-97
Holubar, Alan, 35-39,41,46, 49,50,92,93
Hooper, Bud, 18
Howard, Tommy, 248,249
Huggins, Roy, 159
Hunter, Jeff, 281
Huston, John, 139
Hyslop, Joseph, 82,83

308

Ince, Thomas, 44,152,154
Ingels, Marty, 244
Ingram, Rex, 39,92,94,142
Inventions and developments in film technology
  getting appropriations from Jack Warner for, 112-13
  gobos, 52
  lamp shields, 52
  traveling matte camera, 52,112-13
  triple background projector, 285
  studio's agreement to share standard procedures, 107-8
Iridell, Mr. and Mrs. Russell, 56
Isla de Oro Corporation, 223, 225

Jackman, Fred, 89-90, 106-7, 108,119,120
Jagger, Dean, 189,196
Jaggs, Alan, 176
Jahnke's Tavern, 26
Javal, Ian, 84
Jennings, Gordon, 201,285
Jessel, George, 76-77
Johnston, Jimmy, 18
Jolson, Al, 68-69,77
Justman, Bobby, 280

Kalmus, Herbert, 113
Kalmus, Natalie, 267
Katzin, Lee, 280
Kauffman, Albert, 116
Kaufman, Joseph, 223
Keaton, Buster, 27,198
Keeler, Ruby, 99,101
Kelly, Jim, 81
Kesson, Dave, 70,83,93
Kesson, Frank, 59,88
Keystone Kops, 90-91

King Brothers (see also King, Frank), 246,249,253, 255
King, Frank, 246,247,248,250, 251,253,255
King, Jack, 56
Kirkwood, James, 36
Knowles, Cyril, 81
Koenig, Bill, 98,108,120
Koenekamp, Hans (Kony), 89, 106-7,108,115,120
Krows, Arthur Edwin, 148
Kyne, Peter B., 30

La Marr, Barbara, 56
Labs. See Film labs
Lancaster, Burt, 141,143,144, 145,209,213-15,216, 217
Laughton, Charles, 80,82
Lawrence, Marc, 141,143-44
Lean, David, 181
Lee, Anna, 237
"Leiningen Vs. the Ants" (short story by Carl Stephenson), 219
Lehrman, Henry, 68
Lesser, Sol, 190-91,192,255
Lester, Jimmy, 242-244
Lewis, Bill, 67
Lewis, Jerry. See Martin & Lewis
Liggon, Grover, 90,91
Lindsay, Margaret, 237
Litvak, Anatole, 161-62
Llarinaga Brothers, 110,208
Lloyd, Harold, 44,154
Lloyd, Russell, 183-84
London Symphony Orchestra, 84
Lonergan, Arthur, 263-64
Lonsdale, Frederick, 84
Lovejoy, Frank, 269
Loy, Myrna, 63

Lubitsch, Ernst, 67,129,151
Lundin, Vic, 257
Lyndon, Barre, 204,219
Lynn, Ralph, 80

MCA, 223,225
MGM, 38,39,42,43,66,100,
    101,136,141,149,168,
    200,217,229,249,254,
    164,271,284,286
McAvoy, May, 76
McCrea, Joel, 226-27
McDermott, Jack, 25,34,
    55-56,57,58,101-3
MacDougall, Ranald (Rannie),
    220,221,222
McGann, William, 37
McGhee, Gloria, 232
McLeod, Bonner, 58
McLeod, Norman, 56,58,
    101-5
Macready, George, 237
Madison, Guy, 237
Mansfield, W. Duncan, 44,82,
    83,113,152,153,154
Mantee, Paul, 257,258,
    262-63,267,268
March, Juan, 241
Markey, Enid, 18
Martel, Arline, 234,273
Martel, Christiane, 235
Martin & Lewis, 223,225
Martin, Dean. See Martin &
    Lewis
Marx Brothers, 104-5
Marx, Sam, 55
Massey, Ilona, 237
Matthews, Blaney, 99
Mayer, Louis B., 32,139
Mayo, Virginia, 237
Mdivani, Prince, 27
Meighan, Tom, 196
Meredyth, Bess, 63
Melchior, Ib, 260,264-65
Mellor, William, 159-60

Menzies, William Cameron,
    30,152,259
Metro Company, 35,38,39,41,
    46,92
Mexicana Airlines, 238
Michelina, Beatrice, 18
Mickey Mouse, Limited, 169
Milestone, Lewis, 259
Milner, Vic, 92,94
Mirisch, Walter, 226,228
Mix, Tom, 18
Mohr, Hal, 95,119,120
Mooney, Tom, 20
Moore, Colleen, 27,39,42-43
Moore, Matt, 31
Moore, Phil, 191
Moore, Tom, 31,59,77
Moreheim, Lou, 292
Morrell, André, 209
Morrow, Jeff, 226
Mueller, Richard, 267
Muni, Paul, 52
Murray, Mae, 27
Musquiz, Carlos, 238
Mussmano, Judge M.A., 120,
    123
Musso & Frank, 24-25

NBC, 254,280
Nagel, Conrad, 30
Nat Goodwin's, 26
Nathan, Gabe, 21
Neilan, Marshall, 27-28,31,
    32,44,78-79,84,93,160
Newton, Robert, 176-77,223,
    225,260
Nickelodeons (first film
    viewed by Haskin),
    13-15
Nimoy, Leonard, 281
Novarro, Ramon, 92
Nozaki, Albert, 263
Nyby, Chris, 132

O.K. Freddie, 67-68

O'Brien, Edmond, 187-88
O'Brien, Eugene, 31
O'Brien, Jack, 30
O'Hanlon, James, 229
Oland, Warner, 63
Oliver, Susan, 281
On Borrowed Time (novel by Lawrence Watkin), 166
Orsatti, Frank, 137,139
Orthochromatic film, 87
Osata, Sono, 157

Pacific Cereal Association (see also Albers Brothers Mills; Carnation Mush), 3,5,7,8
Pal, George, 199-200,204, 207-9,219,220,221,228, 230,278,287,291,292
Panchromatic film, 87,88
Pantages Vaudeville, 12
Paramount, 28,104-5,107,134, 140,156,185,188, 199-200,202,206-7, 208,209,220,228,258, 260,261,284
Parker, Eleanor, 220, 221-22,258
Parry, Harvey, 90,98,161
Pathé Studio, 208
Payne, John, 231
Peach, Kenny, 106
Pearce, Perce, 170-74, 175-76,180,183-84,280
Perry, Kathleen, 31
Phillips, Dorothy, 36,37,46, 93-94
Physioc, Louis, 41-43
Pickford, Jack, 56
Pickford, Mary, 25,30,94
Pirates of the Caribbean ride, Disneyland, 180
Pitts, ZaSu, 27,188-89

Playwriting for Profit (by Arthur Edwin Krows), 148
Pleshette, Suzanne, 288-89, 291
Polito, Sol, 95,160
Pomeroy, Alan, 98
Powell, Dick, 99,101
The Power (novel by Frank M. Robinson), 287, 290-91
Pratt, Tommy, 132
Preparedness Day Parade. See Cinematography, B. Haskin
Prevost, Marie, 53,67
Principal Pictures, 46
Producers Association, 116
Prohoska, Janos, 276-77
Projects Unlimited, 278,291

Queen Mary, 170,171
Quinn, Eddie, 56,57
Quinn, Hookie, 56,57

RCA. See His Master's Voice
Rackin, Marty, 223
Rank, J. Arthur, 115
Rank, J. Arthur Company, 115
Reed, Carol, 155
Reid, Wallace, 25-26
Reinhardt, Max, 117,118-19
Rembrandt principle, 86-93
Rennahan, Ray, 285
Rennie, Mike, 287,288,291
Revier, Dorothy, 77
Reynolds, Ben, 71
Reynolds, Burt, 243,245
Rice, Joan, 209
Richmond, Warner, 76
Rigaud, George, 141
Robinson Crusoe (novel by Daniel Defoe), 266,267
Robinson, Edward G., 141

Robinson, W. Simpson, 218
Rockett Brothers, Al and
  Ray, 32
Roddenberry, Gene, 280,281
Roland, Ruth, 55
Rosalind Hotel, Hollywood,
  26
Rosenberg, Frank P., 156
Rosher, Charles, 32,94
Rossen, Robert, 161
Rosso, Lou, 160

Sabu, 158
Said, Fouad, 285
St. Clair, Mal, 59
Samarkand Hotel, Santa
  Barbara, 46
San Francisco Earthquake,
  1906. See Earthquake
  of 1906, San Francisco
Sanders, George, 233
Santschi, Tom, 64
Savoy Theater, 177
Schaff, Monty, 156
Schenck, Aubrey, 208,261,263
Schlichting, Herr and Frau
  (Werner and Isabell),
  256
Schnee, Charles, 141,143,153
Schrock, Ray, 75
Schüfftan, Eugen, 255-56
Science fiction directing. See
  Directing
Science Fiction in the
  Cinema, 289
Scott, Lizabeth, 136,141,
  145,159
Scott, Zachary, 178
Security Savings Bank, 45
Seitz, John, 86,92-94,129
Selig's Zoo Studios, 32,38-39
Selzer, Frank, 231
Selznick, David, 31, 168
Selznick, Lewis J., 31
Selznick, Myron, 31

Semon, Larry, 89
Sennett, Mack, 15, 73,90
Sennett, Mack Studio, 90,91,
  108,246
Serling, Rod, 270,
Shamroy, Leon, 33,163,254
Shotter, Winifred, 80
Siegel, Don, 116-17,
  133-34,146
Smith, Bernard, 217
Sofaer, Abraham, 253,273-74
Sound on film, early days of,
  70-72,84-85
Special effects. See also
  CAPTAIN SINDBAD;
  JULES VERNE'S
  FROM THE EARTH
  TO THE MOON; MID-
  SUMMER NIGHT'S
  DREAM; OUTER
  LIMITS; THE ROAR-
  ING TWENTIES;
  Warner Bros. Special
  Effects Department
 on CONQUEST OF
  SPACE, 229
 montage in WOLF'S
  CLOTHING, 73
 rear projection, 109
 red skies in ROBINSON
  CRUSOE ON MARS,
  262
 trainwreck in DENVER
  AND RIO GRANDE,
  197-99
 traveling mattes in THE
  WAR OF THE
  WORLDS, 201,205,294
 traveling yellow keys,
  109-110
Stark, Mábel, 158
Steele, Pete, 73
Stefano, Joseph, 269-70, 274,
  281

Stevens, George, 160
Stevens, Leslie, 271
Stevens, Mark, 241
Stevenson, Robert Louis, 168, 177
Stevenson, Venetia, 237
Stovall, Mr. (plantation owner in Stovall, Miss.), 125
Strauss, Robert, 241
Stromberg, Hunt, 159
Struss, Karl, 32
Sullivan, C. Gardner, 44,152
Swain, Mack, 90
Sweet, Harry, 56
Swickard, Josef, 63

Tait's-at-the-Beach, 26
Taylor, Estelle, 63
Technicolor, 52,112,113,267
Tedder, Air Marshal, 173
Television
 Editing of films for. See Editing
 Directing for. See Directing
Templeton, Harry, 185
Tetrazzini, Luisa, 12
Thomas, Bill, 99,111,113
Tina Louise, 242
Tinling, Jim, 56,58
Tinney, Frank, 101
Tom Sawyer (novel by Mark Twain), 168
Tondreau, Al, 113
Torrence, Ernest, 39
Totheroh, Rollie, 32, 87
Tourneur, Jacques, 226
Tover, Leo, 159
Traven, B., 137
Treasure Island (novel by Robert Louis Stevenson), 168
Treasure of the Sierra Madre (novel by B. Traven), 137

Tree, Sir Herbert Beerbohm, 231
Trilling, Steve, 137-38
Truart Film Corporation, 55
Tucker, George Loane, 30
Tucker, Forrest, 189
Twelve Little Indians (novel Agatha Christie), 290
20th Century-Fox, 223

UFA, 255
Undercranking. See Film speed
Universal, 35,58,156
University of California at Berkeley, See Education, B. Haskin

Valdez, Ignacio, 234-35
Vincent, Romo, 222
Valentino, Rudolph, 94
Van Enger, Charles, 129
Van Enger, Willard, 88
Vitaphone, 63,87,88
Von Braun, Werner, 230
Von Stroheim, Erich, 188

Wald, Jerry, 131-32,137
Wallace, Edgar, 79
Wallis, Hal, 74,96,99-100,122, 135,136,140-42, 155-56,159,209,223, 278
Walls, Tom, 80,85
Walsh, Raoul, 30,34-35,44
Walthall, Henry, B., 282
Wanamaker, Sam, 272
The War of the Worlds (novel by H.G. Wells), 202-5
Warner, Abe, 66
Warner, Harry, 66,67
Warner, Jack, 27,46,63,66,67, 73,74-75,76,96,97,109, 111-13,132,137-39, 158,212-13,258,279
Warner, Joy, 158

Warner, Sam, 66
Warner Bros. (see also
    Warner Bros. Special
    Effects Department;
    Warner Bros. stock
    company), 32,46,52,53,
    54,59,63,66,68,70,71,
    72,74,90,91,95,97,
    98-99,100,101,106,108,
    127,129,130,137,139,
    156,177-78,208,237,285
Warner Bros. Special Effects
    Department, 73,92,99,
    106-11,112,115,120,
    130,138,207,252
Warner Bros. stock company,
    96,131
Watkin, Lawrence W.,
    166-71,174,176,178
Webb, Millard, 55
Welles, Orson, 203
Wells, H.G., 202-3,204,205,
    276

West, Adam, 268
West, Mae, 206
Western Electric (see also
    Erpi), 63,66
White, Pearl, 204
White, Sam, 292
Wilcox, Herbert, 78-79, 80,
    81,82,83,84,85,255
Williams, Guy, 249,253
Wolfson, Louis, 223,225
Wright, Tenny, 97,139
Wylie, Philip, 146

Yates, Herbert, 160
Yellowtail, Robert, 189-90
Yordan, Phil, 219,220
Young, Frederick, 81, 115
Young, Loretta, 141
Youngerman, Joseph, 233

Zanuck, Darryl, 59,74,75-76,
    109
Zavitts, Lee, 247,249